The Quest for Power

Hobbes, Descartes,
and the Emergence of Modernity

Piotr Hoffman

HUMANITIES PRESS
NEW JERSEY

First published 1996 by Humanities Press International, Inc.
165 First Avenue, Atlantic Highlands, New Jersey 07716

©Piotr Hoffman, 1996

Library of Congress Cataloging-in-Publication Data
Hoffman, Piotr.
     The quest for power : Hobbes, Descartes, and the emergence of
modernity / Piotr Hoffman.
        p. cm.
     Includes bibliographical references and index.
     ISBN 0-391-03924-5 (cloth)
     1. Autonomy (Philosophy) 2. Self (Philosophy) 3. Power
(Philosophy) 4. Violence. 5. Philosophy, Modern—17th century.
6. Civilization, Modern—17th century. 7. Hobbes, Thomas,
1588–1679. 8. Descartes, René, 1596–1650. I. Title.
B808.67.H64 1995
126'.092'2—dc 20   95–16505
                                                                    CIP

A catalog record for this book is available from the British Library.

Printed in the United States of America

The Quest for Power

Contents

Preface

The modern age brings with it a tremendous assertion of man's autonomy and power. With the aid of science and technology, man sets out to realize the project of mastering nature; and the emerging new philosophy both expresses and justifies the new outlook in which man begins to perceive himself as the genuine maker of his world. Slowly but steadily, in spite of many setbacks and resistances, this trend continues to gain strength and to impose itself as the dominant element in the modern view. At its very source we find two thinkers who are the true founding fathers of modern philosophy: Hobbes and Descartes. Almost the entire development of modern epistemology and metaphysics represents a response to the problems identified by Descartes and to the solutions he went on to offer; and the very same observation can be made about the developments that took place in political and moral philosophy after Hobbes. Thus, any attempt to understand the philosophical parameters of modernity must go back to its source in Hobbes and in Descartes.

While on several important issues Hobbes and Descartes remain worlds apart, their philosophical systems take the same point of departure, pursue the same route, and arrive at the same station at least within the domains in which the two thinkers exercised their strongest influence upon the formation of the modern mind. What Hobbes does in political and moral philosophy Descartes does in epistemology and metaphysics. They both start with the notion of an individual human self asserting its autonomy and power. But such a self, they both discover, soon encounters its limit in the will of another self, bent at asserting its own autonomy and power. The emerging human mastery of nature does not erase the self's vulnerability to another self. Thus, in the Hobbesian "state of nature," the individual soon finds himself vulnerable to the violence of other individuals, and the state of nature turns into the state of "war of everybody against everybody." In Descartes, too, the meditating self's drive to put knowledge upon an unshakable basis encounters its most serious limit in the actions of that famous *genium malignum*—the "evil" or "malignant" demon whose will it is to employ his cognitive and practical powers to the end of deceiving the self and blocking its access to the truth.

A historian of scepticism[1] will not fail to notice the radical novelty of this "demonic" doubt and of the "super-scepticism" produced by it: nothing similar was to be found in the arsenal of the ancient sceptics, or even in the collection of sceptical arguments employed by Descartes's immediate predecessors

vii

in the history of scepticism. In making this assessment, the historian will find himself in complete agreement with Descartes's own view of the demon hypothesis. This hypothesis, Descartes tells Burman, goes deeper than the arguments of the sceptics: it is put forward to create "every difficulty that can possibly be raised".[2] By viewing himself as vulnerable to a deceiving demon, Descartes assesses the strength of his cognitive faculties on a worst-case scenario he deliberately adopts.

In political philosophy, Hobbes's point of departure is the same. In a passage of *Leviathan* Hobbes describes his state of nature as a "Chaos of Violence," a most fitting label.[3] The state of nature is the state of chaos, for there is no authority to determine and enforce some common rules for employing such terms as "good" and "evil," "just" and "unjust," and so forth; consequently, there is only a cacophony of individual voices, each of which claims its own authority under the "right of nature." But this chaos is the chaos of *violence*, for the individuals acting out their right of nature soon find themselves on a collision course in practical matters and, under the circumstances, they find it quite rational to engage in anticipatory violence against one another.

In both thinkers, the path of escape from that worst-case scenario turns out to be our submission to a higher power. The Hobbesian "Sovereign" saves the warring individuals from the menace of violent death by imposing peace upon them; and Descartes's God is called upon to guarantee, against the demon, the soundness of man's cognitive faculties and ideas. In both thinkers this escape from the worst-case scenario is presented as a rational move, but on a closer analysis, its alleged rationality may dissolve. The move is undoubtedly rational in the sense that it is of utmost benefit for man to overcome the predicament of the Hobbesian war of everybody against everybody and of that deepest superscepticism imposed upon us by the actions of Descartes's demon. But the means to achieve these benefits may yet turn out to be selected and implemented by an irrational act.

In effect, the ultimate doubt generated with the aid of the demon hypothesis deprives the thinking self of any right to convert most of its evidences into objective truths. Given this utter poverty of the self's cognitive resources at the stage of doubt, Descartes's attempts to reconstruct the knowledge of God are more than likely to founder. Even if it could otherwise be granted that Descartes is not guilty of obvious circularity in his proofs of God, neither the causal proof offered by Descartes in the Third Meditation nor the ontological argument from the Fifth Meditation will withstand a closer examination. Both the causal reasoning and the analysis of the concept (or "essence") of God will fail to lead the Cartesian doubter beyond the realm of his own representations. If this doubter can, in the end, apprehend himself—and hence also his cognitive faculties and ideas—as a creature of God, his raise to this new self-interpretation will not be a rational act, at least not in the sense of rationality allowed for by the strictures of the Cartesian doubt.

And are the Hobbesian individuals capable of escaping from the state of nature by acting rationally? This, too, seems unlikely. Within the state of nature, noncooperation and anticipatory violence may turn out to be quite rational, since the predicament the individuals find themselves in exhibits a clear pattern of the prisoner dilemma—indeed, the pattern of a prisoner dilemma with a huge number of players involved. Under these conditions, the establishment of the Hobbesian Sovereign—and, consequently, man's move from the state of nature to the social state—would have to be viewed as an irrational act.[4] There are, to be sure, the Hobbesian "laws of nature" which counsel us, prudentially if not morally, to choose cooperation. But under the conditions prevailing in the state of nature, these laws are valid, in Hobbes's assessment, only *in foro interno*; they are present in the minds of the warring individuals, but not in the external realm of human interactions, not *in foro externo*. Just like the reference of Descartes's representations to the external world is suspended by the hostile actions of the demon, so too the Hobbesian rules of cooperation may turn out to be inapplicable in the external world due to the conditions of war of everybody against everybody.

We will, in the course of this study, take a closer look at these important issues in both Hobbes and Descartes, and we will try to supply some answers to the questions we have just raised. In pursuing this task we must keep in mind some important aspects of the methods of our two writers.

In constructing his system, Hobbes did not rely only upon his vast empirical knowledge of history and politics, and of human motivation and behavior. He thought he could proceed a priori. In chapter 10 of *De Homine*, he explains how this is possible in political philosophy and ethics. For in these domains of knowledge, we are not concerned, as we are in natural sciences, with explaining the phenomena with some causes which are originally unknown to us and must subsequently be discovered by a process of research and inquiry. Our knowledge in political and moral philosophy can proceed *a priori* for the same reason as our knowledge in geometry. In all these areas, the objects of knowledge—the geometrical figures, the principles and institutions governing human interactions, and so on—are constructed by ourselves. We know them by being their authors; and this "author's knowledge" of geometrical figures or of political institutions gives us an immediate cognitive access to them. This is why we can know them with the *certainty* of an a priori science; and this is why we need not rely upon a posteriori methods alone while studying the political and moral life of man.

But the political and moral life of man is not a matter of principles and institutions alone. The latter are constructed by us in response to the pressing problems created by our passions, desires, and thoughts; indeed, human passions, desires, and thoughts supply the very foundation securing for us the existence and stability of a state with all of its political and moral principles. Thus, our a priori knowledge of man's political and moral life must include an insight into some very basic human motivations. The road to that insight passes through the individual's acquaintance with *his own* experiences. "Read thy self," Hobbes tells us in the introduction to *Leviathan*; and this is, as it were, the Hobbesian equivalent of the cogito. Our grasp of our own thoughts, feelings, passions and so on gives us the point of departure in our reconstruction of the knowledge of political and moral phenomena. This point of departure will prove fruitful, since in "reading" oneself one will also "read" the others—all others—prior to an actual observation of their motivation and behavior. There is enough similarity between ourselves and our conspecifics for such an a priori transfer to take place: "Whosoever looketh into himself, and considereth what he doth, when he does *think, opine, reason, hope, feare*, etc., and upon what grounds; he shall thereby read and know, what are the thoughts, and Passions of all other men, upon like occasions."[5]

Notice must be taken of some important elements in Descartes's method as well. Repeatedly, Descartes counsels us to approach his system through the study of the *Meditations*; and the reason he gives is the priority of the "analytic" method of philosophizing adopted in the *Meditations* over the "synthetic" method of some of his other works, such as the *Principles of Philosophy*.[6] To be sure, the *Meditations* are not the only "analytic" treatise in the *corpus* of Descartes's works on metaphysics. But the *Meditations* are, undoubtedly, the most systematic of them all. They are, in Descartes's own opinion, the key to his philosophical system.

The importance, to Descartes, of the analytic method of philosophizing cannot be overestimated. In the Second Replies, Descartes explains at length how this method alone can lead us away from the unthinking habits and prejudices of common sense toward the properly philosophical viewpoint.[7] The synthetic method consists in presenting and demonstrating the truths in some domain of knowledge without taking into account the process of learning and discovery. For Descartes, a textbook of geometry, with its series of definitions, axioms, postulates, and theorems, is a perfect example of the synthetic method of exposition and demonstration. Here we need not worry how the basic geometrical concepts were forged and discovered. But philosophy cannot dispense with the analytic method. For whereas Euclid's concepts agree with the basic intuitions of common sense, the metaphysician finds himself in a less fortunate position. His concepts and ideas are at odds with those of the common sense. But the metaphysician should not proceed dogmatically against the common sense. To remove the suspicion that his views are unfounded, he must demonstrate their validity by appealing to the ordinary, commonsensical man with arguments intelligible and acceptable to the latter. Descartes's sceptical moves in the First Meditation are a shining example of the analytic method of philosophizing and of its importance to Descartes.

The present study is concerned with the emergence of modern philosophy in the writing of its two founding fathers. As we study some of the key moves made by Hobbes and Descartes, we shall discover in more detail how a certain conception of violence is instrumental both in shaping the framework of their philosophizing and in determining its results. It is true that Hobbes speaks directly about human violence while Descartes makes the human knower vulnerable to the hostile actions of an evil "demon." But the ultimate function of this demon's deceptions in Descartes's epistemology and metaphysics is not very different from the function of the "force and fraud" imposed upon an individual by the others in Hobbes's political philosophy. In both cases, the individual finds himself isolated from the public world, thrown back upon his own resources and enclosed within a private realm from which he can escape only by some truly extraordinary means. We may yet discover that within this condition of human vulnerability and isolation some of the fundamental components of modernity's conceptual framework—the categories of causality, of personal identity, and so on—receive their concrete grounding. Finally, our close look at Descartes's demon will discover in this figure some amazingly human—all-too-human—features.

It would be tempting to pursue this story further; for, in effect, Hobbes's and Descartes's immediate successors may well be viewed as reacting to those worst-case scenarios upon which Hobbes erected his system of political philosophy and Descartes his epistemology and metaphysics. In political philosophy, both Locke and Hume deemphasized the Hobbesian war of everybody against everybody. They argued that the individual's "natural" conduct, guided by either contractarian or utilitarian rationality, need not and will not result in a slide toward universal violence but will of itself secure peace and cooperation. Similarly, there is no trace, in Spinoza and Leibniz, of Descartes's radical scepticism generated by the hypothesis of a demonic will bent at deceiving us. In both Spinoza and Leibniz, the function of the will in general—in God and man alike—is much more restricted than in Descartes, and this removes the very source of uncertainty concerning such important issues as the soundness of our cognitive faculties or the ontological status of the eternal truths. Only with Kant and Hegel will we see again the upgrading of the human will's importance and the reemergence—especially in Hegel—of the problem of violence.

To follow up on these threads would be beyond the limits of this book. Partly, at least, I have tried to do it in my other books.[8] The present work is meant to explore only the origins of modern philosophy in the writings of the two thinkers who laid out the very framework within which the philosophical problems of modernity were to be articulated.

I owe a debt of gratitude to two friends who devoted their time and effort to reading the manuscript of this book. Andrzej Rapaczynski's expertise on Hobbes was instrumental in convincing me that I am not off the track in my interpretation. Bert Dreyfus read the entire manuscript and gave me valuable comments and criticisms which contributed to shaping its present form.

Abbreviations

Works frequently cited have been abbreviated. Full bibliographic information is available in the list of works which follows the notes at the end of the book.

AT	R. Descartes, *Oeuvres de Descartes*
CB	R. Descartes, *Descartes's Conversation with Burman*
De Cive	T. Hobbes, *De Cive*
De Corp	T. Hobbes, *De Corpore*
EL	T. Hobbes, *The Elements of Law*
EW	T. Hobbes, *The English Works of Thomas Hobbes*
HR	*The Philosophical Works of Descartes*
K.	*Descartes, Philosophical Letters*
Lev	T. Hobbes, *Leviathan*

Part I
Hobbes

1

The Self as a Power Center

The first and the most fundamental tenet of Hobbes's philosophical anthropology is his conception of man as a very special part of nature. In spite of the fact that human organisms show a great deal of similarity with animals, they also exhibit certain features which set them apart from the animal kingdom. All of these features are due to a single capacity: the power of speech. Thanks to language, all other human faculties and dispositions "may be improved to such a height, as to distinguish men from other living Creatures."[1] Thus, while animals too are endowed with sense, imagination, memory, and even thought, all of these powers are raised, in the case of man, to a much higher level of performance through their cooperation with the uniquely human capacity to speak. Perhaps "cooperation" is not the right word. It may suggest that we have, on the one hand, certain capacities which remain pretty much the same in both man and beast and, on the other hand, the power of speech, which entertains only an external and contingent relation with those capacities. But this is not the case. It is true that human thought and imagination can entertain mental contents uninformed by names. It is also true, conversely, that man can speak without any reference to the material supplied by those other cognitive capacities. But the penalty for such a disjoining of the various components of human knowledge is severe. Since reason, and hence also the ability to grasp rational connections, emerges only with speech,[2] our reliance upon the prelinguistic modes of cognition does not allow us to order experience in a rational manner. At such a low level of cognition, we can achieve only "prudence," not "science." The order and regularity discovered at this low, prelinguistic level of experience are limited and subject to constant change; our anticipations of the future, not being based on a rational insight into the nature of causes and effects, lack the solidity and the conformity to universal laws which only reason can grasp and for which, therefore, the power of speech is necessary. Conversely, too, the verbal discourse can not free itself from its connection with the material supplied to it by sequences of our mental images and thoughts without sliding into some form of absurdity. For our images and thoughts are derived from objects' impact upon the sense; and so in order to preserve its

3

reference to objects, our "Trayne of Words" must be linked up with the "Trayne of Thoughts." To be sure, the slide into absurdity remains an essential possibility of human speech. For language is entirely conventional: the connections between names and objects are not natural, but man-made, artificial; and this lack of any natural connection between names and objects offers a constant temptation to sever any link between the two, and to employ speech independently of its reference to things. When language is used in that way, some form of absurdity is bound to arise.

On the other hand, the advantages that stem from a sound use of language are immense. By imposing names and grasping connections between them, the human organism ascends to the level of universality. Hobbes's moderate nominalism allows for the existence of similarities in things' qualities and accidents;[3] thus, when a name is imposed upon one particular thing, all other things sharing its qualities find themselves grouped under the same name. If, further, the consequence of *A*s bearing the name *B* is that *A* will exhibit such and such behavior under such and such conditions, then all other particulars falling under *B* will also exhibit similar behavior under similar conditions. Man's cognition becomes liberated from its attachment to the here and the now: "And thus the consequence found in one particular, comes to be registered and remembered, as an Universall rule . . . and makes that which was found true *here* and *now*, to be true in *all times* and *places*."[4] In contrast with animals, then, man does not live in a limited and parochial environment. Language opens up an "universal" environment—a world.

Due to this linguistically induced ability to extract a thing from its particular spatio-temporal context man can consider things from all (merely) possible points of view. And this capacity for an abstract exploration of things is, again, not to be found among animals.[5]

The emergence of a world is, for a human organism, both a blessing and a curse, a source of power and of powerlessness as well. The advantages are clear: by liberating his cognition from the limits of a particular context man can concern himself with all possible contexts thereby preparing his responses to all kinds of threats and dangers he may find himself facing at some future point of his life-history. If, say, a severe drought causes famine in this particular environment I live in and am accustomed to, my rational understanding of the connection between those two events will make me alert to similar dangers under all possible circumstances, wherever I may want to settle. But this also means that a great deal of human energy will come to be dissipated and wasted on worrying about dangers which will not materialize or are extremely unlikely to materialize. For better or for worse—for better *and* for worse, one would like to say—man lives in a "constant anxiety"[6] and a "perpetuall solicitude of the time to come."[7]

Now, this "anxiety" and "solicitude" about the future are a clear indication that man is not related to his future in an attitude of a disinterested contemplation; indeed, given the fundamental parameters of his condition in the world, man can not *afford* to envision his future from the vantage point of a detached observer. For Hobbes[8] man is in a state of perpetual desire, and his happiness does not consist in achieving some state of final and self-sufficient satisfaction, but only in a continued progress in satisfying the ever-emerging new desires. Since, according to one of Hobbes's definitions of "power," the means to satisfy our desires are power,[9] the relentless pursuit of power becomes the only constant purpose of man. And this feverish pursuit of power makes him *concerned* about all kinds of possible future developments which would otherwise fail to affect him in one way or another. For this reason, too, even though the disposition to freely explore the world is curiosity,[10] the motivational engine powering man's unceasing search for causes of things is his anxiety about the future.[11]

So far, however, we have not explained why a truly rational agent could not control his anxiety about the future and would not concern himself only with dangers which are *likely* to occur. Unless an answer is given to this question, an individual's endless effort to accumulate power will remain clearly counterproductive—a useless dissipation of an energy that could have been channeled into more beneficial pursuits—and will be, therefore, a symptom of that individual's inability to adjust to reality. Hobbes does have an answer to our question. The endless striving for power becomes a highly realistic concern on account of one special danger I am not able to master or avoid: the danger of another man. When my powers clash with the powers of another man they are reduced to nothing;[12] and this is due to the fact that the other is, as it were, another me—a creature belonging to the same species that I do and thus endowed with capacities and means that are essentially equal to my own. The effectiveness of my powers—be they "natural" or "instrumental"—is thus cancelled out by the powers of the other, so much so, that Hobbes's second definition of power takes into account that fundamental vulnerability of all my powers to the danger represented by the threat of the other: "Because the power of one man resisteth and hindereth the effects of the power of another: power simply is no more, but the excess of the power of one above that of another."[13] This is why, in the state of nature, my (natural) right to "everything" is soon reduced by the other to what is effectively the right to "nothing." In many passages[14] Hobbes elaborates on this peculiar slide from possessing the riches of "everything" to the anxiety of being stripped down to "nothing"—from, we may say, the wealth of being to the poverty of nothing.[15]

On account of its endless striving for power, the human self is essentially *temporal;* indeed the temporality of the human self is the condition of both the existence and the knowledge of time.

There are several levels at which time appears in the philosophy of Hobbes. Time is, first, the measure of motion insofar as motion is taken only with

respect to what is "before" and "after" in it. This is the sort of time that
Aristotle conceptualized in his *Physics*, and, for once, Hobbes has no qualms
about borrowing from Aristotle and confessing his debt.[16] It may seem that
our measurements of motion, with respect to its "former" and "later" stages,
require that these stages be as real and independent of the measurer as the
motion itself. After all, if the units of measurement—minutes, hours, and so
forth—read off our clocks reflect the objective positions of the pointers, then,
we may presume, the stretches of time represented by their motions must be
objective too. But this is to forget that the *motion itself* does not exist as past
or future: "It is all one to say, motion *past* and motion *destroyed*, and . . .
future motion is the same with motion which *is not yet begun*."[17] Since time is
the measure of motion, and since there is no past or future motion, "the present
only has a being in Nature."[18] As for the past and the future, they exist only
in our minds;[19] and, as we shall see, this inherently mental status of the past is
very different from the corresponding status of the future.

We are thus led to posit the second, and more fundamental, level of the
appearance of time. If it weren't for the human organisms' capacity to store
recollections and form expectations, the external world would not appear within
a temporal frame. On this second, purely internal, level, the past enjoys two
advantages over the future. First of all, our expectation of the future is based
on our recollections of the past: we expect that the present occurrence of *A* in
our experience will soon be followed by the future occurrence of *B,* for these
two types of events are associated in our memory as following each other in
our past experiences.[20] This expectation of the future on the basis of the past
can take more or less sophisticated forms. It can be a form of prudence, where
the association of *A* and *B* in our memory is due entirely to our past observations of their joint appearance in the order of succession. But the expectation
of the future can also be based on a *rational* understanding of causes and
effects. In both cases, however, the expected future developments are projected
on the basis of what we *already* know, that is, on the basis of the past. The
second advantage of the past over the future is, one may say, of an ontological
nature. Whereas the past has a reality of sorts in the human memory, the
future is only a "fiction";[21] it may or it may not occur, and until it actually
does occur, it can not be said to exist. As for our *present* experiences, they are
given through senses,[22] since sensory images are impressed by the presence of
an independent object having a causal impact upon our sensory apparatus. Of
course all kinds of other mental contents—images, thoughts and so on—can
be present too. But by the force of Hobbes's argument, their present position
in a chronological sequence of representations must be established indirectly,
that is, by reference to a present object of the sensory cognition. For example,
since imagination is but *"decaying sense,"*[23] our attention to an image goes together with a feeling of holding onto some sensory content that is already

slipping into the past; and we may then have a problem with discriminating between images and recollections, since, for Hobbes, their difference is merely the one of a degree of liveliness.

Now, if time represented as measure of physical motion is derived from the play of our recollections, perceptions, and expectations, they, in turn, refer to an even deeper level of subjective time; they refer to the temporality of man's perpetual striving for power. As we noted earlier, due to that striving man (anxiously) concerns himself with possible future effects of the presently given causes. But, as we also noted, these sequences of causes and effects make up the content of our recollections and expectations; indeed, Hobbes goes so far as to say that "*all* conception of future is conception of power able to produce something,"[24] where power and cause can be used, in this context, interchangeably. If, therefore, all of our expectations of the future depend upon our conception of the future effects of such and such causes, and if we are disposed to search for causes on account of our anxious striving for power, then this striving is at the root of our disposition to form, store, and constantly expand our expectations.

The link with our concrete expectations and recollections of external events attributes to our striving for power its chronological ordering. The "after" in Hobbes's talk about our desire of "power after power"[25] would be stripped of any chronological meaning if this desire were not dependent, for its realization, upon the actual unfolding of sequences of events. The reason why my desires are arranged in such a way that, say, my desire to buy a house can only be realized *later* than my desire to be granted a loan from the bank is that the second event is situated after the first in a causal sequence I must take into account if my house is to be more than a figment of my imagination. The mere *desire* of power must insert itself into the structure of the external *world,* where, to be sure, only the present is real independently of human recollections and expectations, but where also, given the human organism's capacity to recall and expect, our experience emerges as inescapably chronological; hence the human desires too must be ordered in conformity with the chronological ordering of causes and effects.

The temporality of the human striving for power assumes different forms depending upon whether it expresses itself within the world of violence or of consensus, the world of war or of peace. There is a "time of war" and a "time of peace"; indeed, time belongs to the very *nature* of war and peace.[26] In other terms, war and peace can be distinguished from each other by, among other things, their different ways of laying out the temporal framework within which men express and pursue their desire for power. At a time of war, man pursues power in "continuall feare, and danger of violent death"; his life is, and he perceives it to be, "solitary" and "short."[27] Under such circumstances, there is no firm and secure foundation for our planning of the future, since all our plans—including our very expectation to stay alive—are put under a gigantic question mark by the very present danger of other men's violence. We are sure of our existence only for the present moment, since we can not know if all of our defenses will not prove entirely useless in the moment ahead of us. To give time its continuity, the pacifying and socializing power of the sovereign will be necessary. Man's temporal experience will lose both its solitary character—for man will become a participant in the public temporal rhythm of society—and its momentariness. We will find something very similar to this as we move along the trail blazed by Descartes in his *Meditations*. The threat of an evil demon will reduce the time of my existence to the isolated present moment; and the reestablishment of the continuity of time will depend, ultimately, upon the power of God. In both Hobbes and Descartes, then, the self as a (cognitive or practical) power center finds itself in two kinds of temporal experience: the momentary, discrete, and fragile temporality of powerlessness under a threat, and the continuous, secure, and predictable temporality restored by a power higher than the self in question. Here, as elsewhere, the human experience plays itself out within that spectrum of powerlessness and power.

The self's powerlessness vis-à-vis the other establishes the self as a generalized and indefinite striving for power. As the self aims at the achievement not of this or that power, but of total power—for, in effect, any partial and limited power is vulnerable to the threat of the other—the entire world is perceived as a territory to be mastered and absorbed by the self. It would seem, then, that such a self must live in a solipsistic realm of its own, and that, consequently, there is no sense in which the self at issue could still be said to be a particular item within the world. But this is not the case. For even when we take the self in its single-minded imperialism of its striving for total power, such a self is, and understands itself as being, a self among *other* selves—a particular power center responding to the threat of other such power centers. To be sure, there is a sense—linked up with Hobbes's psychological egoism—in which the self's egocentric attitude toward the world is a fact of human nature. Taken on this primary, elemental level, the impulses of the Hobbesian desire are not unlike the impulses of the Freudian Id—they command unconditionally in the voice of imperatives, without any consideration of prudence.[28] But these elemental, self-seeking impulses of the human desire are entirely different from the generalized desire for power. The former can be checked by prudential considerations of reality; the latter can not be so checked, since the threat to which it responds is real. The self-centered attitude of an agent bent at absorbing everything within his power is due not to a lack of clear awareness of other people's independent standing in the world; rather, it is a way in which the agent responds to the very real and very acute knowledge of the others as power centers representing a constant threat to him. Thus my generalized pursuit of power is predicated upon my awareness of the reality of other selves as (at least) *numerically* different from me. But this difference can not sustain itself as purely numerical and it must become a *qualitative* difference as well. This follows from Hobbes's second definition of power as "excess of the power of one [man] above that of another." Given this second definition of power, Hobbes's first definition ("The Power *of a Man* . . . is his present means, to obtain some future apparent Good") turns out to be merely provisional and insufficient. For the actual reality of those present "means" to some future good will be at once cancelled out by the power of the other *unless* my own power is of such a degree as to secure for me the possession and the use of those means *in spite* of the other. My means to achieve the goods *A, B,* and *C* are real means to me only if the other can not deprive me of them, or neutralize them. They are real and not fictitious power only if my overall standing vis-à-vis the other is such that my power is "in excess" of his—for it is then, and then only, that I can be said to be in a position of securing these means against his own striving for power. Now this implies that I come to know both myself and the other—to know the *qualities* of myself and of the man I confront—by facing up to the threat of the other. As long as I don't measure myself against such a threat, I will live in an imaginary world where the qualities that I attribute to myself may very well be—and, given the human propensity to self-deception, most probably *will* be—unrealistic or altogether fictitious. I do not know myself unless I look at myself in the light of the other's threat to me. If just about everything that matters to me—both inside and outside me—does so only as a vehicle of a certain power, and if I come to know my powers in a confrontation with the powers of other human agents, the real *content* of my self (all of my natural and acquired dispositions, skills, character traits, etc.) comes to my knowledge in the light projected by the threat of the other.

Thus my indefinite and generalized striving for power finds itself situated within a range of *factual* powers at my disposal. Qua pure striving for power I differ only numerically from other such strivings. But then there never *is* a "pure" striving for power. Every particular striving is a *determinate* striving, since it relies upon a set of specific, concrete powers that every individual must bring to bear upon the tasks at hand in order to give his striving some degree of effectiveness.

Insofar as the other emerges as a threat to my power—and, ultimately, to my entire life—he emerges as having a palpable *impact* upon me. Thus *the other is a causal power* in my experience. Moreover, my dependence upon the other is a *necessary* one; I can neither ignore nor escape his capacity to have an impact upon my life; at the very best I can find that dependence of mine rechanneled onto more secure arenas of contest without, however, ever losing my sense of an inherent vulnerability to the powers of another man.

In Hobbes's account, causal necessity is a rational necessity, since the dependence of the effect upon its cause is due to an universal rule of reason. As we recall, reason in general emerges only in human beings, thanks to speech.

In Hobbes's definition, reason is "nothing but *Reckoning* (that is, Adding and Substracting) of the consequences of generall names."[29]. Not all such "reckoning" concerns itself with causal necessity. But a huge part of it does. When we want to know what causes *B* to occur—and most of our cognitive exploration of the world is bent at achieving knowledge of causal connections—we can satisfy this interest of ours in two ways. The first way is the way of "prudence" and "experience" (in the specifically Hobbesian sense of those terms). We observe that the appearance of *B* is always *sequent* upon the appearance of *A*, and we conclude that *A* is the cause of *B*. But the conclusion is not based on an act of reason but, rather, on a mechanical, unthinking association of samples of *A* and *B*—association which leads to the formation of an appropriate habit and has enough strength to form the corresponding expectation of joint appearances of *A* and *B* in the future. There are passages where the text of Hobbes reads like a page from Hume's *Treatise*: "Men that know not what it is that we call *causing* (that is, almost all men) have no other rule to guess by, but by observing, and remembring what they have seen to precede the like effect at some other time, or times before, without seeing between the antecedent and subsequent Event, any dependence or connexion at all: And therefore from the like things past, they expect the like things to come."[30] However, the second, and properly "scientific," way of establishing relations between causes and effects sets Hobbes worlds apart from Hume. In proceeding scientifically, we must proceed in conformity with the method of imposing names upon things, offering their definitions and then reasoning to the consequences of those names and definitions. This is how we come to acquire a higher, properly rational, knowledge of causal relations. Given such and such names and their definitions, the connection between the cause and the effect now becomes purely conceptual, even though in Hobbes's peculiar blend of rationalism and empiricism those conceptually established causal connections must also correspond with the actual causal sequences occurring in the world.

There is no indication, in Hobbes's philosophy, how to close this gap between our conceptions of causal connections and the latter as they occur in the real world, independently of our conceptions. Even in the case of mathematics such a step—the step from the pure to the applied mathematics—is, in Hobbes, highly problematical, in spite of the fact that at least some of Hobbes's teachings on space and time and figures and numbers can be read as an anticipation of Kant and hence also of Kant's approach to the problem of pure versus applied mathematics. When it comes to countless causal statements making up the bulk of our knowledge of the external world we have no choice but to depend upon factual knowledge if we want to test whether this or that conceptual connection between the names of objects corresponds to the factual connection between those objects. But Hobbes himself says that all knowledge of facts is based on sense and memory,[31] and since sense and memory can not supply us with any knowledge of rational, necessary connections, no knowledge of facts can be necessary. The Humean consequences of Hobbes's approach to causality become inevitable.

And yet if our knowledge of facts can not support our ascription of causal necessity to sequences of events occurring in a world independent of our conceptions and definitions, something else can. The knowledge that I have of myself and of the other—of the other insofar as he is a member of my own species and hence, as it were, a duplication of myself—is both certain and in correspondence with an independent reality. As Hobbes teaches us, when I "read myself," I read "all other men"; and as Hobbes also teaches us, this reading of others in myself yields results which are certain. I thus know with certainty that my *conception* of the other corresponds to what he *actually is:* the sort of causal power whose effects upon me are such that I can not avoid them or absorb them, since there is at least one case where I can not preserve *any* independence from the other's impact upon me—and that is simply the case of suffering death at his hands. Under the conditions of the Hobbesian state of nature as the state of war such a death at the hands of others looms as a constant *fate* to which I am exposed: "That miserable condition of Warre . . . is *necessarily* consequent . . . to the natural Passions of men, when there is no visible Power to keep them in awe."[32] The state of war, and hence also my inescapable and ultimate dependence upon the other, is "necessary," given the "natural passions of men"—the passions that I know in others by knowing them in myself. Here, then, the necessary dependence of *A* upon *B* (of violent death upon the natural passions of men) is neither due to an arbitrary definition of *A* and *B,* nor is it simply an ordinary empirical claim open to empirical falsification. *Causal necessity is actually found only in the world of human actions.* When—as in Hume and in Kant—the inescapable vulnerability of human agents to one another is passed over, causal necessity either vanishes without a trace or must be reconstructed with the aid of an idealistic metaphysics of the hidden "transcendental" faculties of human mind.[33]

When we talk about the causal necessity grounded in human agents' essential dependence vis-à-vis each other, some distinctions must be drawn. The main sense of this dependence is simple and straightforward. I am dependent insofar as a chain of events started by the other will, under certain circumstances, necessitate my death. The causal relation here involved is, first of all, purely mechanical: the bullet rushing through the space and hitting my body, the sword cutting into my entrails, and so on. Everything, here, can be studied and articulated in conformity with the conceptual framework worked out by Hobbes in *De Corpore* for the purposes of understanding mechanical causality. But, of course, we may look at the very same causal sequence from a different angle. In pulling the trigger of his rifle, or in driving the sword through me, the other acted purposefully: he aimed at eliminating me as a force standing in his way, and he implemented a strategy to achieve this purpose. And so the causal sequence he originated can be seen as having a final cause too: the other pulled the trigger of his rifle or raised his arm to drive his sword through me "in order to" eliminate me physically. Now, while Hobbes will find it relatively easy to claim that final causes can also act as efficient causes in mechanical processes (since mental events are corporeal events), there is a troubling aspect of this interlocking of teleology and mechanism that must be mentioned and clarified. In effect, if my abilities and skills were, to use Hobbes's expression from *Leviathan,* more "eminent" (if I had been a faster gun or a better swordsman), my power would have been "in excess" of the power of the other, and then the mechanical causal sequence would not have unfolded the way it did. Apparently, then, an individual's vulnerability to the purely physical motions initiated by the other is interlocked, somehow, with the teleologically, and intersubjectively, determined excellence of his powers. Even Hobbes's revealing characterization of death as the "loss of all power" has these two meanings.[34] Death means, first, the total loss of power in the teleological sense: for if I am dead, my faculties' eminence is, for obvious reasons, inadequate to bring within my reach any means to any future apparent good. But death means also the physical extinguishing of my body's ability to cause, through its motions, certain kinds of changes in other bodies (my corpse may still cause some such changes, but these will not be the changes caused by me). Both in life and in death, then, the mechanical and the teleological causalities seem to be interlocked in some sense of that term. This must be cleared out before we proceed further. The theory of mechanical causality is formulated mainly in *De Corpore.*[35]

The relation of causality is, first, the relation between two bodies—one of which is said to be the "agent," the other the "patient." The agent is said to act upon the patient when the former either generates or destroys some accident(s) in the latter; and the agent is said to do this on account of an accident (or a group of accidents) of its own. The accidents generated or destroyed are called the "effect"; and, for this reason, the effect can be said to be situated only in the patient. But it does not follow, from this, that the cause is situated only in the agent. In every instance of causal relation we must distinguish between the "efficient" and the "material" cause. Whereas the efficient cause is located in the agent, the material cause is located in the patient. The efficient cause is the quality (or the qualities) of the agent which, when brought together with the material cause (i.e., with certain quality or qualities of the patient) produces, jointly with latter, the effect. Taken together, the efficient and the material causes represent the "entire" cause (both necessary and sufficient) required to produce the effect under consideration; and, therefore, if the accidents that make up that entire cause are present, "*it cannot be understood but that the effect is produced at the same instant*";[36] otherwise we would have to explain the lapse of time between the cause and the effect by the absence of some partial (efficient or material) causes. It follows from these definitions that an effect's entire cause produces the effect in question with necessity. If it is inconceivable ("it cannot be understood") that if A is given B will not follow, then the occurrence of A necessitates the occurrence of B. The criterion of necessity, then, lies in our inability to *conceive* A as occurring without causing B to occur; and this connection in our conceptions of A and B is taken, by Hobbes, as mirroring the real connections between two events in the world.

Everything we said about causes applies to powers as well, at least inasmuch as the concept of power is restricted to its uses in Hobbes's mechanistic philosophy of nature. Powers are causes viewed in their *future* actions. We say that A is the cause of B if B has already taken place; we say that A has the power to produce B when we refer to some future occurrences of A and B. In the context of such a reference to the future the efficient cause becomes the "active power," while the material cause becomes the "passive power." What is called the effect is called the "act." Every act must have its entire (or "plenary") power which, when given at some point in the future, will bring about the simultaneous and necessary occurrence of that act.

From these definitions Hobbes deduces his strict actualism and determinism.[37] An act the plenary power of which will never take place is an impossible act. Since certain conditions which must be given for the act to occur will never be given, it will be in principle impossible for the act to take place. And this is precisely another way of saying that the act in question is itself impossible. The opposite of what is impossible is possible. Every possible act, therefore, must be produced at some point in the future. If it never is, or can be, so produced, then this can only mean one thing: the conditions (the powers) that are required as the plenary power of its production can never be given; and this, in turn, means that the act at issue is in principle impossible. By the same token, it is meaningless to talk about possible or potential powers. An act, we saw, is identical with an effect. But Hobbes says explicitly that "where there is no effect, there can be no cause; for nothing can be called a cause, where there is nothing that can be called an effect."[38] Now, if every possible effect will occur at some time, if for that act to occur its plenary power must be given and if, further, the act's plenary power is the power which will necessarily produce the act (for the same reason that the entire cause is said to produce its effect with necessity), then every act will occur necessarily. We thus get the strictest possible actualism and determinism: all possible events will actually occur at some point, and they will occur necessarily. There is no room even for a moderate version of indeterminism defended by those who follow the positions of Aristotle's *De Interpretatione*.[39] An event we call contingent is simply an event of which the entire (the necessary) cause is, so far, beyond the reach of our knowledge.

If we now return to human individuals' vulnerability to one another, nothing prevents us in principle from applying to their interactions the concept of mechanical causality. Human organisms are sophisticated machines capable of far reaching anticipation into the future and of responding in complex ways to a huge number of stimuli not given in their immediate physical environment. With this qualification, we have no trouble in applying the categories of mechanical causality to the area of human interactions. Take the case of one man shooting to death another man. Certain mental and physical qualities of the killer (the agent) are the efficient cause (or the active power) of certain qualitative changes, that is, of certain effects (or acts) occurring in the victim of the shooting (the patient) on account of his possession of certain qualities (the frailty of the human body, etc.) representing the material cause (or the passive power). Of course, since the killer and the killed do not come here into a direct physical contact, the action of the killer and the passion of his victim are not "immediate," but "mediate."[40] Thus the killed is the patient and the killer is the agent only due to the action (with respect to the patient) and passion (with respect to the agent) of the gun and of the bullet. But this "progress of causation" is what Hobbes allows for in *all* cases of causality.[41] For example,[42] fire is the cause of heat not only in the bodies immediately adjacent to it but also in such bodies as are adjacent to them. There is no difficulty, too, in applying to human interactions Hobbes's general rule that efficient causes (active powers) are forms of motion: the pulling of the trigger, the firing of the gun, the motion of the bullet all fit into that category. Here, then, is one example to support Hobbes's concluding claim in *De Corpore* that final causes are also efficient causes.[43] Since the purposeful thinking guiding the agent's action of shooting is itself, like all thinking, a form of motion in the brain, it can represent the efficient cause in a chain of mechanical causation culminating with the death of the victim.

Now the interesting thing about Hobbes's analysis of the specifically *human* powers is that the mechanistic account of causes and powers reemerges even within the purely teleological vocabulary adopted by Hobbes for the purposes of explaining human actions as they are viewed by the agents themselves. In the *Elements of Law*[44] Hobbes first speaks of man's natural faculties and powers in a purely mechanistic language. He divides them into faculties of the body and faculties of the mind, and he speaks of them as powers of producing certain future things. On this level, everything here falls under the categories of mechanical causality and can be articulated in these categories. The qualities of mind and body are the "active powers" (the intellectual and the physical capacities of an individual) which, when brought together with certain "passive powers" of this or that patient will produce certain future "acts." When we look at this sequence as being a past one, we need to say, in conformity with Hobbes's terminology, that the act at issue is the mechanical effect of the operation of human faculties viewed as efficient causes. For the individuals themselves, however, the very same causal sequence appears as a teleological one. This is due to the fact that human individuals are interested in bringing about certain *kinds* of effects—the kinds of effects which will contribute to the individuals' ability to stay on the path of continued progress in satisfying their ever emerging desires. From this point of view, something like Hobbes's definition, in *Leviathan,* of natural power as the "eminence" of mind and body becomes indeed indispensable.[45] In both senses, the mechanistic and the teleological, the term "power," when applied to human faculties, refers to the capacity of these faculties to bring about certain future events. But whereas the mechanistic account does not involve any characterization of these powers in terms of a *standard,* the teleological one clearly does. For if my intellectual and physical powers fail to perform at a certain level, they will not be able to bring about the kinds of effects that I find desirable. And so if powers are viewed teleologically (as my "means to some future . . . good"), then their "eminence" becomes part of their definition.

But how do I test that eminence? It is, we recall, a real and not an imaginary eminence only if it withstands the test of measuring itself against the powers of another man. This is why Hobbes defined power as "the excess of the power of one [man] over that of another." The apparent circularity of this definition[46] becomes less troubling in the light of the sentence that follows it immediately in the text and is meant to offer the required clarification; "for equal powers opposed, destroy one another."[47] As it turns out, then, power in the teleological sense is explained through power in the mechanistic sense. My powers can't be genuine powers unless they have a certain *eminence*, without which they would not be able to bring about certain *kinds* of effects. But the powers of the other may prevent my powers from having *any* effects, much less the desirable ones. The other is in a position to do this due to the sheer strength of his brain and his muscle, of his skills and his weapons; briefly, he can do it as an agent in a chain of mechanical causation originating in his motions and culminating in my death. I must define my natural power (*all* my power and hence also my natural power qua eminence of my faculties) as "excess of power" (of power in the sense of sheer mechanical strength that I can marshal) because my essential vulnerability to the mechanical causal chains originating with the motions of the other may nullify all the effectiveness, and hence the eminence, of all my natural powers.

2

The "Chaos of Violence"

Given the natural equality of human agents, their single-minded pursuit of power must degenerate, if not checked by tough political controls, into an open, violent conflict—into that state of war of everybody against everybody characterizing the Hobbesian state of nature.

The equality that Hobbes views as one of the conditions of the universal warfare in the state of nature is the equal vulnerability of individuals to one another. Due to their membership in the same species, human beings' powers and capacities are essentially similar both in the degree and in the quality of their strengths, so much so that the obvious small differences in individuals' natural endowments counterbalance and cancel out each other. Hence the strongest man can be easily overpowered by the force and wiles of weaker individuals. Rejecting Aristotle's claim that superiority and inferiority among human beings are set in nature, Hobbes emphasizes that any such differences can be due only to human intervention, since nature has made all men and women equal by making them equally vulnerable to each other. This equality is, of course, a necessary condition of that universal warfare that Hobbes thinks must break out in the state of nature. Clearly, if some men knew that they are by nature inferior to other men, the former would be unlikely to challenge the latter, and then the state of nature would not be the Hobbesian state of war everybody against everybody. Individuals' equality of condition—their equal vulnerability to one another—is essential to the universality of their conflict, since that equality of condition gives rise to the "equality of hope,"[48] which explains why everybody thinks he is just as good as everybody else—a truly explosive thought, supplying the fuel for the flames of violence in the state of nature.

To the natural equality of men Hobbes adds competition for goods, search for glory, and the ensuing climate of diffidence—working jointly, these causes make the eruption of violence inevitable. Even if some relatively sensible and moderate individuals could manage their competition without a fight, they would be drawn into the latter, if only to defend themselves, by the seekers of glory. And even if they could not be sure whether this or that person is in fact a competitor or a glory seeker, they would still reach for their guns, due to that general climate of diffidence they would be bound to succumb to in the state of nature. And in such a climate of suspicion and mistrust they would be quite rational in striking first, since they would be acting within the prisoner's dilemma type of situation.

But this account—and its various formulations in Hobbes's works—gives rise to several important questions. Is the outbreak of violence due to *reason* or *passion?* At times Hobbes gives the first answer, at times the second, at times both. But the two answers are plainly different, and they seem to be incompatible both in what they mean and in what they imply. For if violence is due to passion—in Hobbes's account the passion at issue is mainly vanity, that is, pursuit of glory[49]—then it seems that the majority of the people in the state of nature would be highly unlikely to succumb to such an irrational behavior, so clearly damaging to their own self-interest. The rational, moderate majority ought to be able to pool their strengths and to control the few glory seekers disturbing the majority's peace and safety. Under such circumstances, however, the state of nature would not be the state of universal warfare: the troublemakers would soon find themselves locked up in prisons and mental hospitals, and the rational majority would go about their business without any need for the Hobbesian Sovereign. On the other hand, if the outbreak of violence is due to reason (i.e., a rational pursuit of self-interest), it does indeed become the fate of everybody, but then reason and pursuit of peace do not go together and this seems to be incompatible with one of the main tenets of Hobbes's philosophy.

The problem is serious, but it arises from a serious, and frequent, misunderstanding of the relation between reason and passion in general and, more specifically, in the philosophy of Hobbes. It is taken for granted that reason and passion are, as it were, two independent and even hostile parts of man. It is assumed, that when I say, "Passion moved me to desire or to do *A*," I mean to indicate that my desire or my action were thoughtless, aiming at the wrong goal or reaching for the wrong means. It is assumed, too, that when I say, "Reason tells me to desire or to do *A*," I mean to say that my rational thought, in its full independence from (and even opposition to) my various passions counsels me to desire or to do *A*. Thus passion is, by itself, blind to reason and thinking; while the latter, when exercised in their proud autonomy, can give me counsels undisturbed by the clamor of passions.

As we shall see in a moment, this picture is entirely at odds with Hobbes's understanding of reason and passion. Passions, for Hobbes—including the passion of glory—are not at all the brute impulses of an individual blind to thinking. They are shot through with a conception and they are guided by their own kind of rationality, adapted to the situation within which they unfold. Conversely, what counts as a rational action is tied up with a certain context which is determined, to a large extent, by the human passions prevailing within it. A change in the agent's way of reasoning about his situation toward other agents is eo ipso a change in his passions; a change in his passions is eo ipso a change in his understanding of what is the rational thing to do in his situation. Considered within this perspective, Hobbes's two ways of accounting for violence— by passion or by reason—are not at all incompatible; indeed, they are the two aspects of one and the same account.

In the *Elements of Law*, Hobbes outlines a theory of passions of the mind as strategies of pursuing and expressing power, strategies endowed with their own rationality. Man is a pleasure-seeking machine, and passions, too, aim at maximizing pleasure and minimizing pain. But the passions of the mind do not search after any pleasure of any kind. These passions bring us (or express) the pleasures and the pains of a particular kind: those that originate in other people's acts of honor or dishonor toward us.[50] Now people honor us when they acknowledge our power.[51] Passions, therefore, both express the power that we have and are ways of achieving more power. For example, laughter expresses the superiority of my power over the power of the other; while the love and fear people feel toward me are additional sources of my power, since those who love me and fear me will offer me service and assistance.[52] Now, if passions are to have this function in my life, every passion I feel must depend upon a *conception* that I have of my power-standing with and among other people. The appropriate conception is not superadded to some "raw feel" of the passion, but is constitutive of the latter. Even the so-called bodily pleasures—which Hobbes opposes to the pleasures of the mind—are, in most cases, dependent upon a conceptual assessment of our power relationships with others. For example, lust and sexual enjoyment are, on the one hand, sensual, but they are also, on the other hand, "pleasure or joy of the mind, consisting in the imagination of the power [men] have so much to please."[53]

Seen within its proper context of a generalized pursuit of power, glory seeking does not seem to be all that irrational. First of all, glory is good in its own right, since its pleasures accompany and express the establishment of my superiority over my opponent.[54] Second, by achieving superiority over the other and inducing him to honor and worship me, I increase dramatically my own power.[55] For this reason the glory-seeking actions, if successful, are highly functional for me. Moreover, the honor and the worship that I achieve by a successful pursuit of glory very often translate themselves into the love and fear others begin to feel toward me—and these passions, as we just noted, represent additional sources of power for me. Even the goods which are merely useful in life are much more easily acquired by dominating and exploiting others than by one's own labor; and hence the acquisition of even those goods is secured more effectively by gaining power over others rather than by cooperating with them in a common effort of work and labor.[56] From every vantage point, then, the actions of the glory seeker are conducive to the increase of his power. Even if he actually kills his adversary in a fight, that action too offers all kinds of gains to the killer. For one thing, the action makes him more honorable in the eyes of others—of the people who have witnessed the killing, or have heard about it, and are therefore prepared to honor the victor. Some-one may reply that in this case it would be useless to the killer to win in an unwitnessed fight. But even this is not entirely true. For a man may very well decide to kill his adversary in order to validate, or to increase, his own self-esteem. This would be one way of showing that his glorying in himself is not based on the illusions of "vainglory," but on the firm facts of life.

It goes without saying that all these ways of pursuing and expressing glory are life-endangering to the glory seeker himself. But to use *this* as the argu-ment for the irrationality of one's passion for glory—on the grounds that the pursuit of glory would be at odds with self-preservation—is to miss the point. To risk one's life may be, under many circumstances, the best way of assuring self-preservation in the long run. The glory seeker is a gambler and he takes a risk which, if successful, will tremendously increase his power and hence also his ability to survive. His choice is not more irrational than the choice of, say, a nineteenth-century California gold digger who had staked everything on an unsuccessful search for gold and who, as a result, finds himself starving on the streets of San Francisco.

To the "irrationality" of glory seeking impulse some commentators usually oppose the "rational" competition for goods. Here, it is claimed, we have a source of conflict which can explain the outbreak of violence not just among (or due to the actions of) a minority blinded by the glitter of glory, but in the bulk of the population. This is not, however, the sort of explanation that can easily be squared with the texts of Hobbes. Whereas *De Cive* puts competition in the first place among the causes of war in the state of nature,[57] in the *Elements of Law* the emphasis is put on diffidence and glory seeking, while competition is relegated to the third, and rather insignificant, place.[58] To be sure, in Hobbes's opus magnum competition is mentioned as the source of war even prior to glory and diffidence.[59] But the term "competition" is then used so broadly as to cover competition for "honor" and "command," that is, that quest for superiority characteristic of glory seeking. And there is nothing surprising about it. For if, relying upon Hobbes's later definition of competi-tion in *Leviathan*,[60] we want to understand by competition our pursuit of "gain," then we will be hard pressed to explain why *this* form of competition (unless taken in the context of an extreme, life-threatening scarcity of goods) would lead to a deadly struggle otherwise than "occasionally" (to use the expression from the *Elements of Law*). Clearly, the "gains" that are needed to secure my self-preservation are not unlimited, and if this is what competition is all about, my very concern about self-preservation will prevent me (and my adversaries) from allowing the competitive contest to get out of hand and slide into an all

out war of everybody against everybody. Conversely, if competition does lead
to such a state of generalized warfare, it is not a competition for gain—but
that other, and much more open ended, competition for honor and superiority, that is, the search for glory. *This* form of contest can expand almost indefinitely and its expansion, although very risky, brings some tangible and visible
benefits to the winners—the service and the assistance of others.

Perhaps the difficulty of reconciling these two Hobbesian meanings of competition will become lesser if it is granted—and Hobbes's argument clearly
points in that direction—that the most deadly forms of what is perceived as
competition for goods are in fact ways of competing for superiority; they belong under the heading of glory seeking. After all, apart from being a "gain"
securing our "commodious living," wealth is also—if not predominantly—a
means of establishing oneself as superior to others. The same could be said
about the other goods of competition listed in *Leviathan,* such as "other mens
persons, wives, children, and cattell."[61] Either one's pursuit of these goods is
limited to the requirements of self-preservation, but then it is hard to see how
(apart from the conditions of extreme scarcity) a life-and-death struggle among
the competitors could be derived from this sort of competition; or the competition for the above-mentioned goods is in fact a channel for expressing one's
drive to assert one's superiority over the others—and only in this case is the
life and death struggle among the participants likely to erupt. But then we are
dealing, once again, with the human impulse to accumulate power by pursuit of
glory. Hegel, it seems, was quite on target in trying to understand the Hobbesian
heritage, for Hegel saw clearly that the seeking of superiority over others is the
cornerstone of Hobbes's view of the state of nature as the state of war.[62]

It can not be denied, of course, that in many passages Hobbes contrasts the
moderate pursuers of self-interest with the immoderate pursuers of glory. Neither can it be denied that the former are often said to be more numerous than
the latter. But there are other passages, and other considerations, which run in
the opposite direction. If glory is of paramount importance only to the few,
then how are we to understand Hobbes's claim that "most men choose rather
to hazard their life, than not to be revenged"?[63] Or what are we to make of
Hobbes's view that ideological differences are the deepest sources of civil war?[64]
Clearly, what is at stake in these ideological conflicts is not some form of
competition for goods, but a threat to one's values and beliefs, that is, a threat
to one's sense of self-importance in comparison with others and hence also a
threat to one's superiority over others, a superiority which is so important to
us, "since all the pleasure and jollity of the mind consists in this, even to get
some, with whom comparing, it may find somewhat wherein to triumph and
vaunt itself."[65] No matter how we look at it, as a source of violence the passion that Hobbes refers to as "pride," "vanity," and "glory" turns out to be
much more important than competition for goods—and not just in intensity

but also in the frequency of its appearance in the bulk of the population.

We can now spell out the connection between passion and reason as far as the rationality of war in the state of nature is concerned. If the majority of individuals—already involved in a competition for ordinary goods—are sucked into the competition for glory, then *diffidence* becomes the prevailing mood of the people. Now, diffidence is a passion,[66] and, like all passions in Hobbes's account, it involves the agent's conception of his power and a strategy to act out that conception. Diffidence belongs to the same family of passions as does despair; despair is one's state (and the corresponding conception) of an absolute privation of hope—that is, of an absolute privation of any expectation of good to come—and diffidence is a degree of despair.[67] But this difference of degree is really the difference in quality. Whereas despair paralyzes an individual, diffidence does give him some active option for coping with his powerlessness. For diffidence is also related to distrust,[68] and the way of distrust is not to place one's expectation of good in the performance of other people but to rely upon oneself.[69] This is why, given the mood of diffidence, it becomes *rational* to engage in preemptive strikes even for the purpose of securing the preservation of one's life and property: "And from this diffidence of one another, there is no way for any man to secure himselfe, so reasonable, as Anticipation; that is, by force, or wiles, to master the persons of all men he can, so long till he see no other power great enough to endanger him: And this is no more than his own conservation requireth, and is generally allowed."[70]

But then how can Hobbes claim that reason will guide people out of the "chaos of violence"? This question itself can be raised on two levels. First, even *within* the Hobbesian state of nature there seems to be enough room for a rational pursuit of peaceful cooperation—Hobbes gives one example of this in his story of the "Foole." Second, the "laws of nature" are precisely the rational maxims meant to light up for us the path of escape from that wretched chaos of violence. On both levels, it seems, reason does not counsel violence but peace and, indeed, some form of justice.

Let us begin with the Hobbesian "Foole"[71] who goes one step further than the original fool from the Bible. While the biblical fool said only "in his heart" that there is no God, the Hobbesian fool says also "there is no such a thing as justice." Even if he is prepared to acknowledge the difference in the meaning of the words "justice" and "injustice," he is not prepared to respect justice in his actions if he finds it detrimental to the pursuit of his goals. If a rational assessment of his self-interest dictates a course of action resulting in a breach of contract, then this is sufficient for him to put aside the considerations of justice as an old wives' tale and to act accordingly, relying only upon his own force and wiles.

Hobbes's first try at educating the "Foole" out of his foolishness is uncontroversial. Hobbes points out that "where there is a Power to make him performe,"[72] the potential violator of the contract would be acting against his own best interest, since he would be exposing himself to legal and legally enforced punishments. This is obvious, but it does not apply to the state of nature, where there is no such "Power" to begin with. It is Hobbes's second reply to the fool that is difficult to square with Hobbes's overall view of the state of nature. For, in effect, Hobbes is now advising the fool to play by the rules even (and especially) in the state of nature; and the argument that Hobbes gives has nothing to do with any considerations of morality, but is couched in a language of a purely prudential rationality. Hobbes first assumes that in the (inherently violent) state of nature no individual will be able to survive "without the help of Confederates"[73]—that is, without becoming a member of some larger defense group meant to guarantee protection to its members. He then goes on to claim that no membership in any such group will be offered to an individual who can be identified as disloyal towards his own (actual or former) confederates. If he breaks a contract with his confederates, word about him will spread around, throughout other defense groups, and he will end up by "not be[ing] received into any Society, that unite themselves for Peace and Defence, but by the errour of them that receive him . . . which errours a man cannot reasonably reckon upon as the means to his security."[74] And so the "Foole" would be well advised to respect the rules within his own defense group.

What are we to make of this twist in Hobbes's argument? Can this reply to the fool be sound given the main outlines of Hobbes's view of the state of nature as the state of diffidence and chaos?

Hobbes tries to convince the fool that the violations of rules he engages in toward members of his own group will become known to members of other groups as well. But how could this happen given the climate of "*perpetual*" and "*general*" diffidence?[75] If Tom does not hold his part of the bargain within his own defense group *A*, why should members of the defense groups *B*, *C*, *D*, and so on believe the stories spread about Tom by members of *A*? Why wouldn't they rather interpret these stories as devious attempts to deprive them of a valuable ally that Tom could become for them? Furthermore, the very reality of such defense groups in the state of nature is highly questionable. Even if they can last for some time, the common bond that holds together their members will be precarious and unstable.[76] Under such conditions it would be quite rational to grab the money and run—as fast as one can, and without any damaging consequences for one's future chances with other (equally unstable and precarious) defense groups.[77] We must conclude that Hobbes's lesson to the fool is incompatible with the bulk of his own theory of the state of nature.

The very same considerations can be brought in to show why the Hobbesian "laws of nature"—those maxims of reason meant to guide us out of the state of nature—can not be implemented even by a *rational* agent as long as there is no change in the underlying situation and in the prevailing passions. When

Hobbes characterizes the state of nature as the state of warfare he does not simply have in mind the outbreak, here or there, of violent clashes between individuals and groups. While *some* manifestations of such clashes must take place, sooner or later, if we are to be justified in our talk about the state of nature as the state of war, much more than that is implied by Hobbes's theory and Hobbes does not shy away from the task of conveying his view in clear and explicit terms. As we recall, the state of war is characterized by its own "time of war"; and this time of war—so different from the time of peace—provides the broadest framework within which *all* human experiences in the state of nature take place. The time of war does not begin with my planning of this or that defense or attack; and the time of war does not end with the ending of this or that battle. The time of war supplies the all-pervasive framework even for the moments free from planning and conducting battles. The way in which I rest, or work, or play is profoundly different at the time of war—when my life is bound to be "solitary, poore, nasty, brutish and short"[78]—than at the time of peace. The passion prevailing during the time of war is the passion of "perpetual" and "general" diffidence.[79] Given this kind of temporal and passionate context defining the state of nature, the "laws of nature" can be no more than desires and intentions of agents thirsting for a better way—rather than the rules of conduct for those agents' actual behavior, even (and especially) if the latter act rationally. In the presocial state, the laws of nature can be valid *in foro interno*, but not *in foro externo*.[80] In the next section I will have more to say about the meaning and the function of the laws of nature as understood by Hobbes. For my present purpose I will limit myself to a brief consideration of some of the arguments that could be made to show that the laws of nature may have at least some actual validity within the state of nature.

One such argument could be built around Hobbes's view[81] that one's nonperformance of the contract is valid only on the assumption of a *justified* fear that the other party will not perform. Sometimes[82] Hobbes puts an even stronger condition upon the fear of nonperformance by one's partner: the fear must be justified by some event that took place *after* the contract was agreed upon. Unfortunately, in the Hobbesian state of nature, every man is the only legitimate judge of what is and is not "justified" for him to fear. Given the mood of diffidence within which every individual views people and events around him, just about anything—a word or a gesture of one's partner, a noise in the woods, and so forth—can give rise to a fear that the individual will consider to be perfectly justified. Can we say, following up on some passages,[83] that it is the "conscience" of the individual that ought to help him to control his inclination to consider all his fears of non-performance by the partner as justified? But Hobbes's entire philosophy shows a deep mistrust of individuals' consciences as guides for action. Even in society, not to mention the state of nature, an individual is capable of justifying anything by an appeal to his own conscience. Hobbes returns to this theme again and again,[84] and his analysis of conscience runs along the same lines as Hegel's later treatment of *Gewissen*.[85] Are we going to say that my conscience would be bound to repress my right to break contracts at least in those cases when my partner has *already* performed first?[86] But even if someone were to be foolish enough to perform first in the Hobbesian state of nature, it would be easy to interpret his move as nothing more than a devious attempt to lull one's vigilance and to take an immediate advantage of this. Given the all-pervasive mood of diffidence, the only question to be considered is the practical one: Who is going to beat whom to the punch?[87]

I began this line of argument in order to show that the separation of "reason" and "passion" is more apparent than real in Hobbes. Under the conditions of the state of nature even the seemingly irrational passion of glory does represent—at least up to a point—a useful strategy of accumulating power, that is, of furthering one's self-interest (including one's self-preservation). Conversely, human rationality is always conditioned by a passion. Given the all-pervasiveness of the passion of diffidence in the state of nature, it becomes quite rational to engage in acts of preemptive violence.

But then our initial difficulty reappears. For if man's reason dictates war in the state of nature, then how can *the very same* reason be depended upon to guide us out of that state? Or do we here confront two *different* kinds of rationality?

I believe we do. The move from the first to the second type of rationality is due to a genuine *conversion* in one's understanding of what counts as rational conduct. It must be added, however, that this radical shift from one type of rationality to another is eo ipso the shift in the underlying passions. This is why it would not be appropriate to describe this shift as being simply "a choice of different rationality."[88] The shift has its "passionate" and its "rational" component. It is a radical, "existential" conversion in individuals' lives. Prior to it, individuals do have an obligation to "endeavor" and to be "ready" for cooperation,[89] but such attitudes can not effect any actual changes in the prevailing state of things.

3

The Laws of Nature

In the depth of the chaos generated by the human bodies' motions in the state of nature, the laws of nature point toward a different, and more effective, mode of human interactions. To the "nothing"—to the constant threat of violent death that was the actual result of every man's unrestricted pursuit of his right to "everything"—there now appears an alternative. An individual may be able to save "something" from the chaos of violence, provided that certain restrictions are imposed upon his and other people's modes of interaction. The pursuit of this new alternative is bound to appear to man as the only way out of the dead end street called the state of nature. This state turned out to be, for an individual, a state of contradiction with himself.[90] His efforts, meant to secure self-preservation under the rule of the right of nature, brought forth the monster of war, where everybody's self-preservation is perpetually threatened by everybody else. Since man continues to find his self-preservation to be of fundamental importance to him, he must be desperately interested in getting out of the state of nature. The laws of nature show the way.

Are they moral or prudential imperatives? After decades of discussion, the Taylor-Warrender interpretation (supporting the first view of the laws of nature) does not look promising.[91] It fails to square with the bulk of Hobbes's writings on at least two counts. It leaves Hobbes's system hopelessly bifurcated, since the deontological and theological layer this interpretation focuses on is at odds with the overall naturalism of Hobbes's approach to man and society. In addition, the interpretation fails to explain the motivational power that the purely moral commands could have given Hobbes's psychology. All indications are that the laws of nature are the imperatives of prudence, even if they are at times[92] called "moral" qua articles of peace.[93]

If this was *all* that had to be said about Hobbes's laws of nature, there would be no cause for any significant controversy around them. But this is certainly not all that Hobbes had to say about his laws of nature. For he also speaks of them as "immutable and eternal."[94] And how could it be that the mere counsels of prudence would ever reach such an exalted status?

This difficulty, some may object at once, stems from a misunderstanding of

Hobbes's terminology. For even though the laws of nature are prudential in the plain, ordinary sense of that term, they are not prudential in the specifically Hobbesian sense of prudence—where "prudence" is opposed to "science"—and hence there is no inconsistency in Hobbes's view of the laws of nature. They are prudential insofar as they indicate the means to our self-preservation, but they are also immutable and eternal, since they are rules of *reason*, and "nothing is produced by Reasoning aright, but generall, eternall, and immutable Truth."[95]

However, the difficulty does not stem from a misunderstanding of Hobbes's terminology. Hobbes himself warns us that reason lacks any substantive content;[96] if we are to avoid falling into the pitfalls of an "absurd" speech we must constantly adapt our reasoning to the material supplied by factual knowledge. But how can *such* knowledge support propositions which deserve to be called "immutable and eternal"?

We have encountered the very same difficulty earlier, in a different context, and we have indicated how it was solved by Hobbes. In the area of *human* interactions, knowledge is both rational and substantive, both necessary and nontrivial. In "reading" myself, I also read the others, and this reading enjoys the epistemic privilege of certainty. If, therefore, the laws of nature could be extracted from such a "reading" of human interactions, then these laws could have the status of eternal and immutable truths without any appeal to the commands of God or conscience (as the Taylor-Warrender thesis would have it).

In the *Elements of Law*, a particularly important law of nature is "*that every man acknowledge other for his equal.*"[97] However, in both *De Cive* and *Leviathan* this law is given less weight on the list of the laws of nature. In addition, in both *De Cive*[98] and *Leviathan*[99] all of the laws are said to express the Golden Rule: "Do not that to another, which thou wouldest not have done to thy selfe"; whereas in the *Elements of Law*, the Golden Rule is also called upon to facilitate the application of what the *Elements of Law* view as a law of nature imposing upon me the obligation to acknowledge the other as my equal.

In spite of these changes, however, the substance of Hobbes's position remains the same. The acknowledgment of the equality of others represents, in Hobbes's ever clearer and unambiguous formulations, a step from an "is" to an "ought": "If Nature therefore have made men equall, that equalitie is to be acknowledged."[100] In the light of the Hobbesian "reading" of others in oneself it becomes clear why the *factual* equality of the other demands a *normative* status. As a member of my own species, the other is a duplication of myself. Thus the very same powers that I have are turned against me in the state of nature. The result is the ever-present threat of death at the hand of the other. It is, therefore, unnecessary to appeal to the framework of pure morality to explain why the other ought to be treated equally. I *ought to* treat him as equal, for he *refuses to be* treated as unequal. I must respect his equality for to deny him that respect is to invite my own annihilation, as I have just discovered by acting out my right of nature in the state of nature. As a force equal to my own, the other forces me to treat him equally. This is what justifies the step from the factual to the normative equality of the other.[101] But to take that step is *precisely* to treat the other in conformity with the yardstick "Do not that to another, which thou wouldest not have done to thy selfe."

The acknowledgment of this equality of the other translates itself immediately into an acknowledgment of his autonomy. As a force equal with my own the other can not be absorbed within my own ends-means sequence. My attempt to treat him, by either force or fraud, as a mere means to my ends will founder, since he is in a position to force me not to treat him that way. I "ought not" to treat him that way since he "is" in principle beyond the grip of all my means. Consequently, whatever uses I may have for him within my own ends-means sequence they can not be bestowed upon him otherwise than through his own consent and agreement. Unlike in Kant, the other enjoys this status of an autonomous being not on account of some "unconditional worth" characterizing him as a "person"; and my acknowledgement of his autonomy is not an imperative of "pure" reason commanding me to strive for the dignity of all persons. The acknowledgment is a response to the equality of forces between myself and the other. This, for Hobbes, is the practical, inescapable foundation of what all moralists have in mind when they teach us, in so many words, that we ought to respect the independence and the autonomy of others. The motivational power behind my acknowledgment of the other's status is indeed prudential: I must take that step from "is" to "ought," since to act on any other assumption is to endanger my life. At the same time, this peculiar step from "is" to "ought" does express some "immutable and eternal" truth about the other. As a force equal with my own he forces me to treat him as an autonomous being.

This is precisely the reason why the master-slave relationship may often prove unstable.[102] As soon as an opportunity presents itself, the slave will challenge the master, his "natural" obligation toward him notwithstanding. Even if it is not quite correct to say that for Hobbes might is right, the obligation of the slave towards the master, although cast in a binding form by the slave's "acknowledgment" of his submission, will be dissolved by the latter as soon as the essential equality of forces between himself and the master reemerges. That the *essence* of their relationship is one of equality is, needless to emphasize, one of the pillars of Hobbes's philosophy. On account of this equality, the master has only two options toward the slave.[103] Either he is prepared to treat the latter as a merely physical force—a force which can be controlled with other such forces (chains, iron bars, etc.)—but then the man in chains has no obligation whatsoever toward the master. Or the master can extract from the slave that "acknowledgment" of his authority, but such an acknowledgment depends upon the master's willingness to give the slave full control over the motions of his body, and, in that case, the master's rule may often come to a quick end.

To conclude again: the normative equality in my relations with the other is grounded in his factual equality with me. I ought not to impose myself upon the other by force or fraud, since he is in a position to force me not to treat him that way. His refusal to be a "means" in my hands imposes upon me the demand to treat him as an autonomous being. For Hobbes, such treatment of the other becomes an inescapable law for me to the extent that I am bent at securing my very being.

This, I submit, is the content underlying and determining all of Hobbes's formal analyses of the laws of nature. Should we sever these analyses' link with their content, we would, inevitably, face faulty or unsupported claims. We would also part with Hobbes's own texts since, as I now propose to show by a close study of these texts, Hobbes never separates his formal analyses from the content they are meant to organize; and, as I will also try to show, only in the light of this essential link between the form and the content of Hobbes's account of the laws of nature can his arguments carry the day.

Hobbes begins his discussion of the laws of nature by contrasting them with the right of nature. The former, he says, are opposed to the latter as obligation is opposed to liberty. Moreover, the obligations expressed by the laws of nature come to be known by us, and become desirable to us, against the background of our better grasp of the right of nature, so much so that the right of nature *itself* is built into the proposition expressing the first law of nature: it is incorporated there as a counsel for the worst-case scenario (if you can't achieve peace, seek war).

I take that to be a very significant indication concerning the status of the right of nature and of its relation to the laws of nature. For if the right of nature can be worded as a proposition which represents a (prudential) ought-statement, then the right of nature itself must be, at least as far as Hobbes's political argument is concerned, a *normative* proposition.

On the other hand, the concept of the right of nature can also be viewed as a purely descriptive concept referring to a human body's unhampered motion in space. This can be gathered even from a careful reading of Hobbes's opening moves in chapter 14 of *Leviathan*. The chapter's first passage can be read as supplying a definition of the right of nature in purely objective terms, without any reference to the normative claims present in the minds of individuals acting on that right. The right of nature is defined as "the Liberty each man hath, to use his own power as he will himselfe, for the preservation of his own Nature; that is to say, of his own life; and consequently, of doing any thing, which in his own Judgement, and Reason, he shall conceive to be the aptest means thereunto."[104] Since the right of nature is defined in terms of liberty—

indeed, "the Right of Nature . . . is the naturall Liberty of man"—and since liberty as here understood is "the absence of externall Impediments,"[105] it seems clear that the right of nature is here viewed as a purely descriptive concept referring to a human body's unhampered motion in space. But there is an obvious difficulty with this: since there never is, or can be, such an unhampered motion in the case of a human body, the concept of the right of nature may turn out to be empty. Hobbes must escape this unexpected difficulty and he escapes it by drawing here in a certain way[106] the distinction between liberty and power. The "externall impediments . . . may oft take away part of a man's power to do what he would; but cannot hinder him from using the power left him, according as his judgement, and reason shall dictate him",[107] that is, in full liberty and in full natural right. Both natural right and liberty (as defined in the present context) are thus beyond any gradation. They are both absolute and admit of no limitation.

As we see, the concepts of natural right and liberty can be interpreted as referring merely to a human body's unhampered motion in space. But the absoluteness of the natural right (and liberty) manifests itself also in a *normative claim* that the agent advances on his own behalf: "Each one not by right only, but even by natural necessity, is supposed with all his main might to intend the procurement of those things which are necessary to his own preservation."[108] In this passage, the "natural necessity" (of human organisms' self-preservative motions) is *contrasted* with the "right" each agent has of securing his self-preservation. As a normative claim, the right of nature is taken by the agent as giving him the permission of actively opposing and excluding other agents in order to assure his being as he sees fit. In the state of nature, the agent will attempt to increase his dominion over other men as much as he sees fit, and "such augmentation of dominion over men, being necessary to a man's conservation, it *ought* to be allowed him."[109] As we shall see later, it is precisely the absoluteness of this subjective, normative claim embedded in the right of nature that generates the political authority as Hobbes envisions it.

The justification of the right of nature qua such a normative claim in the mind of the agent is the proposition that one's being is good, taken together with the proposition that the other is a radical and total threat to one's being. Put in this way, the argument is bound to raise, in the eyes of many, the specter of the forbidden step from "is" to "ought." But this specter would not have represented an occasion for justified fear to Hobbes himself. He would have seen nothing wrong in this move, and he made it quite unashamedly in the last passage I have quoted. It is true, of course, that from the point of view of a disengaged observer—and hence also from Hobbes's point of view as he observes the motions of human bodies—the being or the nonbeing of this or that (or even of every) individual may be a matter of supreme indifference. But for the human agents as they are engaged in the human-life process, such a detached point of view is an abstraction. And so, as observer of men and manners, Hobbes has no qualms in taking the step from *sein* to *sollen:* if death is the supreme evil for me,[110] being is good and (with certain qualifications) it is the condition of my enjoying any other goods. This is the first proposition in Hobbes's justification of the right of nature qua normative claim. Now, death is a threat to my being, but there are all kinds of death. Since my being is finite, its goodness is not incompatible with my "living out the time, which Nature ordinarily alloweth men to live."[111] This kind of death could be found acceptable by individuals as they witness, with ageing, the slow process of decrease of their vitality and zest for life. But there is also another kind of death—that "terrible enemy of nature,"[112] the unnatural, premature and violent death at the hand of the other. This death represents the supreme and absolute evil, for it takes away from us even the finite existence we are given by nature. The other threatens to take away *all* of our being, every bit and shred of it. Since the other is an absolute threat to our being, our right of nature qua normative claim must be absolute too, for it represents only our *response* to that threat of the other: "And *because* the condition of Man (as hath been declared in the precedent Chapter) is a condition of Warre of every one against every one; in which case every one is governed by his own Reason; and there is nothing he can make use of, that may not be a help unto him, in preserving his life against his enemys; It *followeth*, that in such a condition every man has a Right to every thing; even to one another's body. And therefore as long as *this naturall Right* of every man to every thing endureth . . ."[113] In this key passage Hobbes deduces the right of nature from the "condition of Man" and, as a result, he reformulates his provisional definition of this very right. Whereas the opening definition spoke only of the right "of doing any thing" that would preserve a man's life, due to the threat of the other this "any thing" has now become just about "every thing"; and it is *this* definition that is employed by Hobbes in the course of his further argument in the chapter. What does the job for him is precisely the right of every man to literally every thing he can lay his hands on (given the circumstance, that "there is *nothing* he can make the use of, that may not be a help unto him, in preserving his life against his enemys" (emphasis added).

This foundational role, in Hobbes's argument, of every man's right to every thing becomes apparent if we pay careful attention to Hobbes's deduction of the first law of nature: "*As long as* this naturall Right of every man to every thing endureth, there can be no security to any man (how strong or wise soever he be) of living out the time, which Nature ordinarily alloweth men to live. And *consequently* it is a precept or general rule of Reason . . .;"[114] with this "consequently," Hobbes moves on to deduce the obligation to endeavour peace and to seek war only as the last resort measure. Since my being is good, I ought to work toward achievement of conditions under which my being is secure. Such conditions are the conditions of peace. But why, at the present stage of Hobbes's argument, is the opposite of peace—war—a threat to my being ("no security at all")? The answer given in the passage boils down to the unpacking of the status of the other as my ultimate limit. In the condition of war of every man against every man there is no security at all for any man, "how strong or wise he be." No matter how strong or wise I am, I can not enclose the other within my power. And since he is the ultimate limit of my power, he represents—given the conditions prevailing in the state of nature—a total threat to my being. If there is literally "nothing" that "may not be a help" against the other as my enemy in the state of nature, it's because his threat to me is *itself* a total one. If—*per impossibile*—I could exist alone in nature, with all the man-made technologies and weapons left in my hands, I would not confront any enemy who could force me to pass over "nothing" in a struggle with him. Some very definite and limited means would guarantee my security against bears and wolves and fires and snowstorms. However, *nothing* can guarantee my security against a human enemy, and this is why I can afford to neglect "nothing" as a potential part of my arsenal; and even such concern will in the end bring me "no security at all," since any success in my struggle with the other can only be precarious and temporary due to my essential equality with him. As my conspecific, he is a power beyond the grip of all my powers. To ignore that status of his is to invite the loss of my being. Since my being *is* good for me, I am eo ipso obligated to "acknowledge" that equality of the other—not acknowledging it would invite the cessation of my being, that is, something that I "ought not" to allow—and this, once granted, entails the further obligation to treat the other as an autonomous being. But this last obligation is precisely the obligation not to approach the other through force and fraud, but to seek peaceful accommodation with him.

We can now see with more clarity how the step from the factual to the normative equality of the other with me is motivated by the step from the "is" to the "ought" in the case of my own being. Since my being is good, and since treating the other as an element in my own ends-means sequence is a threat to my being—for the other *is* not and *will* not be a mere means to my ends—I am obligated to treat him as an autonomous being. Such a treatment of the other rules out force or fraud and is tantamount to being at peace with him. I therefore have an obligation to seek peace even though in case of lacking any hope of coming to terms with the other I do have the right to assert that "summe of the Right of Nature; which is, *By all means we can, to defend our selves.*[115]

When Hobbes says that his second law of nature is "derived"[116] from the first, he means to say that the content of the second law is already implicitly contained in the content of the first. Such is indeed the case, for the second law makes explicit the idea that was guiding us already in our assenting to the obligation to seek peace and to avoid war as much as we can. War gave us "no security at all" and, Hobbes now adds, "as long as every man holdeth this Right, of doing every thing he liketh; so long are all men in the condition of Warre".[117] And from all this Hobbes will infer the obligation to "*lay down this right to all things; and be contented with so much liberty against other men, as he would allow other men against himself.*"[118] The derivation of the second law is now completed.

The derivation involves implicitly a number of important Hobbesian concepts—of renounciation and transfer of one's rights, of (natural) obligation and justice, and so forth—and it is clear from Hobbes's text that the very meaning of these concepts as *he* uses them is inaccessible outside of the concrete anthropological content they are meant to articulate.

Let us begin with the fundamental ideas encapsulated in the second law of nature as formulated by Hobbes in the passage quoted above. The idea to "lay down this [natural] right to all things" would be meaningless to an individual whose motions would be taking place within a purely natural environment and who would thus be confronted only with non-human, purely natural obstacles. Under such circumstances there would be, of course, certain restrictions and limitations imposed upon the motions of my body—I would be stopped by that huge grizzly bear, would not cross that dangerous river in my way, and so on. But there are different ways of limiting one's motions. The limitations I have just mentioned would not be sufficient to give me the idea of limiting my (natural) right to move anywhere I please. They would represent, at the very best, the temporary adjustments of my body to the equally temporary obstacles hampering its motions within my environment. But I would not view these motions as being hampered *in principle* by such and similar obstacles; in fact, if I were a skilled and well-armed hunter or if I had a boat, my motions would not be hampered by either the grizzly bear or the river. Since my natural right to all things is absolute, to lay down this right I must encounter something that gives me the very idea of the absolute limitation of my motions. Or, to put it differently, to lay down the right to treat every thing as a means to my ends I must first acquire the idea of something that won't be such a means to my ends. And Hobbes is very clear on where this idea stems from: from my discovery of a *human* enemy on my path.[119] Without this discovery I would have, at the very best, the concept of the limitation of my *power*, but—according to Hobbes's opening definition in chapter 14—to view one's power as limited affects in no way one's liberty and hence also one's right of nature. As long as I have *some* power, my liberty and my right of nature are as absolute as ever. Only when, in the light of the threat of the other, I come to see myself as *totally* powerless do I get the idea of being hampered in principle in all of my (actual and possible) motions—and I thereby get the idea of limitation of my liberty. On account of his essential equality with me, the other's power threatens to cancel out *all* of my power, and if all of my power were to be canceled out I would find myself without that "Liberty each man has to use his own power, as he will himselfe, for the preservation of his own Nature". With my power canceled out, my liberty is canceled out too. Thus the liberty I have of using my power as I see fit finds its ultimate and inescapable limit in the liberty another man has of using his power as he sees fit.

In the light of this last statement we can understand Hobbes's definition of what it means to lay down one's right—both the right of nature and, indirectly, any right as well. "To *laye downe* a mans *Right* to any thing, is to *devest* himself of the *Liberty*, of hindring another of the benefit of his own Right to the same."[120] What is involved in that concept of "hindering" the other? How can I divest myself of *any* liberty if, as Hobbes taught me in the opening passages of chapter 14, my liberty is not affected at all by the impediments that curtail my power? To ask these questions is to forget the material introduced by Hobbes in the meantime. I now do have the concept of the limitation of my liberty—and not just of my power—since I have encountered another human power center in my way. Against such a human power center *all* of my powers come to naught, and since in order to have liberty I must have *some* power, I can now conceive of my liberty itself as limited. My liberty (not just my power) is limited by the other. By the same token, my power limits the liberty (not just the power) of the other. Furthermore, this mutual limitation of our liberties refers also (in conformity with Hobbes's definition of liberty) to a certain state of the motions of our bodies in the world: it refers to the objective circumstance that the other may hinder me in, say, taking over that desirable plot of land while I may hinder him in harvesting some trees within the range of my rifle. Thus the mutual limitation of our liberties becomes mapped onto the scale of "more" or "less" where the items measured with that scale are of interest both to me and to the other. For A to "devest himself of the *Liberty*, of hindring" B's benefit of A's right to X, means that A literally "stands out of his [B's] way"[121] insofar as B's motion toward X is concerned. The advantage that B derives from this "is but so much diminution of impediments to the use of his own Right orginall."[122]

We can notice immediately the new, and significant, element in Hobbes's position—his dotting of the i, so to say, on the issue we have just discussed. As of now, the "impediments" are said to diminish or to increase not simply a man's power, but his "Right orginall," that is, his liberty. Whereas, on the first page of chapter 14, Hobbes claimed only that external impediments may "oft take away man's power to do what he would", but would still leave his liberty intact, he now claims that these impediments represent a curtailment of man's liberty; and we have just seen his argument for this claim. Having encountered another liberty competing with my own for such and such range of goods I begin to think of liberty in general as a *quantifiable* thing, as a matter of "more" or "less." Only now do I gain the concept of "divesting" myself of the liberty to lay my hands on this or that good, for only now can I understand what it means to "diminish" or to "increase" my (and the other's) liberty.

This can be done in two ways.[123] I can lay down my right either by "renouncing" or by "transferring" it. I renounce it when I care not about who will benefit from this limitation of my liberty. I transfer my right when the benefit from such a limitation of my liberty goes to a particular person or to a group of persons. When I either renounce or transfer my right I create a (natural) obligation to be "bound" by that renunciation or transfer.[124] And, once again, what it *means* to create and to take up an obligation can only be defined given the underlying material Hobbes has been elaborating upon all along. When I renounce or transfer my right I am "said to be OBLIGED, or BOUND *not to hinder* those to whom such Right is granted, or abandoned, from the benefit of it."[125] Now, as we recall, the very meaning of the concept of "not hindering" the other presupposes the concept of the limitation of one's liberty by the liberty of the other; and that concept, in turn, presupposes the concept of the other as the ultimate limit of one's powers. Such, then, is the context of Hobbes's analysis of (natural) obligation.

When, by a "voluntary act," I lay down my right and create an obligation for myself, it is then my "duty" not to annul that voluntary act of mine by my subsequent actions; should I fail to live up to that duty I will commit "injustice" and "injury."[126] But why must the initial act be voluntary? Certainly not because my commitment ought to originate in an act of "free will"; Hobbes is a firm opponent of indeterminism, and he views a volition as being simply the last, winning, desire in a process of deliberation. If this last desire is (and it is in most cases of our taking up obligations) fear, then fear moves me to lay down my rights and, as Hobbes explains repeatedly in all his major works, I can be said to have done this voluntarily and the obligation is perfectly valid. Why, then, must I make "a Declaration, or Signification, by some voluntary and sufficient signe" of laying down my rights?[127] What is—what could be?— the new element brought into play by any such declaration or signification by words or actions?

What Hobbes refers to as declaration or signification is identical with what he refers to in other contexts as my "acknowledgment" of my renunciation or transfer of a right. Now human beings must acknowledge ("declare" or "signify") the renunciation or transfer of their rights on account of their status as autonomous beings. When *A* grants me a right, he does this in his capacity of a bearer of powers which are essentially equal to my own. In principle, such a power center is not a means to my ends, and so this particular granting of a right ought to be done in conformity with that universal principle even if the granting itself happens to take place on account of my actual superiority. The other must put his "stamp of approval" even when I compel him to grant me his rights by either force or fraud. Thus, when a conqueror enjoys a great deal of advantage over the conquered, a "declaration" or "signification" by the conquered of transferring his rights to the conqueror may not represent much more than an embellishment (although in most cases it does have its own causal efficacy), but it is an important embellishment nevertheless, for it subsumes a contingent, factual relationship of power under the necessary ("eternal and immutable") principle governing the distribution of power among human agents. For this reason, too, all the other forms of laying down one's rights considered by Hobbes (contracts, covenants, free gifts, etc.) must be joined with some way of declaring or signifying one's will.

Let us move on to the next claim put forward by Hobbes as he analyzes the concept of obligation in that densely packed passage of *Leviathan*'s chapter 14. Not only must the laying down of one's rights be a voluntary act, but, in addition, the obligation which I undertake by such a voluntary act can not be made "voyd" by my subsequent decisions and actions.[128] Otherwise, Hobbes goes on to argue, we have something akin to "absurdity," where one's will contradicts "what one maintained in the Beginning".[129] Put in this way, the argument is clearly flawed. I do not "contradict" myself when I renounce my right to *P* in the morning and want to reclaim it in the evening. Not only is there no logical contradiction involved, but even the two acts of will are not incompatible, since they do not occur at the same time. Even *in foro interno*, then—that is, independently of the fact that in the state of nature I would be warranted in resorting *in foro externo* to any "contradiction" in my voluntary acts as long as this way of acting were to serve the purpose of strengthening my security—there does not seem to be any valid reason why the voluntary character of my laying down a right would be sufficient, all by itself, to create a lasting commitment to the obligation thereby undertaken. And yet Hobbes insists that if I annul that commitment I am guilty of "Injustice" and "Injury"—terms which imply clearly some failure to live up to one's duty not simply with respect to oneself (as would be the case in situations where my failure to live up to this or that commitment of mine would not represent any violation of the rights of others), but with respect to other people as well.

Instead of confusing the issue, Hobbes's linkage of the two ideas—of one's failure to endure the course of action taken up by one's voluntary commitment *and* of one's failure to respect the rights of others—allows us to clarify the issue. Let us first pay attention to Hobbes's unmistakable choice of words: when a man has granted his right away, it is then "his DUTY, not to make voyd that voluntary act of his own: and that *such hindrance* is INJUSTICE, and INJURY, as being *Sine Jure;* the Right being before renounced or transferred."[130] The connection couldn't have been made in clearer terms: injustice is not simply a repudiation of one's voluntary act by one's other voluntary acts, but it is such a repudiation inasmuch as it constitutes a "hindrance" to the person(s) who were the recipient(s) of that right. The injustice lies in one's voluntary approach to the other, approach which is here a form of fraud (agreeing not to hinder the motions of the other and then hindering these motions anyway); it is not a formal contradiction, needless to say, but it is the incompatibility in my treatment of the other *given* my concept of him as a being who forces me to treat him as autonomous.

It is still the same context that determines and justifies Hobbes's next, and crucially important, move: whatever we may want to do with our rights, we are in no position to accomplish a valid renounciation or transfer of our right to life and limb. The being and the integrity of our body are thus beyond the pale of any potential bargain.

Hobbes gives at least two arguments for this important claim. Confusing as they are in their own right, they confuse even more insofar as they are applied by Hobbes to what seem to be two independent matters: a man's right to the preservation of his "life" and his right to refuse to suffer "Wounds," "Chayns," and "Imprisonment." It is obvious why these two matters need not go together. A man may find himself in a situation devoid of any danger to his life while sitting in a comfortable prison; and a man may face a threat to his life without running any danger of imprisonment, chains, or even wounds. At times Hobbes considers all of these issues as making up one single case and he gives an argument meant to cover the case as a whole. At times he considers these issues as representing different (if perhaps not independent) cases and he goes on to argue accordingly.

The first argument[131] looks unpromising even when used as a device to convince us not to bargain away our life; and it becomes totally unconvincing when Hobbes uses it to justify our refusal to lay down the right to resist wounds, chains, and imprisonment. The laying down of one's rights is, and must be, a voluntary act. All voluntary acts of the agent aim at accomplishing some good to the agent himself. And so if anyone says, or signals, that he will not resist threats to his life, his words and actions can't be taken at their face value. A sincere renounciation or transfer of one's right to life is a psychological impossibility for man, and hence no man can be understood as engaging in any form of alienation of his right to life. This argument stands or falls with the doctrine of psychological egoism. Since the doctrine itself boils down (especially when tested against cases of voluntary martyrdom for a cause) to being either an empty tautology or an empirically false claim, the argument is unconvincing. Even less convincing is the use Hobbes makes of it to forbid us to lay down our right to hinder the motions of those who are about to impose upon us wounds, chains and imprisonment. Hobbes argues that such motions represent violence against us, and so we can never be sure if they will not result in a loss of our life, the right to which has already been proved (in the first part of the argument) to be beyond the limits of any renounciation or

transfer. Why, we may immediately ask Hobbes, does the threat of imprisonment, chains, or even wounds carry with it the possibility of our death? In
some cases I may actually be better off, in terms of my security, when I sit in
jail, than when I am free on the streets of, say, a city in revolt; and even a
thief having his hand cut off in conformity with Muslim law does not thereby
confront the threat of death. Could it really be, as Hobbes also suggests, that
I could not possibly derive any "benefit" from suffering wounds, chains, and
imprisonment? Certainly I could—sitting in that comfortable jail and watch-
ing the people in revolt from a secure distance.

Hobbes's second argument, however, is built on a much more solid foundation. It represents what is, in effect, a form of transcendental argument unfolding the conditions of possibility of what is involved in the very operation of
laying down one's rights as Hobbes defined this operation at the earlier stage
of *Leviathan*'s chapter 14. The "end" or the proper function of renouncing or
transferring one's rights is one's security. To alienate our right to defend our
life would amount to threatening our security. *Such* an alienation of one's
rights would be incompatible with the very function of one's laying down
one's rights. There would be, of course, no logical incompatibility between the
two, but, given the context of the "condition of Man" in the state of nature
(generalized striving for power in the form of war of everybody against everybody), the condition of possibility of my engaging in *any* laying down of my
rights is my aim to guarantee that minimum of power I will need to secure my
being. We have seen Hobbes's argument for this: if my being is good, and if
the other, insofar as he refuses to be a means to my ends, is a total threat to
my being, then I must treat the other as autonomous and to be ready to come
to peaceful agreement with him by laying down my right to every thing. The
very *concept* of laying down my right was used by Hobbes for the purposes of
articulating the underlying context of the human condition; and, Hobbes now
tells us further, the concept at issue must be linked to that context.

If we accept this last restriction, at least a certain kind of connection can be
seen between Hobbes's refusal to allow us to lay down our right to resist threats
to our life and his refusal to allow us to lay down the right to resist wounds,
chains, and imprisonment. Hobbes himself gives an indication on how to understand this connection in a later passage of *Leviathan*: "No man can transferre,
or lay down his Right to save himselfe from Death, Wounds, and Imprisonment, (the avoiding whereof is *the onely End* of laying down *any* right)."[132]
Thus, the purpose of securing the freedom and the integrity of our body is
here incorporated into the very purpose of *any* operation of laying down one's
right; and this is why, in his earlier formulation of the argument, Hobbes has
defined the "security" that must be left intact by any laying down of rights as
involving also "the means of preserving life, as not to be weary of it."[133]

But how are we to put together all of these claims? In order to secure my being I must have some power, where "power" is a relative and comparative term referring to my standing with and among the others. Now for me to have *any* chance in the race for power, I can not be in a position where my essential equality with the others is destroyed. Were this to happen, I would be *in principle* out of the race for power, since my natural—physical and mental— abilities would be so impaired as not to allow me to participate in the race. But the physical and the mental abilities which make me a viable participant in the race for power are the very same abilities which I have in my capacity as a member of the same natural species as my competitors. They are the (physical and mental) abilities of my *body*. Thus a threat to my body is in principle very different from a threat to, say, my wealth or my weapons. As long as my body is not endangered, I can hope to make a comeback—to make back the money I have lost, or to get another gun, or to lay my hands on some other "means to my future apparent Good." But when my body is threatened, the very condition of my having any power at all is threatened too. This is why[134] Hobbes gives me the right to commit at any moment any crime out of "*Bodily Fear*" while he forbids me—at least outside of the "anything goes" condition of the state of nature—to kill a man who threatens me in any other way. For then the hurt that I am about to receive is "not Corporeall, but Phantasticall";[135] and this, Hobbes thinks, does not represent a sufficient ground for my violent action against the other. Now, to say that a hurt is "phantasticall" can not mean that it is imaginary. If a man steals my new car from the garage, the hurt is by all means real. Neither is the difference between the two kinds of hurt due to the sheer quality of the pain involved; many people would find it preferable to suffer from a wound than from a loss of a parent or a loved one. A damage to my body is more "real" than other damages in the very simple and straightforward sense that my body is the condition of my participation in the only human reality there is—the reality of the race for power. Man is not only a power center, but he is a *bodily* power center; and thus a "bodily fear" is a warning signal that my very capacity to have any power at all is threatened.

Because people have different thresholds of bodily fear,[136] and because the very function of this bodily fear is such that it can not allow the agent the luxury of a long and contemplative assessment of the danger, it is pointless to look for an iron-clad connection between the various restrictions imposed by Hobbes upon the scope of one's laying down one's rights. Rather, these restrictions are to be seen as grouped together as a constellation of circumstances most likely to represent a danger, or an impairment, to our body. It is true that when we think of, say, contemporary Swedish prisons, we have no reason to think of any such danger or impairment. But these are not the kinds of examples that Hobbes had, or could have had, in mind. If he speaks of chains and wounds and even tortures in the same breath that he speaks of prisons, it is because the world around him has established that connection in a fairly convincing way. If the connection is factual—as it obviously is—it is a fact of such a generality that we may forgive Hobbes for not having spent more of his energy on sorting out in imagination the possibilities that he could not have imagined.

It is not my purpose, in this book, to offer a detailed commentary of Hobbes's account of all the laws of nature. They are all applications of the Golden Rule. They all express the demand that the other be treated as autonomous; and, as I have tried to show, this demand is grounded in the other's status as a power center beyond the grip of all my powers. If I am to remain in the race for power, I must respect his equality and independence and act accordingly.

But what does this mean, apart from being merely a thought entertained *in foro interno*? How can I gain any advantage over the other while being confronted with (and having to acknowledge) his autonomy? The entire Hobbesian picture of the human quest for power seems to be a paradox: I must try to gain that coveted "excess of power" over someone whose generic identity with me renders all my efforts to that effect entirely ineffectual. I can not gain any power over the other unless I treat him as fully equal and fully independent; thus in gaining any power over him I can not violate that equality and that independence of his. And this means that I can not have any power in excess of his power—not in any lasting and secure fashion—unless he, in his full equality and independence, puts a stamp of approval upon it. But why would he *want* to do that—to put himself willingly at a lasting disadvantage in the never ending drive for power? And how *could* he do that, since doing so would mean that a force equal to me and independent from me decrees itself out of that equality and independence? But then again: If the other has no incentive and no capacity to acknowledge himself as a force lesser than my own, the entire Hobbesian race to stay ahead of the other turns out to be an absurdity.

The race is an absurdity in the state of nature, but it is not an absurdity in society. The race is an absurdity in the state of nature, and thus the mental attitude of an agent involved in that restless pursuit of power must, sooner or later, appear to him as a violation of the principle of excluded middle. He is aware of the essential equality of the other *and* attempts to make himself unequal with the other. If he is lucid about the situation, he can only act with a paradoxical, "hope against hope" state of mind, which can not last for long; if he is not lucid about the situation, the resistance of others will soon educate him to the reality of their equality and independence.

The absurdity of the human race for power will be resolved within society. The sovereign is the representative of all citizens. Consequently, if *he* validates an inequality between myself and the other, that inequality is eo ipso validated by the other, since the other finds himself in the person of the Sovereign. The equal treatment of the other demanded from me by the laws of nature is lived

up to due to these laws' actual existence as *civil* laws[137] and due to the power
of the sovereign behind them; but the very same factors are also responsible
for the emergence of a framework within which my superiority over the other
can be acknowledged by him. Inequality begins with society, for society is, in
effect, an arena within which what is equal can become unequal.

In effect, as the representative of the other—of all the others making up my
society—the Hobbesian sovereign puts the other's "stamp of approval" upon
what I do and what I have. Insofar as my condition is acknowledged by the
sovereign, it is acknowledged by the other; and this acknowledgment expresses
the status of the other as an autonomous being. Consider, again, the case of
honor. All pleasures of the soul, Hobbes teaches, are derived from having one's
power honored by the other as being superior to his power. But there is a
significant difference between achieving that superiority within the state of
nature and within society. In the state of nature I am free to establish myself
as superior to the other in any way I choose; in society, honor must be achieved
through appropriate channels.[138] Only then will my honor be acknowledged
and recognized by the other. And only then will this honor reflect a solid and
lasting increase of my power. For if I pursue and achieve honors in so many
ways open to me in the state of nature, my achievements will be at the mercy
of any shift in the inherently unstable correlation of forces between myself and
the other. I may either force him or trick him into honoring me, but on
account of his essential equality with me I must count with a constant possibility of seeing that honoring disappear as soon as (and that means, in the
state of nature, at any moment) that equality is reestablished again, after being
temporarily eclipsed by this or that success of mine. In the state of nature,
then, I can not have any lasting acknowledgment of my superiority by the
other, since I can not hold down a force equal to my own. Being essentially
beyond the grip of all my powers, the other refuses to be a means to my
end—in this case, to my end of extracting honor from him. If his honoring is
to have any lasting worth, it must be such an honoring in which, and in spite
of which, the other remains fully autonomous. This happens when I achieve
honor in socially acceptable ways, that is, in conformity with the rules laid
down by the Sovereign or, at the very least, in ways which are implicitly accepted by the sovereign. Since the other finds himself represented by the sovereign, the other's stamp of approval is behind every bit of honor I achieve in
those socially acceptable ways. Only then does the other approve of my superiority while at the same time preserving his status of a force equal to my
own—of a force which imposes itself against me as an autonomous being,
remaining in principle beyond my control.

The very same considerations apply to Hobbes's view of *property* as dependent entirely on the sovereign.[139] In the state of nature I can, of course, have
possessions—a plot of land, a house, and so on. I need not worry about hav-

ing them "recognized" as mine by the wild animals that live in the area. This is not due simply to the fact that bears and wolves do not speak and have no intelligence. My lack of worry stems from their physical inability to do anything that would affect my condition. As long as I have a gun, they are all "means to my ends." The other changes all that, for he matches my gun with his gun, and my skill with his skill. I can't lock up his power in a place where it would not be a danger for what I consider to be "mine." Unless I can be sure that he himself, in his very capacity of a power beyond the grip of all my powers accepts this land and this house as mine, they are not actually mine, but up for grabs in a field of forces where my defenses and controls may be destroyed at any moment. Asking the other to "recognize" my possessions as my property—the recognition which is granted to me by the other through the actions of our common sovereign—is not a luxury of pure morality, mysteriously superimposed upon my ordinary desires. It is a matter of necessity, given the other's essential equality with me.

The obligation to treat the other as equal and independent and to "respect" his autonomy is not a moral obligation if morality is opposed to self-interest. On the contrary, the step from the factual to the normative equality will be taken by me because not taking it would spell disaster for my self-interest. In this sense the obligation is prudential. On the other hand, Hobbes does leave room for some rare "noble" natures[140] whose motivation for justice would be different from prudence. If it is not prudent to treat the other as means to my ends, this is due to an important *truth* about the other; and I may be capable of acknowledging that truth independently of my prudential concerns.

This last circumstance, however, has no bearing upon the problem of how to translate the laws of nature from their shadowy (*in foro interno*) status in the heads of the people onto the firm (*in foro externo*) stage of the public world. Hobbes refuses to cross that abyss on such a fragile bridge as the nobility and generosity of the few (who would, inevitably, share the fate of Don Quixote). We need a firm and solid bridge, supported by the many. But how can such a bridge be built in the state of nature, where the governing passion remains that "perpetual" and "general" diffidence, and where the right of nature reigns supreme? Even if it were granted that the individuals, exhausted and horrified by the trials of war, have already established some verbal agreement to choose a sovereign—*any* sovereign—how would they be able actually to obey him, since he would still lack effective power and since nothing but his effective power could put an end to the prevailing state of war? From a purely rational point of view—and given the kind of rationality operative in the state of nature—a solution to this "coordination problem" is impossible.[141]

Without the emergence of the sovereign, however, the individuals remain in the state of nature, the state of nature remains the state of war, and the state of war remains what it was all along: a state in which an individual views himself as having the right to everything only to end up with having really the right to nothing. This contradiction in the Hobbesian state of nature is very similar to the contradiction in the Hegelian sense-certainty, but it puts the individuals in an even greater bind than the one applied to them by the reversal of sense-certainty in the *Phenomenology of Spirit*.[142] For the blind alley of the Hegelian sense-certainty can be escaped from due to the power of reason alone, drawing the appropriate conclusions from the failures of sense-certainty and proceeding to establish a more adequate standard of knowledge. But the power of reason is inadequate to perform a similar feat to get us out of the Hobbesian state of nature. To be sure, reason can and does observe the contradiction of the state of nature and reason does draw the appropriate conclusions from its observations. But these conclusions (the remedy to the state of nature is the laws of nature) remain valid only *in foro interno*. The new, cooperative rationality will not take root in the objective world of human interactions without a certain special *event* first taking place.

4

The "Mortall God"

As I suggested earlier, the actual emergence of cooperation is due to a radical *conversion* in the individuals' passions and modes of reasoning, so much so that Hobbes is forced to speak of the new "artificial reason and will" underlaying man's social existence.[143] The passion that wins over our diffidence toward each other is the passion of confidence (or trust) in the protection of the sovereign. Analyzing sovereignty by institution, Hobbes says that it takes place "when men agree amongst themselves, to submit to some Man, or Assembly of men, voluntarily, *on confidence* to be protected by him against all others".[144] Now, trust (or confidence) is the opposite of distrust (or diffidence).[145] Since, as we recall, the rationality of war depends upon the underlaying passion of diffidence, the removal of the latter makes possible the actualization (*in foro externo*) of the new conception of what counts as rational conduct. The new atmosphere of trust makes possible the actual emergence of cooperative rationality.

I am not forgetting, of course, the role of *fear* in Hobbes's account of the step from the state of nature to the state of society. Man's fear of death at the hands of others remains the main motivation behind his flight from the state of nature. Still, taken all by itself, the passion of fear is not sufficient to propel man onto the path of cooperation. Reason must show man "a better way," the way of the laws of nature; and for that better way to translate itself from a set of imperatives valid only *in foro interno,* into a set of rules governing human interactions in the public world, another passion is necessary: the passion of confidence. With the shift from diffidence to confidence people are capable of finding a different way of actually *responding* to their fear of violence.

At this point of my argument I can only outline what I think is the correct reading of Hobbes's view of the relationship between the state of nature and the state of society. More detail will be supplied as I move on to analyze some of the key Hobbesian concepts and arguments. Here, then, are the bare bones of what I think is Hobbes's view.

It is true that "*man to man is an errant Wolf*"; but it is also true that "*man to man is a kind of God*"—this is the contrast with which Hobbes begins his *Epistle Dedicatory* to *De Cive.* And he goes on to elaborate: Man is a kind of

43

God to man in a political community, in a state, where "there is some analogy of similitude with the Deity; to wit, justice and charity, the twin sisters of peace"[146]. For the state itself is a "Mortall God," and these Godlike qualities of the state are present in individuals qua citizens.

We are dealing here, it seems to me, with the key metaphors of Hobbes's political theory. These metaphors must be taken seriously and unpacked. The establishment of the state is due to people's coalescence around their sovereign. This coalescence of individuals results from their new way of feeling and reasoning about their self-interest. Individuals now make themselves totally dependent, for assessment and pursuit of their self-interest, upon the sovereign. Since their self-dependence brought them nothing but disaster—indeed, it brought them face to face with the ultimate "nothing" of a violent, untimely death—they leave behind both the passion and the reasoning of that self-dependent way of life. They lose themselves as self-dependent only to find themselves as dependent upon the sovereign: "They cohaere together; but they depend onely on the Sovereign, which is the Soul of the Common-wealth; which failing, the common-wealth is dissolved into a Civil war, no one man so much as cohearing to another, for want of a common Dependence on a known Sovereign."[147] This "common dependence" upon the sovereign appears to represent an exchange of power for powerlessness, but it is, in fact, the very opposite. For the power that the individuals enjoyed in the state of nature soon proved to be entirely spurious, and it was already on its way to becoming that "nothing" closing in on them from within the chaos of violence. To avoid that fate, it was necessary to extirpate its root—the total self-dependence of individuals. But, of course, to do that it was necessary to abolish the entire state of nature. By accomplishing this feat, the individuals have not exchanged power for powerlessness but have created the only conditions under which their power is not totally precarious and momentary.

Accordingly, within the mortal god that the individuals have created, the *time* of their striving for power gains continuity: the sovereign assures a genuine *creatio continua* to lives that would otherwise have remained exposed and vulnerable at any moment. And the *causal necessity* embodied in human interactions—the necessary impact that individuals qua "agents" have upon other individuals qua "patients"—becomes, due to the sovereign's controls, redirected in such a way as to assure the conditions conducive to individuals' secure accumulation of power.

Among the many possible objections that can be immediately addressed against this position, one objection stands out as particularly obvious: if individuals, by what amounts to an irrational leap of faith, place their fate in the hands of the sovereign, then what happens to their unconditional right to preserve life and limb, since Hobbes argues repeatedly that *this* right remains beyond the pale of any sovereign? On the other hand, any refusal to surrender one's right to defend life and limb against the power of the state leaves room for the individual's reliance upon his own private judgment and is therefore incompatible with the newly established authority of the sovereign. For if I can refuse to submit to that authority when *I* interpret its actions as representing a threat to my life and limb, then my judgment is not based on any public standards—for those are established by the sovereign—and then we are back to the state of nature in my relations with the sovereign and, through him, with other members of the community. Thus the cases which, according to Hobbes, give me the right to refuse submission to the sovereign (when I may suffer wounds, imprisonment, torture, starvation, etc.) seem to open Pandora's box. What kind of imprisonment (two days? two years?) would be sufficient to warrant my rebellion? Or where do I draw the line as far as starvation is concerned? Even the fear of wounds seems to be left to my private assessment, since Hobbes holds that people have different thresholds of fear and so my assessment of this or that action of the sovereign as being likely to result in my wounds seems to depend, at least to a signficant degree, upon my private judgment.

If a thinker of Hobbes's caliber has never paid much attention to such an obvious objection, it is because the objection—how can an individual preserve his right to defend his life and limb even while acknowledging the sovereign's authority over him—is misconstrued. It "is not a serious demonstration of the inadequacy of Hobbes's doctrine".[148] There can be no question, of course, of surrendering my right to defend my life and limb, but in some sense, there is no need for such a surrendering. The right is not surrendered, but it is activated only when I see my life and limb actually endangered either by the actions of the sovereign or by his inability to defend me against other men. But under those circumstances the function of the sovereign has already broken down for me in the sense in which we say that "the spell is broken." I then suffer a relapse into my old, pre-social self and, in a Gestalt switch of passion and rationality, I activate my natural right to defend my life and limb.[149] But "while the spell lasts," while the security of my existence is assured within society, that option is put on the back burner and its presence there does not influence my behavior.

The essentially irrational creation of the sovereign—and hence also of society—has recently been analyzed as a phenomenon of self-fulfilling prophecy.[150] Just as the beliefs of many people to the effect that, say, there is a political and economic crisis around the corner may make that belief come true due to the actions undertaken by the people acting on it, so too, many people's actions in conformity with their belief that *A* has the authority to command them will in fact confer such a function upon *A*. The flow of power toward *A* is due not to an independently valid obligation to obey *A* but to certain facts about the human agents involved in the process of establishing sovereignty; and these facts—the human confidence in *A* as their savior from a violence they are bound to unleash against each other without him—come to supply the causal factors needed to explain the emergence of sovereignty.[151]

An immediate advantage of this account is that it allows for a continuity between the natural and the political obligations. Take the slave's obligation toward his master. Hobbes's account of it is, invariably, the same. When, after their struggle, *A* grants *B* the gift of life, and when that grant is followed by *B*'s "acknowledgment" of his indebtedness to *A,* then *B* has thereby taken upon himself a (natural) obligation to obey *A.* *B*'s acknowledgment of *A*'s authority over him supplies a causal factor contributing to the actual establishment of *A*'s right to rule *B.*

The continuity between the natural and the political obligations needs to be stressed, but the discontinuity must be kept in mind, too. While the formation of a political community involves also the twin phenomena of a gift of life by *A* and the acknowledgment of that gift by *B, C, D,* and so on, something else takes place too—something that did not take place in any of the natural obligations and can not be explained as due simply to the huge number of people involved in the formation of the state. Only the latter is a mortal god. Only in the latter does the obligation gain a quasi-religious quality. Only in the latter do we witness the dawn of a new form of life, with that "artificial reason and will" announced by Hobbes in the introduction to *Leviathan.*

It is often said that the political philosophy of Hobbes represents a secularization of Christianity, insofar as some of Hobbes's basic concepts are borrowed from the conceptual framework of Christianity and then reforged within his naturalism. Hobbes's account of political power is an excellent example of how much truth there is to this view. The institution of the sovereign, says Hobbes, is "like a creation out of nothing by human wit";[152] and, he adds immediately, this human *creatio ex nihilo* takes place when man finds himself in "an estate of enjoying nothing."[153] When the chaos of violence turns out to be a dead end street, when the people are brought face to face with the "nothing" of a violent death, they are shaken down to their very foundations, and then, in a radical conversion of their feeling and thinking, they create, through their own beliefs, the mortal god to save them from the chaos of violence.

This Hobbesian secularization of religious concepts is behind some of the key moves and positions adopted by him in the course of formulating his theory.

Let us take his argument for the absolute power of the sovereign. The argument[154] relies upon a demonstration of the practical impossibility of attributing only limited power to the sovereign. Hobbes first explains what he means by absolute power: it is the kind of power each and every individual has over himself in the state of nature. Given this understanding of absolute power, Hobbes goes on to outline the main body of his argument. The argument boils down to a demonstration of the impossibility of a regress in the distribution of power. If *A* were to exercise power within a state, and if *A*'s power were to be limited, then somebody else would have to impose these limits upon *A*. If the power of the limiting authority (say, *B*) was in turn limited, then somebody else (say, *C*) would have to limit it. But in this case we either have a vicious infinite of a never to be completed series of powers, or we must come to the actually given final term which, qua final, can only be endowed with an unlimited power. Why, one may ask immediately, couldn't the infinite regress be stopped by some laws and regulations everybody would be bound to obey? Given Hobbes's view of man, this question has hardly any meaning. Who, after all, would be the enforcer and the interpreter of those laws and regulations? Either there would be one single authority to do this—but then *it* would enjoy the unlimited, absolute power (it alone would determine the moral standards, the policies to be pursued, etc.)—or there would be several seats of authority checking and balancing each other, but this, for Hobbes, is an invitation for anarchy and civil war. Since no cooperative behavior between individuals and groups is possible if they are given the opportunity to use their power as *they* see fit, any fragmentation of power bears the seeds of a slide toward the chaos of violence; and hence to avoid that slide the sovereign's power must be absolute in the sense in which Hobbes has just explained it to us: as absolute as the power of the individual over himself in the state of nature.

But this absoluteness of the sovereign's power is defined by Hobbes in still another way. It must be, he says, "as great, as possibly man can be imagined to make it".[155] How are these two definitions of absolute power related to each other? Could not a sovereign enjoy absolute power in the sense of the first definition while still falling short of the standard set down by the second definition? Or are the two definitions equivalent?

They are indeed. As Hobbes told us, within a state individuals "cohaere together; but they depend onely on the Sovereign . . . the Common-wealth is dissolved into a Civil war . . . for want of a common Dependence on a known Sovereign".[156] This passage allows us to grasp the link between Hobbes's two definitions of absolute power. Insofar as I act within the state of nature, I am the ultimate authority in determining and pursuing whatever power I deem necessary to secure my interest. In converting to society I divest myself of my "natural" self-dependence by making myself dependent upon the sovereign. I must do this *without holding back* any part of that self-dependence, since I would then relapse into exercising my private judgments about determining and pursuing power, and this would bring me on a collision course with the others and hence also, as Hobbes sees it, on the path to civil war. And so, given the human condition as seen by Hobbes, his two definitions of absolute power are not logically independent: (1) the sovereign does have the kind of power that man enjoys in the state of nature, and (2) his power is the highest

men can possibly make, since they endow their sovereign with every shred of
their independence by making themselves dependent "onely on the Sovereign."
They *lose* themselves (entirely) as self-dependent only to *find* themselves as
depending (entirely) upon the sovereign.

We can discover the very same line of thought running through Hobbes's
treatment of the concepts of "authorization" and "representation"—two key
components of his account of sovereignty. The way in which Hobbes uses
these components to build his account, the functions that he assigns to them
in supporting his entire theory of sovereignty reflect his need to find a conceptual
articulation for man's conversion into a social being. Even the central claims
that Hobbes puts forward are incomprehensible when taken out of that context.

This applies, first of all, to the very meaning of Hobbesian "authorization."
The authorization that he speaks of is not an ordinary authorization. The political authorization is very special, for its conditions are such that *all* actions
of the sovereign are recognized as *our own*.[157] We do not view them as an alien
necessity we are helpless to master even though, at the same time, we do not
keep some right to "dismiss" the sovereign. Now, to endow the sovereign with
this kind of authority, the underlaying authorization must be, says Hobbes,
given "without stint": "Every man giving their common Representer, Authority from himselfe in particular; and owning all the actions the Representer
doth, in case they give him authority without stint: Otherwise, when they
limit him in what, and how farre he shall represent them, none of them owneth
more, than they gave him commission to Act".[158] When we put together the
claims encapsulated in this remarkable passage we don't need any extended
commentary to find ourselves on the terrain we have become familiar with
while analyzing Hobbes's argument for the absolute power of the sovereign.
Two claims are involved here. First, the power of the sovereign does not hover
over and above the individuals as a fate alien to their own lives. The sovereign's actions are *my* actions (if only because I am said to "own" them); and,
far more important, this identification with the sovereign applies not just to
this or that action that he takes, but to everything he does qua sovereign; it
applies to *all* of his actions qua sovereign. Second, I can achieve this kind of
identification with the sovereign only when I (and the others) authorize him
"without stint", that is, without holding back the slightest shred of authority
over my actions. For were I to hold back some independent authority of my
own, I could always fall back upon that island of authority and to judge the
actions of the sovereign from a transcendent standpoint—but then it would
not be the case that I would have to identify with *all* of his actions; I could
very well disavow some of them if I were to find them wanting in the light of
my own standards. The authority of the sovereign is to be total, and so to
establish it I must abdicate all of the authority *I* have—at least for as long as
the sovereign will continue to discharge his function of guaranteeing my secu-

rity. Thus the two claims we have just seen put forward by Hobbes are not logically independent. If I am to find myself (entirely) in the sovereign, I must lose myself (entirely) as the self-dependent agent that I am in the state of nature.

But there is more. The sovereign is not only an extension of myself (insofar as I identify with *all* of his actions), but he is, in a sense still to be defined, a posit, or a product, of my activity of authorizing him. It is in this "creative" sense that I am the "author" of the sovereign: "Every particular man is author of all the Soveraigne doth and consequently he that complaineth of injury from his Soveraigne, complaineth of that whereof he himselfe is Author".[159] I am the one who—together with other members of my community—brought the sovereign *qua* sovereign into being. And, once again, the idea of this truly creative process of setting up the sovereign must be viewed as indispensable in Hobbes's acocunt of sovereignty. For if I must divest myself *entirely* of that old, asocial self that I was, or continue to be, as a self-dependent, state-of-nature agent, then the identity I am about to take up must be a newly created identity. This is why Hobbes describes the institution of the sovereign as a true feat of the human *creatio ex nihilo*.

The medium of that feat is language. The distinguishing mark of *every* linguistic representation is, we remember, its lack of any natural connection with what it represents. Whereas a sensation, an image or a thought can be traced back to objects acting upon our sensory apparatus, names are imposed upon objects by acts of human will. When A becomes nominated ("named") sovereign, his function of "representing" $B, C, D \ldots$ is attributed to him through the linguistically conditioned process.[160] But this attribution is not an *ordinary* attribution of a name to an object. The lack of any natural connection between words and things is here seized upon and used as an opportunity for manufacturing a thing from the power of words. The word becomes *constitutive* of its object; and thus the human capacity for absurd speech brings unexpected fruits. In the plain, ordinary sense, every individual is the only authority on the issue of his security. There can be no *natural* connection between my (or anyone else's) security and the sovereign's function of guaranteeing that security. But in spite of that, the very process of many people "naming" A to be the guarantor of their security has led to the actual emergence of A in precisely that capacity. The word has become flesh; and, for once, the human propensity to make "absurd" speeches has proved to be instrumental in bringing about what is in fact man's greatest achievement, since the creation of the political community "resemble[s] that *fiat*, or the *Let us make man*, pronounced by God in the Creation."[161]

Given this general background of Hobbes's moves, it becomes possible to sort out the details of his theory of representation and authorization. The concept of representation is used by Hobbes to explain the idea of a "person," which he defines as follows: "A Person, is he *whose words or actions are consid-ered, either as his own, or as representing the words or actions of an other man, or of any other thing to whom they are attributed, whether Truly or by Fiction.*"[162] When my actions and words are considered as my own I am, Hobbes goes on to explain, a "natural" person; when, in contrast, my actions and words repre-sent the actions and the words of someone else, I am an "artificial" person. In both cases the word "person" refers to one's presence (one's "persona") on the stage of the public, intersubjective world. Furthermore, when the words and the actions of an artificial person (of *A qua* representing *B*) are "owned" by the man he represents, the former is said to be authorized by the latter and the relationship between them is said to be the one of an "author" to his "agent."

The authorization of sovereign by his subjects shares its formal structure with the cases of ordinary authorization, but its content is entirely different; and, I shall argue, it is the content, not the mere form of political authoriza-tion, that plays a decisive role in Hobbes's theory.[163]

We have already noted how individuals' beliefs concerning the capacity of *A* to act as their savior from violence materialize themselves in an actual emer-gence of *A* in precisely that capacity. Through this process, we must now add, individuals set up a power that changes *them* from what they were as initiators of the process; thus the individuals are literally products of their own activity of authorizing the sovereign. They are changed from a "multitude" into a "unity;"[164] and this unity emerging from the process of political authorization is not the merely verbal unity of particulars falling under a common name ("the British", "the French," etc). The unity here accomplished is even "more than Consent, or Concord; it is a reall Unitie of them all, in one and the same Person."[165] We have encountered this "real unity" before. It is the same unity due to which individuals were said to "cohaere together" in their dependence "onely upon the Sovereign."

In order to impose that real unity upon a multitude of individuals, the sov-ereign must be a particular entity—preferably one person, at the very least an assembly of persons—set over against them. Individuals can not achieve a real unity on their own. While Hobbes was toying with this possibility in the *Ele-ments of Law*, he came to abandon it altogether in his later works. At the root of this progressive clarification of Hobbes's view is, of course, his nominalism. For if Hobbes—like Hegel and Marx later on—were to allow for the possibil-ity that individuals themselves might coalesce into a real unity, then human individuals could not be viewed as mere particulars, but they would have to be viewed as endowed with a social, universal dimension. The difference between the state of nature and the state of society would then have to be toned down, if not altogether abolished, and Hobbes would find himself on a slide toward the Aristotelian view of man as a social being, even if that social essence of man were to be conceived—contrary to Aristotle and more in line with the spirit of modernity—as emerging from a historical process. But Hobbes is emphatic in rejecting any view of man as essentially social, and he gives a long list of reasons to support his position.[166] Thus the real unity must be imposed upon individuals by a particular power center acting upon them from outside. And this is precisely the function of the sovereign as he is posited by the individuals themselves through the process of political authorization.

The process itself takes place when individuals *"conferre all their power and strength* upon one Man, or upon one Assembly of men, that may reduce all their Wills . . . onto one will."[167] Now, this idea of individuals' "conferring" all their powers upon the sovereign constitutes the very core of the Hobbesian view of authorization. It also gives rise to a serious difficulty which can not be removed without taking into account the specific content of the political authorization.

By the time Hobbes begins to speak of authorization as a process of "conferring" powers upon the sovereign, he has already introduced a host of closely related, but still insufficient, notions—especially the notions of renouncing and transferring one's rights. In some sense, the authorization of the sovereign does involve individuals' renouncing and transferring their rights to the sovereign. The rights that are renounced and transferred through the authorization of the sovereign boil down to a single "Right of Governing my self."[168] This right does not represent any new addition to Hobbes's conceptual arsenal but is identical with the right of nature. Hobbes had already explained, at an earlier stage, the difference between renouncing and transferring one's right in general. When I simply renounce my right to *P*, I do not care who will inherit or take over that right. But when I transfer my right to *P*, I mean to give that right to a specific person or group of persons. When we apply these definitions of renouncing and transferring to the process whereby we yield our right of nature to the sovereign, we still fall short of that "conferring" of our strengths and powers upon the sovereign. By renouncing or transferring (granting) my right, I am only obliged "not to hinder those to whom such right is granted."[169] It is enough that I refrain from impeding the motions of the sovereign for the renunciation and the transfer of my right of nature to take place.

As I noted, in some sense this renouncing and transferring of one's right of nature to the sovereign is the necessary condition of the emergence of the sovereign. But it is not yet its sufficient condition. It is the necessary condition of the sovereign's emergence, for unless the sovereign enjoys the "unimpeded" motion within the state, he can not discharge his function of protecting men from each other. It is not yet the required sufficient condition, for the activities of the sovereign within the state appear to me not simply as motions which I have no right to impede, but as being in some sense *my* motions, since I am somehow positively involved in all the actions of the sovereign—all of them are *my* actions. Thus the power of the sovereign is *my* power; and this should not come as a surprise to us, since we have already explained how the power of the sovereign does not represent, to individuals, an alien necessity, but, instead, the anchorage of their own identity as they "cohaere together" in their newly established real unity.

The difficulty involved in Hobbes's talk about individuals' "conferring" their power and strength upon the sovereign can now be fully brought out. The flow of power away from the individuals and toward the sovereign is not a natural, physical process, since power itself is not something that could be conferred in such a direct, natural way.[170] Now if the setting up of the sovereign by individuals consisted only in their renouncing and transferring their right of nature, then the difficulty would be manageable, for the shift of power toward the sovereign would amount to no more than individuals' readiness not to impede the motions of the sovereign. But authorization qua "conferring" of power upon the sovereign involves more than that. It does not merely represent a voluntary limitation of one's motions vis-à-vis the motions of the sovereign, but a positive involvement of one's power in the activities of the sovereign. But then the difficulty reemerges. For if the flow of my power toward the sovereign can not be understood as a physical process, what kind of process is it?

The difficulty is real enough and it is even unavoidable if the relation between the sovereign and myself is seen as sustained by an *ordinary* authorization—by the sort of authorization where the author and the agent are brought together in an external relation established for some limited purposes and operating under some specific and restricted rules. In all such cases, the agent's doings remain firmly under the author's control. Now, it may be that for some the ordinary meaning of authorization and representation is the only one that ought to be allowed—and then the specifically Hobbesian meaning of those terms can only give rise to an astonishment.[171] And there may even be good reasons in Hobbes's own philosophy of language to take such a dim view of the way in which he handles the concepts of authorization and representation when he uses them to explain the emergence of political authority. On the other hand, Hobbes's political philosophy as a whole ceases to be comprehensible unless we allow for a possibility of words becoming flesh in the process of the human *creatio ex nihilo* of the sovereign. And whereas the ordinary meaning of authorization and representation does not allow us to conceptualize that process, it is Hobbes's hope to be able to build upon those words' ordinary meaning and to deepen it to such a degree as to allow his readers to achieve a measure of understanding of how it comes about that by "naming" *A* as their savior from the chaos of violence and by acting on that belief, individuals do in fact "confer" all of their power upon *A* and thus succeed in producing him as their sovereign—an event which acts back upon its makers and remolds their multitude into the real unity of a people.

5

Obligation and Liberty

Once again, I will begin by outlining the approach I will be taking in interpreting the relevant parts of Hobbes's system.

In the process of political authorization, the individuals confer upon the sovereign an authority meant to be as absolute and unconditional as the authority they enjoy over themselves in the state of nature under the rule of the right of nature. Under the right of nature, every individual has the right to "every thing," and the ways of implementing this kind of right are spelled out by Hobbes in terms which leave no room for doubt or ambiguity. An individual acting under the right of nature will know no boundaries and no limits in trying to impose his mastery over persons and property. Such an individual will aim at mastering, by whatever means, all men he can until there is no one representing a threat to him,[172] and since, in the state of nature, every man is viewed as a potential threat to one's life, the individual will not rest until all men, their dependents and their property are firmly under his rule. Every individual acting under the right of nature views himself as the center of the universe; his aim is, quite simply and quite clearly, to become a small "god among men," to use Plato's phrase.

This is the sort of authority that individuals, driven into a corner by the "contradiction" in the state of nature—they were aiming at "every thing," they ended up with "nothing"—now confer upon the sovereign. The sovereign's right to rule is as absolute and unconditional as the right each individual had over himself. Each individual sees in the sovereign the seat of absolute and unconditional authority, each of them considers the sovereign the center of his social world. Since the sovereign's authority is absolute, his commands must be obeyed "no matter what" and "come what may." But submission to such a higher power issuing unconditionally binding commands is nothing else but submission to the properly moral authority. Thus the emergence of the sovereign's action of conferring the "real unity" upon the "multitude" of individuals is tantamount to the emergence of the specifically moral obligation shot through with that quasi-religious quality that makes the state into a "mortal god." Hobbes's philosophy is about men's fall into the "chaos of violence" and about their earthly salvation by the sovereign. As their savior, the sovereign imposes upon them obligations of an entirely new type—the specifically moral obligations.

These obligations are new, in the first place, with respect to what man is, or could ever be, in the state of nature. For the authorization of the sovereign is a process of the human *creatio ex nihilo*; and hence the obligation resting on the authority of the sovereign is very much *un*like anything that can be found among the obligations binding (be it even *in foro interno*) in the state of nature.[173] It does not fall under any category of the natural obligation—the directly physical obligation, as in "being obliged" to stay at home since the doors are locked from outside; and the obligation resulting from one's granting one's rights to another person—and it alone confers (retroactively) a morally binding status upon the social compact itself. The emergence of this new obligation does not imply, needless to say, the destruction, or even the suspension of the self-preservative impulse of human individuals. Quite the contrary: for the sake of assuring their self-preservation individuals entrust their fate to the sovereign that they themselves have created. Should he fail in discharging that function individuals will, inevitably, lapse back into the state of nature.

Let us now supply more detail to this outline. The new and the original type of obligation imposed upon individuals by the sovereign is the obligation toward "Justice." This word, of course, has several meanings in Hobbes. Most of them are to be found in the laws of nature. But the justice that begins with and flows from the actions of the sovereign is an entirely different type of justice. The shift is not merely from what is present *in foro interno* to what takes place *in foro externo* (in the sense that one and the same conception of justice can now guide not only people's intentions and desires but their actual behavior), but it concerns the very conception of justice. Whereas the laws-of-nature conception of justice implies the equality and the independence of the individuals involved, according to the new conception "they shine no more than the Starres in presence of the Sun."[174] And whereas we can accuse our partner of violating the laws-of-nature standard of justice, no such accusation is meaningful, much less justified, when raised against the sovereign.

The justification that Hobbes supplies for this claim in *Leviathan* is connected with his theory of authorization. Since "every" subject is the author of "all" actions of the sovereign it follows that "whatsoever" the sovereign does, cannot be viewed as violation of justice; indeed, injustice or injury in its "proper signification" can have no place in the actions of the sovereign toward the citizens.[175]

Let us contrast this immediately with the meanings of justice embedded in the laws of nature. The first time Hobbes mentions justice is in connection with one's obligation to live up to one's voluntary act of transferring a right to someone else. We have already analyzed Hobbes's support for justice in this sense. In conformity with the Golden Rule, individuals must acknowledge their equality and independence; they must refrain from treating one another as mere means. Given this rule I have a duty not to go back on my voluntary commitment to not hinder the other's motions toward such and such goods; and a violation of that duty is injustice.

Injustice and justice in this sense receive a separate and special treatment in the third law of nature, although Hobbes's argument there is not free of some confusion that must be cleared up. It must first be pointed out that the third law of nature ("*That men performe their Covenants made*") is said to "follow"[176] from the second law. The reason given is simple: without living up to their covenants men return to the state of war. Thus, from the very beginning, and quite explicitly, the third law of nature is justified by its function of preventing the slide toward that total loss of power represented by the threat of human violence.

Hobbes has already defined covenants as a subset of contracts during the course of his analyses of the second law of nature. When one of the contractors (a contract being defined as the mutual transfer of rights) has already performed his part of the bargain and is expecting the other party to perform at some future time, or when both parties promise to perform in the future, the agreement between the parties is called a covenant. Given this definition of covenants, Hobbes can then justifiably claim that "INJUSTICE is no other than *the not performance of Covenant*".[177] For if (1) the mutual transferring of rights is done immediately and without any promise of future performance, there is no opportunity for violation of the agreement between the parties. The transfer of rights consists, in such a case, in a physically perceptible exchange (say, *A* giving the good *X* to *B* and *B* giving the good *Y* in exchange); and thus the required mutual acknowledgment by both parties of the agreement between them translates itself at once into a physical, perceptible process. And if (2) the transfer of rights is not mutual, the transferring itself is not a contract but a "free gift" and is the ground not of justice but of "gratitude."[178] Consequently (3), when Hobbes now defines justice as the not performance of a covenant he is at least not inconsistent with his earlier use of the term "justice" in chapter 14 of *Leviathan*. For me not to live up to the obligation I have created by my granting of my rights to the other boils down—practically if not logically—to my failure to live up to the promise of the future performance of a covenant with the other.

If it is sometimes possible to view the obligation to keep one's promises to one's partners as a deontological imperative commanding us not to contradict ourselves,[179] it is because, as I have indicated earlier, the demand to treat the other as an autonomous being may be taken from two angles. Its motivational power is, in most cases, purely prudential: to try to absorb the other within my ends-means sequence is to find myself on a slide toward violence, that is, toward the ultimate threat to my self-interest. But, on the other hand, this demand is grounded in an important truth about the status of the other. As a power center beyond the grip of all my powers the other "is not" a means to my ends. Some ("noble" and "generous") individuals may be able to acknowledge this status of the other as a truth to be taken in its own right, and without any prudential calculations. For the same reason,[180] the obligation to keep one's covenants (i.e., the obligation not to break one's promise of the future performance of the terms of the agreement) can be looked at from two points of view. Its motivational appeal is, for the most part, prudential; for, as Hobbes teaches us, without respecting our promises we will find ourselves in the state of war, which is eminently at odds with our self-interest. But the obligation to keep promises *may* be found binding independently of those prudential considerations. If the violation of the promises toward the other is, as a form of fraud, incompatible with treating him as an autonomous being, I may be able to refrain from violating my promises merely on the grounds of doing justice to the status of the other as such an autonomous being. I would then be refusing to commit what Gilbert Ryle once called a "category mistake" (in this case: treating as a mere means a being who demands to be treated as autonomous) quite independently of the circumstance that my committing such a mistake is also damaging to me in prudential terms. In this sense—and as we recall from our earlier analyses—it is indeed possible to talk about a "contradiction" involved in one's violation of one's promises. *Given* the concept of the other as an autonomous being, and (only) in the light of that concept, there is an incompatibility between promising A to do X and then violating that promise.

The definition of justice as the performance of covenant is followed immediately by another definition of justice put forward by Hobbes as he deduces and discusses his third law of nature: and it is this second definition that creates some confusion in Hobbes's account of (natural) justice. For Hobbes now quotes approvingly the scholastic definition of justice as "the constant Will of giving to every man his own,"[181] and, he goes on to claim, since what is man's "own" refers to his property, it follows that where there is no question of property there can be no question of justice.[182] Moreover, Hobbes does not view this second definition of justice as differing in substance from the first definition. The missing link is supplied by the sentence in which Hobbes claims that to fulfill covenants is precisely to make good that "Propriety, which by mutual Contract men acquire, in recompense of the universall Right they abandon."[183]

Let us look more carefully at the context of Hobbes's analysis. Injustice was first defined as one's going back on one's voluntary granting of a right to someone else. This granting of a right, in turn, was defined as an act whereby the grantor commits himself to literally "stand out of the way" of the grantee in the latter's motion toward this or that good or set of goods. Now whatever goods may be parted with through some operation of laying down and transferring one's rights, it is out of the question to lay down one's right to life, limb and corporal liberty. Furthermore, the special case of slavery aside,[184] the Hobbesian transfer of rights takes place among partners who have already taken the step from their factual to their normative equality. They treat each other as autonomous beings. Since honor is a reflection of an individual's power in the eyes of other individuals, the individuals involved in the Hobbesian laying down and transferring of their rights honor one another equally. They have achieved a state of mutual recognition of their equality and independence; and their willingness to limit their liberty for the sake of one another—a willingness which is a condition of possibility of any laying down or transferring of rights—is predicated upon that mutual acknowledgment of their equal share in honor. Honor can be distributed unequally only in two cases. The first case of such an unequal distribution of honor can be observed in the state of nature, where some individuals succeed temporarily in imposing themselves upon other individuals. But such forms of achieving superiority are unstable and precarious. Sooner or later— and rather sooner than later—the essential equality of individuals is bound to reemerge and to wipe out whatever ephemeral superiority this or that individual may have gained over the others. If such a development did not represent the norm in the state of nature, Hobbes would not characterize the latter as the state of permanent insecurity for each and every individual, "how strong or wise soever he be." The second case of an unequal distribution of honor is to be found in the social condition of man— in the differences of rank and order defining individuals' social standing toward each other. But, as we recall, this form of inequality is built upon the foundation of the previously acknowledged equality. The sovereign, who alone has the right to distribute honor in society, is the representative of all individuals qua equal and equally honored participants in the social compact; and thus whatever inequalities may emerge within society, they will all emerge on the basis of the underlying equality of all citizens. Therefore, even in conception (i.e., *in foro interno*), there can be no just transfer of honor among individuals who honor themselves equally by acknowledging their equal vulnerability and powerlessness vis-à-vis each other.

Now, in this respect the right to property is entirely different. For Hobbes, the transfer of property rights from *A* to *B* does not affect *A*'s and *B*'s essential equality. Such a transfer (at least as long as it does not threaten *A* with starvation; if it does, Hobbes forbids it in categorical terms and gives *A* every right to take all the steps necessary to avoid death by starvation) is not only compatible with that Hobbesian "End" of all laying down and transferring of one's rights, but is, in fact, instrumental in bringing about precisely that end: the security of equal and independent individuals. This is why only the rights to property can be transferred in any covenant I may make with the other under the laws-of-nature standard of justice. And this is also why, *given* the context of Hobbes's analyses, the two definitions of justice formulated in chapter 15 of *Leviathan* are not independent. Justice as the performing of a covenant boils down to justice as the will of giving each man his own (property), since nothing but property *can* be transferred through covenants. Only the political covenant is different in this respect, but the political covenant goes over and above the conception of justice laid down by the laws of nature.

After this brief digression we may return to our task of contrasting justice in the sense of the laws of nature with justice as determined by the sovereign. If "he that fulfilleth the Law" was said to be "Just"[185] even prior to the emergence of the sovereign, the justice at issue was meant in the sense in which we speak of "doing justice to reality." The man who was endeavoring to fulfill the law was trying to do justice to the reality of the forces involved; he was trying to treat the others as autonomous, since they refused to serve as means to his ends. The others had to be treated equally, since the equality of their forces imposed such a treatment upon, and against, the will of the individual. Precisely for that reason, however, there was a *standard* of justice—"the Originall of Justice", as Hobbes called it[186]—which could not have been changed without violating the reality of the relations between human agents. And although that standard of justice remained valid only *in foro interno*, it did supply us with a yardstick in terms of which we could judge certain actions as "unjust."

If no such labels can be applied—be it even *in foro interno*— to the actions of the sovereign otherwise than due to a conceptual confusion, it's because the relationship between the sovereign and the subjects is not a relationship between autonomous partners.

As we saw earlier, the "conferring" of powers upon the sovereign does involve the laying down and transferring of rights by the subjects; and this operation, like all others of its kind, boils down to the voluntary act by means of which individuals undertake the obligation not to hinder the motions of the sovereign. But—and this is the first reason why the relationship between the sovereign on the one hand and his subjects on the other hand goes over and above the category of the mutually acknowledged autonomy of partners—whereas the subjects do promise not to hinder the motions of the sovereign, the sovereign makes no such promise to the subjects. While the laws of nature demand that the physical and social space be so divided among the individuals as to allow them to move without the menace of a deadly collision, the sovereign is not a part of that space at all. His liberty is not a matter of "more" or "less," for it is not meant to be limited by the impediments represented by any other liberty within a given state. To sum it all up: the obligation to treat the other as autonomous was undertaken by me since I could not enclose the other within my ends-means sequence; in contrast, my position toward the sovereign does not leave me with any independent means of my own: whatever means I do have, they are all derived from the authority of the sovereign. And even though in the state of nature my means were all cancelled out by the means of the other, the laws of nature gave me at least the *concept* of "my" means—as over against the means of the other. This concept is now changed almost beyond recognition due to the emergence of the sovereign. Insofar as the sovereign secures the existence of a framework within which I can pursue and accumulate power with a relative security, I can, for the first time, gain a measure of lasting control over some means to my future apparent good. But the property that I have, or may have, the honors that I achieve, or may achieve, are all dependent upon the sovereign. Taken as a self-dependent unit, apart from the sovereign, I have nothing and I am nothing, since both what I have and what I am are then exposed to the violence of others. I have gained a secure access to some means to my future apparent good for, to begin with, I agreed not to claim anything as my means over against the sovereign. Thus the entire laws-of-nature conception of justice is inoperative, on logical grounds alone, when it comes to describing my relations with the sovereign.

To this first, merely negative, reason why the laws-of-nature conception of justice can not govern the relationships between the subjects and the sovereign one must add the second, and positive, reason. It is not simply that I have forfeited any right to any means of my own, held independently of the sovereign, but, in addition, all of the actions of the sovereign are *my* actions. Since I authorized all of his actions, *I* am their author. Thus, I can not accuse him of injustice if he punishes me, for his punitive actions against me are the actions he undertakes in his capacity of my agent; they are, in this sense, my actions, and it is I who am being unjust (in the present sense of justice), since to be punished by one's own authority is precisely to be unjust.[187] This claim seems strained, but it makes perfect sense given the function of the political authorization as Hobbes envisions it. Under the right of nature I have the authority to determine what is right and wrong, just and unjust. This authority I now—unconditionally and with no reservations—confer upon the sovereign. From now on, then, if he determines that my doing X or Y or Z merits punishment, it is as if I determined by my own authority, that my own actions of doing X, Y, Z merit punishment. The only change is that my own authority of defining the normative standards and meting out punishments as I see fit is now located outside me and, in the case under discussion, it becomes turned against me. But it remains *my* authority nonetheless; and, for the same reason that it makes no sense to accuse the sovereign of injustice (the reason being precisely my authorization of all of his actions) it is necessary to recognize oneself as unjust when receiving punishment from the sovereign.

Both the negative and the positive reasons for the sovereign's status as the source of the new, and the specifically moral, sense of justice are at work in Hobbes's account of the social covenant. The covenant itself represents the meeting point between the natural and the specifically social and moral conceptions of justice. As a pact entered into by individuals in the state of nature, the social covenant exhibits the structure that can be found in any natural agreement. The social pact is a "Covenant of every man with every man . . . as if every man should say to every man, *I Authorize and give up my Right of Governing my selfe, to this Man, or this Assembly of men, on this condition, that thou give up thy Right to him, and Authorize all his Actions in like manner.*"[188] In this pact, the natural conception of justice guides the individuals insofar as they agree to lay down their right of nature. We have already analyzed the meaning and the function of any operation of laying down one's rights. In encountering another man in my way I run up against the ultimate limit of my powers and I thereby form the concept of limitation of my liberty. My liberty finds itself dispossessed from its exalted status of being the center of the world by the appearance of another liberty. I thus begin to think of liberty as a divisible item; I think of it as divisible for I am forced to do so by the irremovable obstacle of the liberty of the other. If I refuse to think of liberty as divisible—if I continue to cling to the thought that my liberty absorbs the whole world—I will bring upon myself the "loss of all power" at the hand of the other and hence also (since, as we recall, to have any liberty at all I must have *some* power) the loss of my liberty. And so I must come to terms with and acknowledge the divisibility of liberty—I must be prepared to talk about my (not to mention the other's) liberty in terms of "more" or "less." By the same token, and on account of the fact that the right of nature is defined in terms of natural liberty, I must be prepared to talk about the limitation of my right to "every thing." My exercise of that right and of that liberty consists in my motions toward certain goods. I must therefore voluntarily restrict these motions of mine. For this reason, the subsumption of my liberty under the scale of "more" and "less" expresses itself in certain restrictions imposed upon the motion of my body and in certain openings given to the motions of the body of the other. The entire operation of laying down my rights is guided, from the very beginning, by my acknowledgment of the equality of the other. It is precisely because I could not enclose the other within my own ends-means sequence that I decided to treat him as autonomous (i.e., to give his liberty as much room as I gave my own). Everything, so far, conforms to the laws-of-nature conception of justice.

What goes over and above that conception—and what constitutes the first, the merely negative, reason for the novelty of the justice flowing from the authority of the sovereign—is my giving up my right of nature "to this man, or to this Assembly of men." To be sure, this operation too is sustained by my treatment of the others as autonomous and by my demand to be treated by the others in the same way. The operation is carried out by equal and independent power centers ready to limit their natural liberty vis-à-vis each other.

But—and this is the new element—their reciprocal limiting of their liberties is implemented through the channel of the sovereign. They limit themselves (in part) vis-à-vis each other by limiting themselves (entirely) vis-à-vis the sovereign. Or, again, they limit the motions of their bodies in a common space by agreeing not to limit any motions of the sovereign in that space. Moreover, practically if not theoretically, the two operations are inseparable. Without the sovereign, I can have the *concept* of treating the other as an autonomous being, but I can not implement that concept as an effective rule governing my actions; the very attempt to do so would put me immediately in jeopardy. The translation of natural justice from the *in foro interno* to the *in foro externo* realm demands the submission to the sovereign and to the justice originating with him. The (still merely negative) reason why this new conception of justice does not fall under the laws-of-nature conception of justice becomes clear now. Insofar as the sovereign must implement the limitations of individuals' motions in space, *his* motions ought not to be subjected to limitations at least within that space. For this reason alone he can not be accused of not justly dividing that space together with (and as one of) the individuals involved. And this is another way of saying that he can not be accused of injustice in the laws-of-nature sense of that term.

The second—the positive—reason for the difference between these two senses of justice is also spelled out in Hobbes's formula of the social covenant. Individuals not only give up their rights to the sovereign, but they also "authorize all his Actions." It's not just that the motions of the sovereign are unconstrained, but—at least in some sense, and as long as my life and limb are not actually endangered—they are also *my* motions. Since whatever the sovereign does, he does it through my authority, and since the latter is defined, under the right of nature, as absolute and unconditional, it follows that whatever the sovereign does has an absolute and unconditional claim upon me. Nothing that anyone does, or could do, under the laws-of-nature conception of justice resembles even remotely this new standard of justice. The second law of nature is clear in this respect: any limitation of my right and my liberty goes hand in hand with the limitation of the right and the liberty of the other. I abolish my claim to every thing only if the other abolishes the corresponding claim of his own; and I therefore reserve the right to judge whether the motions of the other in the space I share with him reflect that abdication of his claim to every thing. No such abdication is expected of the sovereign quite the contrary. Now, to be sure, I authorize all of the sovereign's actions "on condition that thou" authorize him in the same way. But the condition applies to other participants in the covenant; the condition does not apply to the sovereign. This part of Hobbes's formulation only brings out with more clarity both the continuity *and* the discontinuity between the two concepts of justice. Insofar as the authorization of the sovereign is a covenant between the individuals involved, this authorization must conform to the standard demanding that the individuals treat each other as autonomous beings; thus, if I am willing to authorize all of the actions of the sovereign and limit myself so radically, I have the right to demand that you limit yourself in the same way. But this *conditional* limitation of our rights vis-à-vis each other is implemented by the *unconditional* limitation of our rights insofar as we authorize the sovereign to be the bearer of our "Right of Governing" ourselves.

To the two kinds of justice resulting from the social covenant there correspond two kinds of obligation; or, rather, since these two kinds of obligation are inseparable, the political obligation as a whole is a "double obligation": "The government is upheld by a *double obligation* from the citizens; first, that which is due to their fellow-citizens; next, that which they owe to their prince."[189] It is, of course, the obligation toward the sovereign ("the prince") that represents here the specifically moral obligation. Moreover, although this new obligation emerges from the process of political authorization, its justification *qua* moral does not rest on its origin in that process. Quite the contrary, the very acts of authorizing the sovereign begin to oblige morally as a consequence of our submission to the sovereign. Through their own actions, men have posited an authority which changes its makers and confers a new status upon the very actions of making that authority itself. There can be no question about reversing that relation between the acts of authorizing the sovereign and the specifically moral obligation. For if we were morally obliged to the sovereign merely on the grounds of our own acts of authorizing him, then it would make sense to talk about the new, specifically moral, sense of justice quite independently of the actions of the sovereign; morality would be embedded already in our acts of authorizing, and this is not, most emphatically, the case in Hobbes's account, since what creates the unconditionally "just" and "right" are the commands of the sovereign. The moral authority of the sovereign does not flow from our authorization but from the sovereign himself qua finished product of that authorization. Once posited as our savior from the chaos of violence, the sovereign commands us to follow him unconditionally; but his commands are morally obligating because they are *his* and not because *we* have established him as the supreme authority to be obeyed.

The same observation can be applied to the element of promise present in the social covenant; indeed given Hobbes's definitions of these terms, we are dealing here with a purely logical connection: to the extent that we are allowed to speak of a covenant at all we must also speak of a promise involved in making it, since a covenant just *is* a contract based on a promise of future performance. The two promises involved in the making of the social pact are, then, as follows. First, the promise made by each individual to the other participants in the pact. Through this promise, I signal my willingness to refrain from hindering the motions of the other merely on my own authority; from now on, if such a hindering from my side is to take place, it will have to be done on the authority of the sovereign. The promise I give to the other expresses both my acknowledgment of him as an autonomous being *and* my willingness to practically implement that acknowledgment through the mutual submission to the sovereign. And my declared willingness to submit to the sovereign constitutes the second promise involved in the making of the social pact. Whereas the promise I make to the others conforms to the laws-of-nature standard of justice, the second promise goes over and above that standard. It is not that I commit myself not to hinder the motions of the sovereign on condition that he refrain from hindering my motions, but I deprive myself of the right to move at all unless given the (explicit or at least implicit) permission by the sovereign. While the promise to the other is reciprocal, the promise to the sovereign is one-sided. But there is also something that both promises—to the other and to the sovereign—have in common. Taken on their own, they both lack the moral quality. The double pledge I have given to the other and to the sovereign represents only a practical device for dealing with the supremely undesirable consequences of the universal exercise of the natural freedom of men. To be sure, this device itself (the social pact as a whole) is entered into when individuals "convert" to a new way of feeling and reasoning about their self-interest. The individuals "let go" their attachment to their right-of-nature, self-dependent form of life and they decide to "give peace a chance" by coalescing around the sovereign. But the conversion *itself* has no moral sanction, except in retrospect and through the authority of the sovereign who emerged from it. The sovereign commands obedience to society, with all of its laws and institutions; and since everything the sovereign commands is "just" in the new, properly moral, sense of the term, our obligation not to go back on the social pact itself (i.e., on the pledge involved in our conversion from the natural to the social condition) gains itself a moral sanction. By the same token, the promise we made to each other in entering the social covenant becomes endowed with a moral quality too. To break the promise of not hindering the motions of the other without the sovereign's permission means, as of now, violating a moral imperative expressing the will of the sovereign.

The two kinds of justice have led us to two kinds of obligation; the two kinds of obligation, in turn, imply two kinds of *fear*. Fear remains the motivation behind *most* human commitments to what is just; and although the "noble" and "generous" natures that Hobbes mentions, now and then, are capable of taking up and fulfilling obligations independently of fear, the solidity of the web of obligations regulating human interactions depends upon the strength of fear. Fear in general is, for Hobbes, the expectation of evil. But there are different fears, since the evils expected may be greater or smaller and the expectations of those evils may be stronger or weaker. The fear of death prevailing in the state of nature is so high that it barely falls short of the ultimate limit of fear, which is despair. Nonetheless, the state of nature is not the state of despair, but the state of diffidence; and the diffidence prevailing in the state of nature is, we recall, that "perpetual" and "general" diffidence which makes violence inevitable. What happens, though, if in this condition of universal diffidence and war I enter a covenant with someone for fear of losing my life? Hobbes gives an example of this: when, in the state of nature, I agree to pay ransom, or to perform a service, to my enemy in exchange for my life, the covenant remains valid and I am obliged to perform in conformity with its terms.[190] But what kind of validity is it? The covenant is valid according to the standard of justice determined by the laws of nature. However, in the state of nature the laws of nature themselves are valid only *in foro interno*. It follows that the present covenant, too, remains valid only *in foro interno*. It is pointless to reply that the enemy has "already" performed by not taking my life away and that, therefore, my obligation to deliver the goods I promised must be fulfilled. For the state of nature remains the state of universal diffidence and war where force and fraud are permissible, even advisable. Therefore, whether I *actually* (*in foro externo*) keep my part of that bargain with the enemy will depend only upon my assessment of the risks and dangers involved in my refusal to deliver the promised goods or services. But this possibility of refusal is a realistic option to me, only because my fear of this particular enemy is limited in space, in time and in the power of its cause. The fear sustaining the obligation toward the sovereign is entirely different in this respect. The power of the sovereign is everywhere and his threat is conveyed to me not just by the sound of the police cars' sirens and by the sight of county jails, but, in point of fact, by all of the social institutions and by the people who work there, since the social fabric as a whole rests on the fear of the sovereign. Due to this all-pervasive fear of the sovereign the civil laws are the "artificial chains."[191] which I carry with me along all the paths and trails laid out within the social world. Thus, the fear sustaining a natural obligation is always limited; the fear sustaining the political obligation is, for all intents and purposes, unlimited. Furthermore, there is also the second—the positive—reason for the difference between these two kinds of fear. In fearing an enemy in the state of nature I do not fear my own authority. In fearing the sovereign—I do. For my enemy's actions are (only) *his* actions, while my sovereign's actions are (also) *my* actions. Thus, I am unable to escape the fear of the sovereign in the double sense of that term: I can't escape the sovereign's power of hindering my motions, and I can't escape the authority vested in that power, since the sovereign's power remains my own power at least as long as it does not threaten my life and limb.

The sovereign secures peace by implementing its "articles": the laws of nature. But the laws of nature oblige differently when we view them as general rules of action counseling us to treat the others as our equals, and when they are commands issued by the will of the sovereign. Once again, Hobbes secularizes the conceptual framework of Christianity: "Think not that I am come to destroy the law, or the prophets: I am not come to destroy, but to fulfill."[192] The actions of the sovereign too are meant to realize the *law*. But the law is—and can only be—realized through *his* actions. In following the sovereign—our earthly savior from violence—we must put aside all doubts about the interpretation and the application of the laws of nature and we must submit to *his* guidance. As long as the social world within which we live and move does not break down—as long as our life and limb are not endangered—we must follow the sovereign come what may and no matter what. In this sense it is not incorrect to say, as one commentator does, that the commands of the sovereign oblige "beyond reason."[193] But, of course, this "irrational" obedience to the sovereign is itself highly functional— and, in this sense, highly rational—in terms of our self-interest. The laws of nature are conducive to our self-interest; and since it is impossible to implement the laws of nature through our own judgments and actions, it is imperative that we let them be implemented by the sovereign. As long as we are self-dependent, the universality of the laws is stained, and brought to naught, by the particularity of each and every individual (his "conscience" notwithstanding) trying to live by them. Since, on the other hand, the laws of nature have no power of their own to shape our conduct, they must be realized in the judgments and the actions of a *particular* agent. And this agent can not be an *ordinary* individual among other ordinary individuals; his particularity must express the particularity of each and every member of the community. Otherwise, the law would be perceived by individuals as an alien necessity; whereas the law is their own law insofar as they recognize themselves in the sovereign. The law is universal, but (1) it can come to life only in the actions of a particular being and (2) the particular being at issue—the sovereign—is not an ordinary individual, but the depository of all individuals' identity.

What is often called Hobbes's "legal positivism" depends precisely upon that identification of the (actualized) law with the will of the sovereign. Hobbes's argument is simple.[194] The laws of nature become *actually* laws only in society and due to the sovereign's authority behind them. Taken in their social, actual form, the laws of nature are *civil* laws. This dependence of the laws of nature upon the civil laws can be understood in at least two senses. First, the laws of nature would have no efficacy at all if they were not realized in the civil laws of a given society. Second, by being thus actualized in the civil laws, the laws of nature are changed from abstract formulae into a set of more concrete rules and regulations: the sovereign determines for us what counts as a break of contract, a nonequitable treatment of persons, and so forth. Since the civil laws express the will of the sovereign, and since the laws of nature gain their actuality only as embodied in civil laws, it follows that the laws of nature can present us with the *actual* (and not simply *in foro interno*) obligations only qua civil laws. The change that takes place in the status of the laws of nature as they become civil laws is so profound, that only now can they be called "laws" in the proper sense of that term. Prior to their actualization in the civil laws, the laws of nature were only "qualities" or "conclusions" or "theorems" disposing men to peace and obedience, but they were not yet "laws." For a law is a command, and a command obliges us only (and merely) as expression of the will of someone who has the authority over us in this or that respect. Since civil laws secure the very existence of the social order, and since the sovereign alone has the authority over that order, civil laws are commands of the sovereign. But civil laws are precisely the (actualized) laws of nature. And so as commands, the laws of nature oblige us qua expressions of the will of the sovereign.

Given all this it comes as no surprise to us that "no law can be unjust."[195] Civil laws are laid down by the sovereign, and whatever the sovereign does is just. Hobbes's legal positivism is now unavoidable. We may still ask whether a law is "good" *provided* that we mean by this no more than whether the law at issue is either needed or understandable to the people; but under no conditions whatsoever can we question the moral sanction of each and every law laid down by the sovereign.

The statement "no law can be unjust" draws a clear, and merely logical, line between the laws-of-nature conception of justice and justice as defined by the sovereign. The laws of nature do supply the "Originall of Justice," but they themselves can not, on the grounds of logic alone, be evaluated in terms of that standard. In *its* terms, only the evaluation of people's actions and intentions is possible. The laws *themselves* can be said to be "just" only insofar as they are embodied in civil laws, flowing from the will of the sovereign.

The danger implied by this position is clear. If no law laid down by the sovereign can be unjust, and if sovereignty is always bestowed upon a "Man" or an "Assembly of men," then what happens in cases when the bearers of sovereignty begin to pass laws meant to secure their particular interests? The sovereign not only is, but must be, a particular being if he is to impose the real unity upon the multitude of asocial, or even anti social, individuals. Now, the particularity of the sovereign would be a mere word if it did not imply that the sovereign is more than the *function* attributed to him by individuals in the process of authorization. Were he to be no more than that function, his particularity would be absorbed within the social whole; whereas, for Hobbes, the human multitude becomes (and remains) a whole only on account of the actions of the sovereign qua particular being external to that whole. Or, to put it still differently, the sovereign is not defined (merely) by his internal relations to individuals and institutions making up the social whole. He is, to be sure, the "Soul" of the commonwealth, but he can discharge this function only qua particular being. The power and the authority flow to him from within the *social whole* he sustains; but the power and the authority flow to *him* qua this or that man (or assembly). We have already indicated the source of this tension in Hobbes. The sovereign fulfills the *law* but he fulfills the law as *this* particular being, and the very presence of his particularity opens up the possibility of distortions and abuses of the law. And yet, without the particularity of the sovereign, the law cannot take root in actual reality.

There are several ways in which Hobbes attempts to solve this difficulty—if indeed the difficulty can be solved at all. We can appeal, first, to the identity of the sovereign's particular interest with the interests of the people; it would then follow, that by discharging to the best of his abilities the social function of securing the people's interests, the sovereign would also contribute most effectively to his own interest. And so Hobbes tells us that the glory and the wealth of the sovereign depend upon the power and the wealth of his subjects.[196] But this connection is far from obvious in factual terms; as a historian, Hobbes should have known, and must have known, better. History offers us many examples of rulers riding to wealth and glory by abusing, rather than by furthering, the interests of their subjects. It is possible, of course, to reply that the connection at issue is not factual but definitional: the hardships, the mass starvation, the violent deaths resulting from, say, a long and costly war of conquest or from an ambitious social transformation undertaken by the ruler would all contribute, by definition, to the wealth and glory of the nation. But it is highly dubious whether Hobbes would buy such a tautological defense of all the activities of the ruler, including those which seem to be so clearly at odds with the purpose of guaranteeing peace and security to the citizens.

Can we then put our bets on some form of a moral or religious obligation to uphold the laws of nature that the ruler himself would acknowledge? Once again, there are texts to back up this suggestion.[197] But the problems created by it are severe; indeed they are the same problems we have already encountered, only they are now being pushed one step further. The ruler remains, and must remain, a *particular* being; and the danger is that the influence of his particular interests will distort his performance of the tasks and functions attached to the office of the sovereign. If he is capable of living up to a moral or religious obligation as this particular being that he happens to be, then there is no reason why other individuals could not be trusted to do the same in the state of nature, and then no (Hobbesian) sovereign is needed to pull them out of that state. But if he, as a particular being, is incapable of living up to those moral or religious obligations, then the entire difficulty reemerges: since no law can be unjust as expression of the will of the sovereign, and since the sovereign's will may be influenced, not by a sense of moral or religious obligation to uphold the laws of nature, but by his own particular interests, we may find ourselves in a situation where we are morally obliged to follow a law devised to advance someone's (the sovereign's) particular interest.

Raymond Polin has suggested what seems to be the best way of dealing with the difficulty.[198] The sovereign is, for all intents and purposes, omnipotent. As omnipotent, the sovereign has no *need* to assert his particularity independently of his social function. He knows no obstacles and no limits and he is thus free of any *lack* that would set off his own private striving for more power. The omnipotence of the office of the sovereign renders unnecessary such a private striving for power of his occupant. Thus the discrepancy between the social and the particular aspect of the sovereign's existence loses its menacing potential. The sovereign's particular interests will not diverge from the public interest, for his omnipotence, or near omnipotence, removes the need for an independent assertion of his interests; for the same reason, the sovereign's will has no incentive to legislate for his own good, in opposition to the good of the community. It is true that no empirical sovereign is, or can ever be, actually omnipotent in this sense. But at least we are given some explanation as to why the particularity of the sovereign need not be at odds with his own social function. As for the outstanding part of the difficulty—as long as the sovereign is not fully omnipotent he may find it desirable to assert his independent interest—the ultimate response remains Hobbes's consistently held view that the inconveniences of the state of nature are far worse than those resulting from our submission to any sovereign.

Can this omnipotence, or near omnipotence, of the sovereign find itself limited by the people's beliefs in an omnipotent God? In answering this question we need not concern ourselves with the broader issue of the *theoretical* possibility of man's obligation towards God in the system of Hobbes.[199] It will be enough to show why, in purely practical terms, the worship of God not only does not diminish the power and the authority of the sovereign, but, if anything, contributes to strengthen them significantly.

The first reason as to why there should be no conflict, in people's minds, between the power and the authority of the sovereign and the power and the authority of God lies in the incomprehensibility of the divine being. Reason can demonstrate the *existence* of God. But the divine *attributes* remain an impenetrable mystery to reason, since our rational faculties are too limited to comprehend the infinity of the divine being.[200] It is not possible to reply to this that we have the *concept* of infinity and that, therefore, we ought to be able to grasp the attributes of God by employing that concept. For, as Hobbes points out in *De Cive*,[201] our having the concept of infinity not only leaves us with no capacity for understanding the infinite being, but is in fact the expression of our incapacity to achieve such an understanding: when I apply the concept of infinity to an *X*, this is, for me, tantamount to a confession that *X* is beyond the grasp of my understanding. Reason can tell me that God has no passions (since they all involve a degree of dependency), that he is beyond space and time, that he has no senses, and so forth; but reason can not tell me, in positive terms, what are the attributes of God. Now, we worship God precisely in his attributes, and the meaning of these attributes is embedded in our words. Since we have no knowledge of the divine attributes, their meaning is established merely by human linguistic conventions and agreements. But these conventions and agreements can not be, on penalty of confusion and civil war, established by particular men, but only by the sovereign: "It followeth, that those Attributes which the Sovereign ordaineth, in the Worship of God, for signes of Honor, ought to be taken and used for such, by private men in their publique Worship."[202]

This may not yet be enough to rule out the possibility that religious beliefs will be called upon by some "private" men to justify their opposition to the sovereign, or an outright rebellion against him. Some of those "private" men may turn against the sovereign even (and precisely) on the grounds of a religious belief as defined by the standards laid down by the sovereign himself. Hence Hobbes's second reason for a (still stronger) subordination of religion to the state. The main premise of his argument is simple: there are no men on earth with spiritual bodies, and hence there can be no spiritual community on earth.[203] Given this very simple fact, no claims of spiritual allegiance can override the claims of a temporal authority meant to regulate the interactions of human bodies. Religious beliefs should serve to strengthen that authority—indeed, it seems to be Hobbes's view that some form of religious justification of political power is necessary for a state to function properly—but they can not be allowed to undermine it under any circumstances. This is relatively easy to achieve in Christian communities, since the governments of those communities are themselves ruled by the principles of the Christian faith. But even under non-Christian sovereigns there can be no question of trying to oppose the government on the grounds of religious convictions. Should a Christian find himself in a situation where he feels he must oppose his government for religious reasons, Hobbes has no hesitation in advising him to choose martyrdom.[204]

Our analysis of the concept of obligation allows us to return to the concept of liberty; indeed, liberty, in Hobbes, can best be understood through its contrast with obligation. There are two kinds of liberty in the philosophy of Hobbes; and these two kinds of liberty differ by their respective standing toward (natural and political) obligation. There is, first, the "natural liberty"—the liberty of man as he is, or would be, if he acted independently of society and in conformity only with the right of nature—and there is also, second, the political liberty, the "liberty of subjects" as Hobbes calls it, which is the kind of liberty enjoyed by men acting within the web of social obligations and constraints.

A free man, says Hobbes, "*is he, that in those things, which by his strength and wit he is able to do, is not hindered to do what he has a will to do.*"[205] This is Hobbes's full definition of freedom in general and it represents the fruit of his reformulation of the relationship between freedom and power. As Hobbes explains in the opening passage of *Leviathan*'s chapter 21, freedom is the absence of external impediments to one's voluntary actions, while power can be curtailed by the impediments rooted in the internal constitution of the agent. Thus,[206] when a prison's walls and chains prevent a man from fulfilling his desire to walk, their physical presence represents an impediment to his liberty; but when a man is fastened to bed by an illness, the impediment curtails not his freedom, but his power to move.

This is Hobbes's standard understanding of liberty and of its relation to power. We recall, however, that in the opening passage of *Leviathan*'s chapter 14 Hobbes was talking about "power" in terms which do not seem to square with his present use of the concept of power. For in that earlier chapter Hobbes was telling us that the external impediments may curtail a man's power, but they will leave his liberty intact. The very opposite seems to be the case at the present stage of Hobbes's argument: while the external impediments are said to represent limits upon a man's freedom, they do not affect in any way the same man's power; the latter can be expanded or curtailed only by the differences in the man's internal constitution.

However, in spite of a terminological confusion, there is no inconsistency in the substance of Hobbes's views. The liberty that Hobbes talked about at the beginning of chapter 14 was not different from the right of nature, viewed both as a descriptive concept and as a normative claim in the mind of the agent when he interprets his position vis-à-vis other agents. That claim, and hence that liberty, were absolute and unconditioned; they knew no limits and no constraints. Hobbes did allow these external impediments to limit a man's power, but not his freedom. By the time Hobbes's argument has reached the stage of the opening moves of chapter 21, he has already introduced the concept of the limitation of liberty itself—I found my natural liberty limited by the appearance of other natural liberties in my world—and he is now in a position to talk about the impediments to both liberty and power.

This new distinction between what impedes a man's actions from "inside" and from "outside" should not obscure the connection between these two kinds of impediments. Let us take Hobbes's own example. If the prison walls are said to be the "external" impediments to my actions, it's because I am not strong enough to break through them or to pull them down—and this lack of muscular strength represents here the limit of my power, that is, the "internal" impediment to my actions. Had I had stronger muscles, then, perhaps, I could have broken through these prison walls. Similarly, as one commentator points out if I can not really deliberate whether I should or should not fly, it's precisely because flying is not within my power.[207] And yet all such "internal" impediments modify and change what counts as "external" impediments to my actions (if I had stronger muscles, the prison walls would not have been an external impediment to my actions; if I had wings, that huge ravine in front of me would not have impeded my motion forward, etc.). Thus, the impediments that are said to limit my liberty (the external impediments) depend, in the last analysis, upon the impediments said to limit my power (the internal impediments). This dependence of the limits of liberty upon the limits of power may supply one reason why, in the *Elements of Law*,[208] Hobbes chooses to call our natural liberty the "natural power" of man: liberty is not opposed to power as what is curtailed by the external constraints to what is curtailed by the internal constraints, but liberty "is" power at least to the extent that an effective exercise of our natural liberty is also, qua effective, an exercise of our power. A man without such "liberty" viewed as "natural power" is "no better than an inanimate creature, not able to help himself."[209] To say that such a man cannot "help" himself means simply that he has no appropriate power to implement his desires; thus the possession of natural liberty becomes more than a subjective claim in the mind of the agent only to the extent to which liberty is translated into some power. By the same token, a limit upon a man's power (i.e., an "internal" impediment) is also, eo ipso, a limit upon a man's liberty, since it makes that liberty less effective in coping with various "external" impediments. It must be noted that in the passage I am analyzing Hobbes is talking only about our natural liberty to deliberate and (on this basis) "to do and undo";[210] he considers *that* aspect of natural liberty to be identical with natural power. But this is of no great consequence to the point I am making, since in Hobbes the process of deliberation concerns only what we think is *possible* for us to accomplish[211]—we are "able to help" ourselves through this kind of liberty (to deliberate, to do or undo) only because, when exercising it, we have sufficient power at our command; and this is a clear indication that liberty itself may very well be considered as increased or diminished by the presence or absence of the impediments to our power.

If there is some confusion in Hobbes's various uses of the concept of power, no similar confusion can be detected in his concepts of will and voluntary action. It is clear why Hobbes needs these concepts to formulate his theory of liberty. If our liberty was merely the absence of external impediments to actions which remain within our power, then a man pushed off a cliff would be falling freely. Something, then, is needed to explain why this man's fall differs significantly from the fall of a man who himself jumps off the cliff; and the difference seems to be that the second man takes the plunge "of his own will," that is, "voluntarily."

But what do these expressions refer to? Certainly not to some uncaused acts of "free will"; Hobbes's determinism does not allow for anything of that sort and Hobbes has nothing but the proverbial scorn and ridicule for those who understand volitions in that way. For Hobbes, volition is nothing other than the last desire in the process of deliberation—the desire that precedes immediately the action itself. The process of deliberation, in turn, is composed of the following elements. There is, first, the bundle of various passions we feel to-wards the result of the action we deliberate about and towards the means lead-ing to that result. There is a play of hopes and fears, of appetites and aversions, and this play is terminated when one of our passions asserts itself as the mo-tive inducing us to act or to refrain from acting in some particular way. But, second, the victory of this or that desire in the process of deliberation is due not only to that desire's sheer strength, but is due also to a favorable cognitive appraisal of the chances of success of the anticipated action, of the action's consequences and of their place on the list of our priorities and so on. Thus the element of thought is always present in deliberation; and while our thoughts are "Scouts and Spies" to our desires,[212] the reports of the former modify the direction and the ordering of the latter. In the special case of human agents—the case is special for beasts too can and do deliberate—this contribution of thought to the outcome of deliberation can not be overemphasized. Our far-reaching anticipation into the future, our conceptual, linguistic, understanding of countless possibilities laid out in the social world weigh heavily in the pro-cess of deliberation and produce outcomes which could not have been ex-pected to occur without the participation of those highest cognitive functions of man. In the third place, the process of deliberation concerns only things that we think possible for us to do; thus the assessment of our power is im-plicitly, and often explicitly, present in every activity of deliberating. Finally, as we already pointed out, the termination of a deliberative process puts an end to our liberty of doing or undoing something.

Now, if the will is the last desire in the process of deliberation, then, to begin with, our will too is shot through with a conceptual assessment of the situation within which we act—with the assessment of the ends, of the means, and of the circumstances of the action. For this reason, every voluntary action involves some form of reasoning.[213] How, then, does our will differ from rea-son in action, and how can we reconcile the account given so far with Hobbes's refusal to identify will with practical reason?[214] Hobbes seems to have two answers to this question. He says, first, that the language of deliberation (and hence also the reasoning guiding all voluntary actions) "differs not from the language of Reasoning, save that Reasoning is in general words; but Delibera-tion for the most part is of Particulars".[215] But it is difficult to see how this claim could be sustained given Hobbes's account of reason and of rationality in general. If, as we recall, man's reasoning amounts to the grasp of some universal rules, how can deliberation "reason" at all if its mode of reasoning is to concern itself—be it only "for the most part"— with mere particulars? Even our practical skills—swimming, riding a bike, and so on—are not free of some understanding of universal relations between various elements present in a par-ticular context of an action. The sort of intelligence guiding us in the exercise of such skills can not be reduced to Aristotle's practical syllogism, but it does, nevertheless, involve our grasp of some general patterns and relationships; only on account of this circumstance our practical knowledge, when fully operative, is transferrable to an almost infinite variety of similar contexts and situations. In any case, there seems to be no room for such an account of practical intelligence within Hobbes's overall account of reason. But Hobbes gave us another clue as to how we ought to distinguish between will and reason: "The Definition of the *Will* given commonly by the Schooles, that it is a *Rationall Appetite*, is not good. For if it were, then could there be no Voluntary Act against Reason."[216] But this too is far from clear, for it can't mean that in acting voluntarily "against Reason" a man acts blindly and without being guided by some form of rationality. Even the actions of a madman, insofar as they are voluntary, can be said to follow from a wrong ("vain-glorious") assessment of his power;[217] and this means that in such cases at least (as opposed to cases of involuntary, physically induced, madness) the will of the madman is not at all free of thought and conception. Presumably, then, when telling us that voluntary actions are "against Reason" Hobbes uses the term reason as equivalent with what he calls "the right reason"—that is, with that special kind of rationality which allows us to appraise objectively our power and, on this basis, to determine the course of action best suited to serve our interests.

Apart from the difference between will and reason another important feature of all voluntary acts must be noted. If liberty means the lack of external impediments to actions which I have the will (and the power) to do, and if my will is only the last desire in the process of deliberation, then a change of that desire means a change in what counts as my free action. If, in a given situation, I had had a different desire, then what I felt as the external impediment to my action in that situation might not have been an impediment at all. If, say, I enjoyed losing part of my fortune since I saw in this loss an opportunity for proving that I can make a financial comeback, then the loss would not have represented an impediment to my motions—even though, in an obvious sense, it would have deprived me of the possibility to spend an otherwise pleasant year in Paris. Thus, whether I label an action "free" or "unfree" depends upon my desires, at least to the extent that no description of what counts as external impediment can be given independently of the corresponding description of my desires and inclinations. Even some life-threatening situations may not be seen as impediments to my liberty if I am one of those rare "noble" and "generous" natures willing to sacrifice their life rather than to frustrate their desire to act justly. To sum up: whether this or that aspect of my environment is viewed as contributing to the freedom of my actions or as constraining them depends upon the desire causing the action to occur; and this means that what counts as an external impediment to my action depends upon the direction of my will.

What does not depend upon the will is the will itself. "Appetite, fear, hope,

and the rest of the passions are not called voluntary; for they proceed not
from, but are the will; and the will is not voluntary. For a man can no more
say he will will, than he will will will, and so make an infinite repetition of
the word will; which is absurd and insignificant."[218] To say that the will can
not "proceed" from itself means that the will can be neither produced nor
constrained by itself. If I act voluntarily I act as I desire, but I do not voluntarily give myself my desires, since my will itself is a desire; and thus, even if
I succeeded in voluntarily producing a desire in me, my will itself, being as it
is another desire, would have to arise in me (on penalty of "infinite repetition") simply on account of some causal interactions between my organism
and its environment. For the same reason, my will can not be constrained by
itself: to say that I voluntarily repress this or that desire of mine means only
that another desire wins out in the process of deliberation; and this new, winning, desire just *is* the will itself.

There is one special case, though, where the will does depend upon the will
itself, for there is one special case where what impedes my actions is incorporated into my will. Such is the case of the "artificial chains" of laws impeding
the "liberty of subjects."[219] The bonds of laws are not physical bonds, and the
liberty of subjects is not "natural liberty"; in fact, if laws and liberty were to
be construed here as being equivalent to physical impediments and natural
liberty, Hobbes would be in no position to make the statements he is making
in the present context. Moved by their desire to live in peace, men have made
those "*Artificiall Chains*, called *Civill Lawes*, which they themselves, by mutuall
covenants, have fastened at one end, to the lips of that Man, or Assembly, to
whom they have given the Sovereigne Power; and at the other end to their
own Ears. These Bonds in their own nature but weak, may neverthelesse be
made to hold, by the danger, though not be the difficulty of breaking them."[220]
Thus, the bonds of law impede our motion in spite of the fact that they do so
due to our own fear of them, that is, due to our own will. But how can this
be? Let us take a better look at the case at hand. Hobbes's definition of freedom as absence of external obstacles to one's voluntary motions was meant to
cover all cases of free action; and, as we saw, in terms of that definition what
counts as an external obstacle to my action depends upon the direction of my
will, that is, upon the desire preceding and producing the action. But my fear
of the sovereign—for he is the "danger" that I fear when I want to break the
law—falls into a separate category. This fear is *my* fear and, nevertheless, the
civil laws and the power of the sovereign behind them are still considered as
constraints upon my action. Thus when this fear wins in the process of deliberation and I decide not to oppose the sovereign and his laws I find myself
constrained *even though* my action is voluntary. But if it is *my* will (*my* fear) to
obey the sovereign and the civil laws, how can I be acting under a constraint?
In all other cases whether this or that was an obstacle to my freedom depended

only upon the direction of my will: there was no part of my external environment which might not have been seen as not impeding my motions if only my will had changed its direction. But this case is different: here my action is voluntary (for I act out of my own fear of the sovereign) and, at the same time, constrained by the "chains" and "bonds" of the civil laws. It can be replied at once that in the present case the constraint upon the will is due to the circumstance that what I fear is the end of all willing—the death that the sovereign is likely to impose upon me should I choose to break the laws in some important ways. But this can not be the correct reply. For in all other Hobbesian cases when I act due to my fear of death— as in the case when I give money to the thief to save myself, when I throw my goods into the sea to prevent my ship from sinking with me on it, and so forth—I am said to act voluntarily and, therefore, acting under the pressure of one's fear of death is not at all incompatible with acting *without* having one's will constrained. And yet there is one special case in which the agent's will is constrained when he acts out of his own fear of death—and this is the case when what threatens him is the power of the sovereign.

We discover here what is perhaps the main paradox involved in Hobbes's theory of freedom as a whole.[221] In effect, Hobbes's standard definition of freedom as absence of external impediments to one's voluntary actions seems to break down in the case of political freedom. Hobbes speaks of that political "liberty of subjects" in terms which are clearly incompatible with his general definition of freedom. The "chains" of laws are said to impede my freedom and they are said to do so by the danger involved in my breaking them. Now, if my anticipation of this danger inclines me to avoid the actions that may provoke it, it's because the danger at issue is perceived as the cause of certain evil consequences for me. Any anticipated evil is an object of fear. And so it is my own fear of certain events and developments (the sheriff arresting me as I am in the process of robbing that neighborhood bank, the county jail, the jury deliberating my case, etc.) that makes me refrain from a certain course of action which I would otherwise have taken. So far, everything conforms with Hobbes's standard definition of liberty. In terms of that definition, my liberty can be impeded by external obstacles, but it can not be impeded by my own desires, whatever they may be. This is why, on numerous occasions, Hobbes explains that when I act under the pressure of fear, I act freely. Free action is voluntary action, and will just *is* the last desire terminating the process of deliberation. It follows that if a deliberative process is terminated by fear and if fear is the cause of the action, then fear is here identical with will and the action itself is done voluntarily and, therefore, freely. If my fear of anything could be an impediment to my action, then my will would have to represent an obstacle to itself; my will would block the action which I would otherwise want to perform, and this seems to be impossible given the Hobbesian account of freedom. But then how can the civil laws "chain" and "bind" me by the danger of breaking them? As I contemplate that open and empty space between myself and the bank I see no external impediments to my actions. Neither am I impeded by a lack of power, since I have all the (natural and even instrumental) "means" to carry out the robbery. What impedes me from moving in on the bank is a mental image of the sheriff and the fear provoked by that image. But if, when I give my money to Hobbes's "Theefe"[222] due to my fear of his actions, I do it freely in spite of that fear, and in spite of the fact that the thief's threats may be conveyed to me in the physical shape of a knife he holds to my throat—why would I be less free when I refrain from robbing the bank merely on the grounds of a fear arising from some possibilities (I may get arrested, go to jail, etc.) I go over in my head? If the thief's dagger does not, apparently, transform my relation to him in a "bond" or a "chain," what is so special about the sheriff's shotgun that my fear of it makes me think and act as if the civil laws *were* "bonds" or "chains" of some kind?

But this is to forget that in positing the sovereign we have subjected ourselves to a constraint which is not an ordinary "external impediment"—for the sovereign was posited by *us*—but, nevertheless, does represent a limitation to our *political* liberty. At the same time, if the civil laws are the "artificial chains" as far as political liberty is concerned, they are no chains at all as far as natural liberty is concerned: "A man sometimes pays his debt, only for *feare* of Imprisonment, which because no body hindered him from detaining, was the action of a man at a *liberty*. And generally all actions which men doe in Commonwealths, for *feare* of the law, or actions, which the doers had *liberty* to omit."[223] In this passage Hobbes is talking about a man exercising his *natural* liberty toward the law. Such a man does not view himself as the author of all actions of the governing authority. Since he does not recognize himself in that authority, *his* fear of the laws (when he decides, out of that fear, to repay the debt) is simply his last desire in the process of deliberation; and, in this sense, his action of repaying the debt is done voluntarily and with no compulsion. Thus the laws are "chains" and "bonds" to the will of the *political* man, but they are neither "chains" nor "bonds" to the will of the *natural* man. And this ambiguous status of the laws is reflected in Hobbes's description of them as "artificial chains." To the extent that they *are* chains they can be said to represent genuine obstacles to men's voluntary motions. But to the extent that they are *artificial* chains, an individual has the option of avoiding their "bondage" by simply activating his natural liberty, that is, by refusing to think and act in conformity with the demands of the social pact.

Part II
Descartes

1

The Demon and the Doubt

With the aid of the hypotheses of a "deceiving God" and an "evil demon" Descartes achieves two purposes.[1] First, he generalizes his doubt about perceptual cognition as a whole. If there was any hope that we could weed out dream illusions from veridical perceptions by relying upon our ordinary cognitive powers, the hope is now gone, since those powers are, as of now, under the influence of a powerful deceiver; and so the very criterion we ordinarily depend upon to separate dream illusions from perceptions (the "coherence" of the latter) must be regarded with suspicion. Second, the doubt is so far-reaching, that it encompasses even the "simple and universal" ideas of mathematics—ideas whose objective validity was left intact (at least qua pure mathematics) by the degree of methodical scepticism generated by the argument from dream illusions.

Thus, the supposition that our cognitive powers are defective due to our dependence upon some powerful deceiver is essential for producing the universal doubt with which Descartes concludes the First Meditation. But why does Descartes use *two* different hypotheses to give us reasons to doubt the reliability of our cognitive powers? He starts out by appealing to the notion of a deceiving God (who has created us cognitively defective), he then finds this notion somehow dissatisfying and goes on to offer us the demon hypothesis. As one commentator puts it, these two hypotheses "do not differ in any respect of epistemological significance"[2]—they perform the very same function of undercutting whatever confidence we may still have in our cognition by making the latter vulnerable to the power of some great deceiver. But if the two hypotheses are epistemologically equivalent, why does Descartes feel the need, at least in the First Meditation, to substitute the hypothesis of the demon for the hypothesis of the deceiving God?

One possible answer suggested by the text of the First Meditation is as follows. Descartes has just considered the deceiving God hypothesis. He then moves on to consider still another possibility: we might have been born cognitively defective due to some accident or fate at the very origins of our being. He then concludes: "but it is not enough to have made these remarks, we must also be careful to keep them in mind. For . . . ancient and commonly held opinions still revert frequently to my mind, long and familiar custom having given them the right to occupy my mind against any inclination and rendered them almost masters of my belief."[3] Since our philosophical meditation can be conducted only if those common, ordinary opinions are set aside and our commitment to methodical scepticism remains constant and steady, and since the deceiving God hypothesis can not exercise such a strong influence in this respect, we need another, and stronger, hypothesis to do the job; and the demon hypothesis may be precisely what we need.

This may be part of the answer, but it is not the whole answer, and it is not even the most important part of the answer. For it is not just those commonly held opinions and familiar customs that are behind our refusal to endure in methodical scepticism induced by, among other things, the deceiving God hypothesis. It is Descartes himself who endorses the *right* of these opinions and customs against the sceptical outlook we have managed to generate so far: "So long as I consider them as they really [*revera*] are, i.e. opinions in some measure doubtful, as I have just shown, and at the same time highly probable [*valde probabiles*] . . . there is much more reason to believe in than to deny them."[4] Now this is very different from simply bowing to custom, habit and natural inclination. For Descartes tells us that the deceiving God hypothesis—even when joined with that other hypothesis about fate or accident at the origin of our being—has only succeeded in casting *some* measure of doubt upon our ordinary convictions; and this very modest degree of doubt is not enough to give us the *reason* for parting with those ordinary convictions. Thus, what is preventing us from suspending our allegiance to our ordinary convictions (to our conviction that our cognitive faculties are sound, that we do not go wrong whenever we add two and three, etc.) is not the sheer weight of habits and natural inclinations and the mental comfort we find in following them, but the lack of sufficient *justification* for such a departure from the ordinary patterns of belief. In spite of the doubt generated by the hypothesis of a defect at our origin (in God, fate, or accident), the ordinary beliefs remain "highly probable" and, apparently, this probability of theirs, when compared with the very modest measure of doubt we have generated so far, seems to give us sufficient reasons for discarding our hypothesis and for sticking to the everyday opinions. When Descartes—as a thinking individual, not as a member of the unthinking crowd—considers these opinions, he concludes that their high probability gives him a reason strong enough to put their established wisdom above any suppositions that his origins might have him defective in his cognitive powers.

But, perhaps, this very situation of having to assess his options with the yardstick of probability is precisely the reason why Descartes finds himself dissatisfied with the deceiving God hypothesis. And, in effect, this is one of the main arguments brought out by the scholars who emphasize the radical difference between the deceiving God hypothesis, and the demon hypothesis.[5] On this interpretation, the main shortcoming of the deceiving God hypothesis is that the reasons for doubt it has produced are not yet compelling precisely because they remain merely probable when cast over against the ordinary opinions. Since we fail to be entirely swayed by the persuasiveness of the deceiving God hypothesis, the doubt generated with its aid can not impose itself upon our minds.

But why should we fail to see sufficient strength in the deceiving God hypothesis? Descartes's main rule in the *Meditations* was, and remains, "to withhold [his] assent from matters which are not entirely certain and indubitable."[6] Given this rule, Descartes's saying that the ordinary opinions and beliefs are still "highly probable" after the deceiving God hypothesis, amounts to his saying that they are *only* highly probable. Whatever may be the measure of doubt that we have cast upon them with the deceiving God hypothesis, we did succeed in casting *some* doubt upon them. And this ought to be enough to give us the *reason* to suspend our allegiance to them, at least to the extent that we are prepared to endorse Descartes's rule to rid ourselves of all beliefs found wanting in absolute certainty. The question remains: why do we continue to assent to opinions which are *only* highly probable and may well be false in the light of the deceiving God hypothesis, even while engaging in an inquiry conducted in conformity with Descartes's main rule of rejecting all opinions which are not entirely certain and indubitable.

Or, perhaps,[7] it is our *will* alone which fails to endure in the sort of doubt generated with the aid of the deceiving God hypothesis? But this would be putting the cart before the horse. For if the reasons to doubt generated with the deceiving God hypothesis had the required clarity and distinctness to our intellect, our will would follow suit—this, at least, is Descartes's doctrine in the *Meditations*. Now according to Descartes's own standard, demanding of us to reject all opinions which are not indubitable and certain, the reasons to doubt generated by the deceiving God hypothesis ought to be strong enough to justify our repudiation of the ordinary views. If the will would not follow suit in such a repudiation of the ordinary views on the strength of the deceiving God hypothesis, then we would have to conclude that that hypothesis, when compared with the (competing) ordinary views is found inadequate in meeting the standard employed by our *intellect* itself. So even if we were to allow here for some failure of the will, we would not put our finger on what Descartes himself viewed as the main shortcoming of the deceiving God hypothesis. He found it wanting not because—or not mainly because—it failed to sustain his will on a steady course of doubt, but because he himself decided that the ordinary views and opinions remain more probable. *This* is why he decided to come up with another hypothesis—with the hypothesis of the demon. Having just told us that he himself finds more reason to believe in the everyday opinions than in the sceptical view produced by various hypotheses concerning his origins, he explains that *that is why*[8] he will take the further step of allowing himself to be deceived by a supposition that he may be at the mercy of some evil or malicious demon. Apparently, the demon hypothesis gives our intellect more compelling reasons to doubt than the deceiving God hypothesis, at least at the present stage of Descartes's argument in the First Meditation.

The entire paradox remains what it was. At the very beginning of the First Meditation Descartes committed himself to a general rule commanding him to withhold his assent from all beliefs which are not entirely certain and indubitable. The deceiving God hypothesis does succeed in casting some measure of doubt upon our ordinary opinions and beliefs. This ought to be enough—given the general rule adopted by Descartes—to suspend our assent to those ordinary opinions and beliefs. Yet Descartes refuses to do so precisely on the grounds that our ordinary opinions and beliefs still remain highly probable—as if he was unaware that in the light of him main methodological principle he ought to be repudiating the ordinary view precisely on account of its mere probability. Within a few paragraphs Descartes has succeeded in committing himself to stamp out all merely probable beliefs and in violating that commitment.

Moreover, we cannot take the easy escape route and claim that the reasons to doubt produced by the deceiving God hypothesis have been found wanting only from a psychological point of view. For if Descartes could not keep his mind steadily committed to the doubt generated by the deceiving God hypothesis, it was precisely on account of the ordinary opinions high probability as assessed by Descartes himself when he compared them with the scepticism generated by the supposition that he might have been created by a deceiving God (or fate, or accident). The upshot of Descartes's assessment was that the deceiving God hypothesis failed to sustain doubt on account of the hypothesis's insufficient probability when measured against the "high probability" of the ordinary views. It was *that* failure of the deceiving God hypothesis which was at the root of its failure to act as the psychologically adequate motive for Descartes's will. Somehow, the doubt generated by the deceiving God hypothesis is *theoretically* less persuasive than the doubt generated with the hypothesis of the demon; and the demon hypothesis's stronger appeal to our will is the result of that theoretical superiority of the demon hypothesis over the deceiving God hypothesis. It is in this sense that the demon hypothesis seems to be doing a better job at competing with the high probability of the ordinary opinions.

This can only mean one thing. At the present stage of the *Meditations*—although not everywhere in Descartes's philosophy—the demon hypothesis must be, in some sense and for some reasons, more "probable" to us than the deceiving God hypothesis. For if the issue is how to overcome the high probability of the ordinary opinions and if the demon hypothesis succeeds where the deceiving God hypothesis has failed, then the demon hypothesis must have a higher degree of "probability" than the deceiving God hypothesis. Somehow, the demon hypothesis must be less farfetched and more plausible at least at the present stage of Descartes's argument.

But why should this be so? After having considered the two hypotheses concerning his origins (he might have been created by a deceiving God or by some accident or fate crippling him forever in his cognitive powers) Descartes describes these reasons to doubt as very powerful and maturely considered.[9] What else, then, do we need to oppose the probability of the ordinary opinions? Conversely, in the Third Meditation, where Descartes takes up again the deceiving God hypothesis, the reasons to doubt generated by that hypothesis are said to be "very slight" and yet, in spite of that, they seem to be quite adequate to remind Descartes of the threat of doubt, so much so that he tells us he cannot be certain of "anything" until he removes that hypothesis.[10] In the First Meditation, then, the deceiving God hypothesis—even when strengthened with that other hypothesis about a possible "accident" or "fate" at our origins—is not sufficient to sustain the required doubt; in the Third Meditation, the deceiving God hypothesis turns out to be fully adequate for the task. It is as if Descartes was contradicting himself in his assessment of the persuasive power of this hypothesis.

To suspect Descartes of contradicting himself on so basic an issue would be silly. The only place where the demon hypothesis is clearly preferable to the deceiving God hypothesis is on the ascending ladder of doubt in the First Meditation. The distinctly "demonic" features of the deceiver are still present at the beginning of the Second Meditation[11]—we have arrived only recently at the stage of doubt and we still need the most convincing device for keeping us there—but already in the Third Meditation, where philosophical thinking has long passed the threshold of overcoming the ordinary views, Descartes seems fully comfortable with the deceiving God hypothesis. And the demon hypothesis is not used at all in the "synthetic" unfolding of Descartes's system in the *Principles of Philosophy*. It seems, then, that the demon hypothesis is better at generating doubt only at the initial stages of our philosophical journey in the *Meditations*, and especially in the First Meditation.

The special status of the First Mediation is not difficult to identify. We must keep in mind Descartes's own distinction between the "analytic" and the "synthetic" method of deploying his philosophical system and the importance of this distinction for the present issue. Entering upon the "analytic" path of the discovery of truth in metaphysics, the First Meditation must appeal to the ordinary, everyday consciousness and to *its* ways of looking at knowledge and reality.[12] And this is precisely what is being done in the First Meditation. Descartes himself characterizes the First Meditation in this way: "The author is considering at this point the man who is just beginning to philosophize."[13] Descartes starts with simple, ordinary cases of sensory perception—he recalls how he was misled, now and then, by his senses; he considers himself as he sits there by the fire, with paper in his hands, he dismisses the experiences of madmen as extravagant and (as he will put it elsewhere) unacceptable to an "honest man"[14] and he focuses on the cases of dream illusions which he has had and which he thinks all people must have had since he has had them merely on account of being human.[15] His philosophical journey starts with a reflection upon his everyday epistemic predicament, and he is careful not to reject the claims of the ordinary opinion by turning against it all kinds of facts, that the ordinary opinion itself is prepared to acknowledge without being prepared to acknowledge the sceptical conclusions that the philosopher may want to draw from these facts. There are of course, sensory illusions, but we do not conclude from this that the senses will deceive us when we perceive our object at an appropriate distance, under good perceptual conditions, and so forth. This is what any ordinary man would say by reflecting upon his sensory illusions and this is what Descartes says too.[16] His path of doubt is the path that begins with the ordinary persons' claims and takes all the care to make doubt plausible to them. On this path—and on this path *alone*—the demon hypothesis proves more useful than the deceiving God hypothesis. Once this path is behind us, the two hypotheses become equivalent (and, we may suspect, any other hypothesis concerning some possible cause of an inherent defectiveness of our cognitive faculties—we may be at the mercy of some superior intelligences, or we may represent a total genetic mishap—would do just as well in this respect).

As a tool for generating methodical scepticism the demon hypothesis is more persuasive than the deceiving God hypothesis only within the context of that educational journey, in the First Meditation, from the plain, ordinary standpoint to the sceptical standpoint. The demon hypothesis is clearly preferable as we begin to reflect upon our everyday epistemic predicament; the demon hypothesis allows us to overcome that predicament while the deceiving God hypothesis is found wanting in this respect. The superiority of the demon hypothesis lies in its stronger appeal to the intellect (and not just in its stronger influence upon the will), but only to the intellect of the individual who sets out on that journey from the ordinary to the philosophical point of view. From the vantage point of a reflective, thinking individual who examines his ordinary beliefs and who is willing to part with them only if he does not have to violate their "high probability" without having sufficient reasons for doing this, the demon hypothesis is satisfying. For *such* an individual, this hypothesis is persuasive enough to make him suspend his own ordinary opinions. We should not be surprised at the implicit demand that such a suspension of the ordinary opinions be carefully pondered and prepared. After all, what is at stake here is the suspension of even such beliefs (in mathematics, etc.) in which, as Descartes himself once thought, "it is scarce *humanly possible* for anyone to err except by inadvertance."[17] We must now consider even those beliefs as *in principle* (and not due to mere "inadvertance") doubtful; and for a man beginning the journey of philosophical education such a step is extraordinary indeed. It can not, and it should not, be taken lightly; and, in this respect, the demon hypothesis conveys a message

which is more plausible and more convincing than the message of the competing hypotheses, including the hypothesis of the deceiving God.

From this point of view—and from this point of view alone—some striking
differences can indeed be detected between the demon hypothesis and the deceiving
God hypothesis. These differences must yet be spelled out, but the change in
Descartes's thinking as he reaches out for the demon hypothesis is immediately
noticeable. Having explained to us his reasons for refusing to adopt the sceptical
viewpoint on the strength of the hypotheses concerning his origin (in God,
fate, etc.) he concludes that instead of relying upon them he will *deceive himself.*[18]
The demon hypothesis is the device with the aid of which Descartes deceives
himself ("I shall suppose not that God . . . but some evil genius," etc.).[19] Thus,
Descartes's will to deceive himself will emerge as a reason to doubt when he
considers himself as being vulnerable to *another* will to deceive—the demon's
will—operating outside him and against him.

Descartes wills to be deceived and this deliberate, voluntary character of his
doubt is made possible by the supposition of another will to deceive bent at
destroying the integrity of his cognition. Descartes thinks that *this* conception
of his epistemic predicament will prove more plausible and less far-fetched
than the other hypotheses at least on that path of the philosophical education
in the First Meditation. Viewed from this angle, the differences between the
deceiving God hypothesis and the demon hypothesis are considerable. In the
first place, the hypothesis of the deceiving God was *found* by Descartes rather
than *created* by him. He has "long had fixed in [his] mind the belief"[20] that an
all-powerful God had created him and he simply wonders if that God might
not have created him cognitively defective. In contrast, the figure of the demon
is constructed by Descartes himself and with the aid of the resources (the will
to deceive) that he— and every thinking individual—finds real enough in his
own experience. In constructing this hypothesis Descartes presupposes very little; and this is a clear advantage in comparison with the deceiving God hypothesis. Second, the will to deceive may be impossible to reconcile with the
quality of supreme goodness (to say nothing of perfection in general) which
we also attribute to God. Such a reconciliation may still prove feasible in the
end, but there is room for uncertainty and hesitation in this respect and this is
enough to make us prefer the (immediately acceptable) hypothesis of the demon.
We can't wait until those uncertainties and hesitations are resolved by a philosophical analysis for we are still at the stage of liberating ourselves from the
ordinary opinions and we need a hypothesis which is immediately acceptable
to us precisely at this stage. And there is nothing surprising about this particular
difference between the two hypotheses. When Descartes thinks of God he can—
at the very best—make an effort to suppose that God is a deceiver, but he
must also take into account the other features of the divine being (such as
goodness, perfection, etc.). God may be a deceiver, but (on account of those

other features) he may not. But the demon is immediately acceptable in his role of a powerful deceiver, since he was deliberately constructed by Descartes himself in order to play precisely that role. Finally, while the deceiving God is thought of as the author of my being to whom I assign my very origin, the demon hypothesis involves me in no speculation about my origin. I need not postulate that I have been created by demon, but only that I am being deceived by him. Elsewhere, Descartes will entertain the possibility that he who created him might also be deceiving him,[21] but in the First Meditation he refrains from doing so, since such a supposition would immediately reestablish, in the mind of the ordinary knower, all the hesitations and uncertainties connected with the deceiving God hypothesis. The entire argument of the *Meditations* will soon corroborate the soundness of this initial decision of Descartes to separate, in the First Meditation, the concept of his deceiver from the concept of the author of his being. For Descartes will soon show us how the idea of our creator contains the idea of infinite perfection and how that idea, in turn, is incompatible with a will to deceive. Since we have some foreknowledge of this already in the First Meditation (otherwise Descartes would not acknowledge the tension, in the notion of the deceiving God, between the supreme goodness and a will to deceive), it is best to separate the idea of our deceiver from the idea of our creator if we are to supply the most plausible reasons to enlist the ordinary knower under the banner of philosophical scepticism.

Let us conclude this part of the argument. When Descartes tries to educate himself out of the naive realism of the ordinary views he finds the demon hypothesis a better tool for generating his doubt than any other hypothesis competing to do the same job. Once the job is done, however, the other hypotheses become equivalent to the demon hypothesis. The demon is still present at the beginning of the Second Meditation (for the thinking self has barely liberated itself from the ordinary views and it still needs the most powerful stimulus for holding onto methodical scepticism), but even in the Third Meditation, which continues to use the "analytic" method for attacking its own problems, the stage of the self's rise to methodical scepticism is so far behind, that Descartes feels free to use the deceiving God hypothesis to sustain him in his doubt. In the *Principles of Philosophy*—where Descartes employs the "synthetic" method from the very beginning—the demon hypothesis can, and does, disappear altogether, since it is not the purpose of the *Principles* to first raise the ordinary consciousness to the level of philosophical discourse.

In the First Meditation Descartes finds the figure of the demon more appealing, for in positing the demon he only "deceives himself"—and he is certain both that he can do at least this much and that his doing this can best overcome the claims of the ordinary views. But his exercise in self-deception opens up a new difficulty which must be resolved. The reasons to doubt Descartes wants to generate cannot be produced by a psychological projection of some experiences peculiar to Descartes himself. If Descartes has rejected the claims of the insane as insufficient grounds for generating scepticism, it's precisely because these claims were mad and, were he to take them seriously, he himself would think like the insane.[22] Clearly, then, Descartes does not think that his concern with the demon is mad or peculiar merely to him. The reasons to doubt generated by the demon hypothesis are not idiosyncratic, otherwise they would not be given the place they are given in the First Meditation, where they are introduced as the most convincing means for producing scepticism. *After* we have confronted, and liberated ourselves from, the sceptical menace, our view of its "demonic" cause will become much more detached and relaxed; thus Descartes himself will, at some point in the Seventh Replies, speak half-jokingly of those miners who are in the habit of ascribing their troubles at the mines to some "spectres or evil spirits inhabiting the subterranean places."[23] But this detached, Olympian point of view is available to Descartes only when he succeeds in putting the threat of scepticism behind him. Looking back at his sceptical arguments, looking back at *all* of them, he will be quite ready to call them all "doubtful" and accepted as valid only as long as certainty and knowledge are beyond his grasp.[24] But this is the assessment he will be able to offer only at the end of his road away from scepticism. He can't afford such a luxury while he is still engaged in the struggle of securing, against the demon, the integrity of his cognition. At *that* stage—at the stage of the First Meditation—the threat of the demon must be taken seriously as a genuine, real issue the ordinary knower must concern himself with. And so if a will to deceive can be posited outside us in the figure of the demon, and can be taken seriously in this capacity, we must suppose that there is some aspect of reality that allows for such a state of affairs to take place.

To my knowledge, the French thinker Hamelin was the first to confront the issue head on. He tried to show that "the demon is not a phantasy of Descartes."[25] To Hamelin, the demon was the personification of the external, hostile influences exercised by an irrational universe upon the human spirit;[26] it was a metaphor in which Descartes tried to express a constant menace, to our cognitive faculties, of the blind forces of nature. But, we may ask, if the demon symbolizes the blind forces of nature, why is he presented to us as an intelligent, inventive, and free agent whereas nature, for Descartes, is void of both will and intelligence? Any account of the demon must come to terms with these features of the demon—with the very same features that Descartes finds in himself as he decides to "deceive himself."

Let us then apply to the demon the Hobbesian method of "reading" the other in oneself. Immediately, the demon ceases to be a mere projection of the workings of the philosopher's own mind. The will to deceive is found in me, but—since in reading myself I also read what is outside me, I read the *other*— the very same will is also the will of the other. Since the other is a member of my own species, certain characteristics that I find in myself will be, quite naturally, mirrored in the other. It is true, of course, that a valid philosophical inquiry could not take off with Descartes finding in himself and then attributing to the other certain traits and characteristics which are peculiar or idiosyncratic. This is why Descartes did not want to anchor his inquiry in the experiences of the insane. But the will to deceive, at least qua temptation, is no peculiarity of Descartes or of anyone else. It is a generic feature of human individuals qua intelligent but free beings. No one can deny a great plausibility of this view within both the philosophical and the ordinary standpoints. Thus, in being told to look at his own will to deceive embodied outside him, as the will of another free and intelligent agent, and in being asked to consider that will as a menace to his cognitive faculties, the commonsensical man is not asked to explore and assess a speculative theory concerning his origins. The external menace to his cognition that he is now being asked to consider is made up of the same stuff that he finds in himself qua intelligent and free being.

This human, anthropological content of the demon has not escaped the attention of commentators.[27] In section 4 of the present chapter I will take a closer look at a passage from the *Principles*[28] in which Descartes himself will finally give us the much needed explanation: if he denies that God may have a will to deceive it's because, he will tell us, he knows that *among men* such a characteristic testifies to various imperfections and weaknesses, and is therefore incompatible with the essence of the divine being. By the same token, Descartes feels free to attribute to the demon the very same characteristic—the will to deceive— found in human individuals and in himself qua human individual. If, in the figure of the demon, this human characteristic is aggrandized and isolated from others, this should not be viewed as a sufficient reason for denying its anthropological content.

It will be objected immediately that the will and the intelligence of a *human* agent bent at deceiving me would, inevitably, lack the *power* to induce in me the sort of (almost unlimited) doubt produced in the First Meditation. But this is by no means clear. If, in Descartes's own judgment, even some unfortunate "accident" at my origin might have crippled my cognitive capacities, why couldn't a human agent do the same right now? Let us consider again the environment of a generalized human violence, where the Hobbesian "Force and Fraud" take precedence over any rules. Under such circumstances, a man may find himself powerless to shelter his cognitive faculties from the impact of, say, drugs or physical and psychological pressure applied to him with the aim of disrupting the normal operation of his mental powers. There is no reason why, under such circumstances, he might not always fail in performing elementary substractions and additions (like in Descartes's own example of going wrong whenever we add two and three); and there is certainly no reason why the normal operations of his senses and memory could not be disrupted, including his very ability to recognize even the individual(s) who put him in such a condition. If moments of lucidity were to return to him, he might even find himself in the state of Cartesian doubt—he might wonder if what is happening to him and around him is "real," if his memory (with the images of his childhood, his town, his family life, etc.) is not altogether deceptive, and so on. As long as the Cartesian demon's task is not to create the truth, but only to mislead us in our apprehension of it—as long as Descartes's theory of the creation of truth is kept firmly separated from his account of man's sceptical predicament[29]— a human agent encountered in an environment of force and fraud seems fully capable of performing it.

Sometimes it is almost taken for granted that Descartes's deceiver could not mislead us the way he does without being omnipotent. But this assumption is at odds with Descartes's overall position on the issue of scepticism. For he thinks he can generate his methodical scepticism by thinking that we might have been created cognitively defective by something *less* than omnipotent—by an accident, or blind fate, indeed by a very *imperfect* "author" of our being.[30] Apparently, he does not think that the cause of our cognitive defectiveness needs to be omnipotent. And there is no good reason why omnipotence would be needed for such a cause, be it "demonic" or not.

Moreover, the textual evidence for the omnipotence of Descartes's demon is not unambiguous. Some time ago, a lively debate took place on this issue, with each of the two participants defending tenaciously his view to the exclusion of the other.[31] The fact is, the evidence cuts both ways. On the one hand, in the key passages of the Second Meditation, the French expressions used to describe the demon's power— in a translation of the *Meditations* approved by Descartes himself—picture him as "very" (*trés*) and "extremely" (*extrêmement*) powerful.[32] Clearly, these expressions imply that the demon may well be *less* than omnipotent.[33] On the other hand, even in the passage in the First Meditation where our encounter with the demon first takes place Descartes switches, at some point, to a talk about "this arch deceiver, however, powerful and deceptive he may be."[34] Here the suggestion is that the demon may well be all-powerful; and, of course, the deceiving God is endowed with the quality of omnipotence.

But even when Descartes speaks of the deceiving God in the *Principles* he refers consistently to what *may* be the case. Descartes is capable of suspending his assent to doubtful and uncertain beliefs "even supposed that He who created us employed His unlimited powers in deceiving us in every way,"[35] or "even should he prove to be all-powerful and deceitful."[36] Thus, far from proving that the deceiver must be omnipotent, some of the key passages in both the *Meditations* and the *Principles* indicate only that he *may* be omnipotent. The possibility remains that he *need not* be omnipotent.

No one can deny, of course, that Descartes does concern himself with the possibility of being at the mercy of an omnipotent deceiver. But the passages just quoted are clear in at least one respect: in all three of them Descartes claims only that nothing would change in his epistemic condition if the deceiver who is causing him to err were to be omnipotent. Whether he actually is, or must be, omnipotent is quite another matter. No support for such a claim can be found in those passages; and the claim is in conflict with Descartes's consistently held view that all kinds of less-than-omnipotent causes could have made us sufficiently defective to induce us to mistrust in principle our cognitive faculties.

But then why does Descartes even bother to explore the possibility that the deceiver may be all-powerful? He must do this, for he cannot know *beforehand*—that is, prior to his exploration of that possibility—that the omnipotence of the deceiver would in no way affect his epistemic condition. He is in a state of the universal doubt due to the actions of a deceiver. He thinks that under such conditions he can still keep his thinking free of deception at least by suspending his assent to doubtful or uncertain beliefs. But to prove that his optimism on this issue is not illusory he must consider what would happen to him if his deceiver were to be omnipotent. His epistemic situation, he concludes, would be unchanged in the two respects that really matter: (1) the increase of the deceiver's power would not produce any additional reasons to doubt and (2) Descartes would still be able to escape the net of deception by suspending assent to unfounded beliefs.

It is necessary for Descartes to deal with the possibility that the deceiver may be all-powerful, but it is not necessary for the deceiver to be all-powerful. Even if he is only "very powerful" or "extremely powerful" he can induce in us the state of universal doubt *and* give us the opportunity to discover the autonomy of our thinking through the "suspension" of our judgment in doubtful and uncertain matters. The doubt is achieved through my discovery of my own powerlessness vis-à-vis the deceiver; the autonomy I regain through my suspension of judgments is a (very modest, to be sure) reassertion of my power against him. But my initial powerlessness does not imply the omnipotence of my deceiver. He must be powerful enough to make *me* powerless—powerless to secure, against him, the normal functioning of my ordinary faculties—but he need not be all-powerful. And if he needs to be only "very powerful" or "extremely powerful," the door is open for a discussion of just how powerful he must be to have the capacity to cripple my cognitive grip upon the world. As I have suggested earlier, the power of a *human* agent acting against me in an environment of violence is fully adequate to bring about the state of Cartesian doubt.

The figure of the demon is human, but it shows some human, all-too-human features in an aggrandized and hypostasized form, and in isolation from other human characteristics. The temptation is then natural to detach the demon from his anthropological roots. Elsewhere, I have tried to follow up on such an interpretation of the demon and I have tried to show how, on such an interpretation, the demon generated doubt will fail to meet the paramount requirement of "plausibility" to the ordinary knower.[37] As a result, philosophical scepticism will emerge as totally alien to the standards, indeed to the very vocabulary, of ordinary consciousness. The path is then cleared for a criticism of philosophical doubt undertaken in the name of ordinary consciousness, or the ordinary language, and so on.

But, it may be objected, to give the demon back his human features may open up a new difficulty. For if I know that my sceptical attitude is due to the supposition of another human will operating outside me and against me, then I do know quite a bit about the world, and then my epistemic condition is far from being so desperate as I thought it to be. And this seems to invalidate the very scepticism the hypothesis was meant to generate in the mind of the ordinary knower.

However, our adoption of the demon hypothesis need not represent a self-refutation of scepticism. For our formulation of the hypothesis, and the kind of knowledge that goes into making it, may still render all the rest of our knowledge—indeed, all of the knowledge that we ordinarily take for granted—inherently doubtful and uncertain without thereby undercutting the sceptical outlook itself. This solution can be defended even while we recognize the human identity of the demon. For even in this case my knowledge that I am vulnerable to the other's will to deceive need not depend upon, and take for granted, my knowledge of the world (with its physical objects, its concrete social grouping, etc.). To be sure, I have no other way of knowing the other as an object within my experience, but I need not rely upon *this* knowledge in order to know that I am an object for the other; and it is highly significant that in our own century a sophisticated Cartesian system has been constructed in which these two orders of our knowledge of the other are entirely different in precisely this respect.[38] I need only look into myself to understand what it would be like to be vulnerable to a deceiving human self set outside me, since in apprehending my own temptation to deceive I apprehend a characteristic generic to me as man.

In this respect, the demon argument may even show some strengths when compared with the other sceptical arguments from the First Meditation. In effect, if we have to depend upon the occurrences of sensory or dream illusions to build the case for scepticism we face a serious difficulty in trying to extend our scepticism to the whole *background* of perceptual cognition—to the background within which, and against which, we experience the illusions. Our very *concepts* of sensory and dream illusions seem to be forged within, and against, such a background of perceptual cognition. The soundness of this background is not only taken for granted but indeed presupposed by our confusions—actual or possible—of illusory with veridical perceptions.[39] We confront no such difficulty while attempting to generate methodical scepticism with the aid of the demon hypothesis. For the figure of the demon is built from the materials Descartes finds *within himself*—from his own will to deceive. To be sure, the demon is posited outside Descartes, as a powerful will *other* than Descartes himself. But Descartes does not posit the demon outside himself by trying to generalize from some features of the perceived world (thereby presupposing the veracity of his perception); he posits the demon as external by reading the other in himself.

The demon is not only posited outside me, he is posited there as affecting me, as having an impact upon me. To the extent that I am subjected to his actions I am passive; indeed, the breakdown of my ordinary cognition under the impact of the demon is the sort of occurrence which has me as a patient and him as an agent. Accordingly, and in conformity with Descartes's own understanding of causality,[40] I think of myself as *causally dependent* upon the demon. Within the very depth of the Cartesian subjectivity, where all of our ordinary beliefs are suspended, and all of our ordinary ties (to the world, to the others, etc.) are severed, the demon emerges as a causal power.

Thus, the suspension of our ordinary beliefs is due to our conception of ourselves as causally dependent upon a hostile will. The sceptical predicament results from an *event*: we find our ordinary grip upon the world undercut by the power of a "demonic" will. This ordinary grip is not merely theoretical but practical as well and its destruction must take place on *both* of these levels. Descartes's demon is "powerful" not simply in the sense of being able to disrupt my cognitive processes, but also—and in the first place—in his sheer ability to remain beyond my control. For were I to be able to control the demon I would not have to worry about any threat, from him, to the integrity of my cognitive faculties. Only because the demon is in a position of force vis-à-vis me do I have to face the issue of being subjected to the deceptions he may be imposing upon me.

This presence of force and fraud deployed by the deceiver comes out clearly in Descartes's final characterization of the sceptical predicament at the end of the First Meditation: "I shall then suppose . . . that . . . some evil genius not less powerful than deceitful, has employed his whole energies in deceiving me; I shall consider that the heavens, the earth, colours, figures, sound, and all other things are nought but the illusions and dreams of which this genius has availed himself in order to lay traps for my credulity."[41] It should not be supposed, as it is sometimes done on the ground of this passage, that our mathematical ideas are suddenly rendered immune from the demon hypothesis. For the very task of this hypothesis was to do a better job at supporting the doubts—*all* of the doubts—generated with the deceiving God hypothesis, and hence also the doubts concerning our mathematical knowledge. And so when Descartes, at the beginning of the Second Meditation, reviews the doubts generated with the demon hypothesis in the First Meditation, he declares flatly that body, figure, extension , movement, and place are now "but the fictions [*chimerae*] of the mind."[42] He cannot mean that figure or extension remain sound at least as purely mathematical concepts (as the pure "essences," as he will call them in the Fifth Meditation), for he would then refrain from calling them fictions (since the Fifth Meditation will sharply separate genuine essences from fictions of our mind). And he would not conclude this brief review of the demon generated scepticism by telling us that, as of now, he may well be altogether separated from the truth.[43] The deceiving "demon" has severed entirely Descartes's link with the world. Accordingly, Descartes's attempt to overcome the sceptical predicament will amount to a power struggle with the deceiver: "I shall remain obstinately attached to this idea, and if by this means it is not in my power [*potestas*] to arrive at the knowledge of any truth, I may at least do what is in my power [i.e., suspend my judgement] and with firm purpose avoid giving credence to any false thing, or being imposed upon by this arch deceiver."[44] In response to the deceiver's threat Descartes declares a total and unwavering mobilization of the powers of his will and his intellect.

2

"I Am a Something"

In the Synopsis of the *Meditations* Descartes prepares us for a rich harvest to be gathered, eventually, from our experiment with scepticism—provided, of course, that that experiment is properly set up and conducted. With the aid of our "liberty" we must adopt a certain general attitude toward the world: we must treat as non-existent all things the existence of which is in any degree doubtful and uncertain.[45] Thus, the act of freedom, although not incompatible with the data of the intellect, is here given an important function of its own. The intellect does assess our beliefs about the world as uncertain and doubtful; and, on the grounds of this assessment, we are fully justified in suspending our assent to those beliefs. Even in achieving this result, we depend upon a contribution of our liberty: Descartes makes a deliberate, voluntary decision to "deceive himself" (although, of course, this voluntary effort at self-deception would have foundered if Descartes had not been able to support it with a valid *reason* found in the idea of the deceiving demon). The ultimate, "demonic" doubt does not befall his passive cognition, but is produced by Descartes's own decision to assess the worth of his beliefs by a free adoption of the worst-case scenario of the most extreme deception possible. But the contribution of our liberty becomes even more pronounced in our adoption, at the end of the First Meditation, of the general attitude toward the world demanded of us in the Synopsis. The intellectual assessment of the damages inflicted upon our cognition (all our beliefs concerning the world turn out to be doubtful and uncertain) is converted, with the aid of our liberty, into an apprehension of the world as non-existent. Once again, we make a deliberate decision to think on the basis of the worst-case scenario. This time, however, our effort will pay off.

In effect, Descartes continues in the Synopsis, in apprehending the world as non-existent, I come to discover my own existence: it is "absolutely impossible" that I who apprehend the world as non-existent could fail to exist (at least while I apprehend the non-existence of the world). If my decision to view the world as non-existent is a serious one, then I must also take seriously the reality of that decision and of the ensuing attitude: the reality of my own apprehending of the world as non-existent. To put it the other way round, if

I can't take seriously the reality of my own apprehending of the world as non-existent then the world itself cannot be present to me as non-existent. Thus, the apprehended non-existence of the world throws me back upon the existence of my own apprehending of that non-existent world.

The Cartesian knower is well equipped to apprehend the non-existence (of the world or of anything else). Already at the stage of writing the *Rules for the Direction of the Mind* Descartes was well aware of what is required for such an apprehension to take place: the non-existence itself must be comprehensible to human intellect. Descartes met the requirement head on. "For it is quite as genuinely an act of knowledge by which I am intuitively aware of what nothing is . . . as that by which I know what existence is."[46] This need not imply that we can actually represent the "nothing." Such a thesis is untenable and Descartes would not have needed Bergson's ingenious experiments in imagination to become aware of that. Only he would have deemed any such experiments entirely irrelevant to the issue. Again and again, he will explain to us that nothing is a "privative" and "negative" concept.[47] If it is comprehensible to us, it is not because we can succeed at a childish attempt in picturing or representing nothingness or nonbeing, but because we ourselves participate in nonbeing to the extent that our own being is characterized as a lack.[48] Since, as Descartes will explain in the Third Meditation, we aspire to the infinite perfections contained in the idea of God, our own endowments are, inevitably, seen as failings when assessed in terms of that high standard to which we aspire. The strategy is at work beginning with the First Meditation. We aspire to absolute certainty in matters of knowledge; in the light of this aspiration, the demon hypothesis is put forward and adopted as the worst-case scenario we must take into account since, quite clearly, we cannot hope to reach absolute certainty without subjecting ourselves to, and withstanding, the menace of absolute doubt. We then face the possibility of the non-existence of the world, since our cognitive faculties are found wanting in the light of the demon hypothesis. By making us comprehend our cognitive faculties as a lack, the demon makes us comprehend that we lack grounds for attributing existence to the world. Moreover, if our cognitive faculties are, thus far, failing us in a confrontation with the demon, it's because the demon remains beyond our *practical* capacity to control him. Thus, our apprehension of the non-existence of the world results from our general (cognitive and practical) *lack of power* to secure, against the demon, the reality of our world. Were we to have enough power to thwart the demon's actions, we would not be confronted with the very real danger that he may be changing our world into an illusion. Due to the demon's power and our own powerlessness, we are brought face to face with the collapse of the world. But, by the same token, we discover ourselves (and our own existence) as witnesses of that collapse. For in order to apprehend the collapse of the world, I, who notice it and report on it must be its survivor.

We can now offer some comments on Descartes's main argument for his own existence in the Second Meditation. Having left us, at the end of the First Meditation, with the thought that all "external things" are only illusions caused by a demon bent at destroying our cognitive access to the real world, Descartes now tries to see if some reality may not remain within the reach of our knowledge in spite of the deceiver's actions. Descartes's attempt is carried out in two steps. He first reviews the devastations the demon brought upon the *world,* and he then concludes that he, Descartes, insofar as he witnesses these devastations, must be real: "I was persuaded that *there was nothing in the world,* that there was no heaven, no earth, that there were no minds, nor any bodies: was I not then likewise persuaded that I did not exist? Not at all; of a surety I myself did exist since I persuaded myself of something."[49] But this, Descartes thinks, does not yet go far enough. For even if he already knows that he exists, in spite of the world being transformed into a collection of illusions, how does he know that *his own* existence, inasmuch as he appre-hends the nonbeing of the world, is not one more of these "illusions" caused by the demon? In the second part of the passage Descartes takes up this further challenge: "But there is some deceiver or other, very powerful and very cunning, who ever employs his ingenuity in deceiving me. Then without doubt I exist also if he deceives me, and let him deceive me as much as he will, *he can never cause me to be nothing as long as I think that I am something* [aliquid]."[50] Thus, even while I entertain the possibility that some powerful deceiver may be trying to take my being away from me—by changing it into one of these illusions he set up for me—the proposition "I am, I exist" is necessarily true every time I think it.[51] In fact, even if I attempt to deny that proposition I still find myself assenting to its truth. For if I try to think that I am indeed the "nothing" the deceiver is bent at making of me I still discover myself as being: it is just as impossible for me to witness my own nonbeing while not enjoying actual ex-istence, as it would be to report on my own death. My being unable not to witness my own existence and my not being able to witness my own non-existence—this is the irremovable object on the path of any potential deceiver.

Put together, then, the two parts of Descartes's argument in the Second Meditation boil down to his attempt to test his existence, and his knowledge of it, against the power of an intelligent and free deceiver. If this demon causes the world to be non-existent then Descartes discovers that he himself, insofar as he apprehends the world as non-existent, must be a "something." And he remains such a "something" even on the more radical assumption that the demon may be trying to mislead him in his very thinking that he, Descartes, exists. In both cases the apprehended danger that reality is collapsing around him throws Descartes back upon the presence of his own thinking as he witnesses that collapse. Thus, whatever the demon does to Descartes, he can't take away from Descartes at least one possession: Descartes's own thinking at that precise moment when the philosopher envisions and tests the limits of the demon's power. As owner of this possession (or "attribute") Descartes is a "something" or a "real thing" (*res vera*)[52] in a way closely related to what we have in mind when we say of someone that he "amounts to something" in this world, or else that he is a "somebody," or, perhaps, that he is "for real." Descartes's thinking is "for real"—try as he may the demon can not take that away from Descartes—and thus Descartes himself is for real too.

Descartes is real if the power of the demon to deceive him has really been tested. Has our test been properly performed? In asserting himself against the deceiver Descartes attributed to himself "thinking" and "existence." Did he know the significance of these ideas? And why did he show full confidence in their objective validity—even while he refrained from attributing such a validity even to mathematical ideas? If a powerful deceiver can be strong enough to "mislead" one about mathematics, how can one be certain that the ideas of "existence" and "thought" are not under the very same threat? To be sure, in his struggle with the demon Descartes comes to realize that his attributions of both thinking and existing to himself are, in some sense, *self-verifying*: if he is being misled by the demon in his very thinking (in his thinking that there is a world, or that he exists, or even—and especially—that he is thinking) he still finds that he must be actually thinking and existing.[53] But this does not yet solve the difficulty. Let us look more carefully. When Descartes thinks that the demon misleads him in, and about, his own thinking, he realizes that he is thinking. But in order to realize this he must fall back upon his knowledge of what "thinking" is and how it is to be recognized in his experience. And why does he think that he can take for granted such a knowledge?

Descartes did acknowledge and address this question. In the Sixth Replies he gives the most significant statement of his answer. Our knowledge of what thought is, and what existence is, does not require any reflective cognition or demonstration: "It is altogether enough for one to know it by means of that internal cognition which always precedes reflective knowledge, and which, when the object is thought and existence, is innate in all men; so that, however overwhelmed by prejudice and attention to the words rather than their signification (*significationes*), though we may feign that we do not possess that knowledge, we cannot, nevertheless, really be without it. When, therefore, anyone perceives that he thinks and that it thence follows that he exists, although he chance never previously to have asked what thought is, nor what existence, he cannot nevertheless fail to have a knowledge of each sufficient to give him assurance on this score."[54]

Thus, prior to and independently of any reflection or demonstration we have what amounts to a *pre*reflective knowledge of the notions of thought and existence. We have, in addition, an actual perception of our own thinking; indeed, as Descartes explains a bit later in the Sixth Replies, "We cannot help *experiencing* within us that we think."[55] These two components of our cognition—the intellectual grasp of the notions of thought and existence joined with an actual perception (or experience) of our own thinking—can't fail to give us the knowledge of our own existence qua thinking beings. It is important to realize that both components as well as their joint operation take place on the prereflective level. Anyone who perceives that he is thinking (and everyone has this perception at every moment) cannot fail to recognize that he thinks and that he exists, even though he has never reflected upon the meaning of the notions involved and/or upon the legitimacy of their application in this particular case—in the case of his own thought and existence. Apparently, the knowledge of what existence and thought are as well as the knowledge of myself qua thinking and existing is so basic to me that I need not acquire it through reflective cognition.

But if my awareness that I think and that I am takes place already on a prereflective level, and if this awareness is deemed by Descartes himself to give me the sufficient knowledge that I think and that I exist, then Descartes must confront a further difficulty. After all, what he himself is doing in the Second Meditation as he ponders his condition and discovers that he thinks and exists represents, undoubtedly, a process of *reflective* cognition. In the first place, then, it is clear that in some sense one can discover reflectively one's thought and one's existence. And, in the second place, this reflective, meditative discovery of one's thinking and existing is presented to us precisely as a theoretical demonstration that our knowledge that we think and that we exist is justified. For what else does the Second Meditation prove if it doesn't prove that? Not only is such a demonstration supplied by the Second Meditation but, more important, it represents the foundation of the *Meditations'* entire project of putting our knowledge upon a secure basis. Either, then, I can be said to know that I think and that I exist already at the ordinary, prereflective level, but then the reflective approach of the *Meditations* is altogether unnecessary, or the reflective project of the *Meditations* is indeed indispensable to supply me with the badly needed demonstration that I think and that I exist, but then the claims we have just seen put forward in the Sixth Replies fall to the ground.

The difficulty becomes even more acute if we focus on the relevant outlook of the prereflective consciousness and compare it with the corresponding outlook of the reflective consciousness of the philosopher. The latter discovers his own thought and existence as he apprehends the non-existence of the world. This is how Descartes himself describes, in the Synopsis, what will take place in the Second Meditation. But, of course, the everyday, prereflective consciousness does not apprehend the world as non-existent. And yet this consciousness is said to give us sufficient knowledge that we think and that we exist. But if this is so, why do we need the reflective, meditative test of apprehending ourselves over against a world sinking fast into non-existence? And, even more important, if for some reason we do need such a test, then the plain, prereflective consciousness can not give us the sufficient knowledge of our thinking and being, since the plain, prereflective consciousness does not apprehend the world as non-existent.

But then what *is* the purpose of the philosophical meditation over against our ordinary prereflective knowledge? "By meditation and observation we are able to bring about a change from mere indeterminateness and confusedness in our knowledge to clearness and determinateness."[56] This is Descartes's general answer to Meno's paradox, and it is quite helpful in solving the present puzzle. The philosophical meditation does, to be sure, liberate the plain consciousness from various habits and prejudices, but it does so by digging out those "significations"[57] which are already understood, however vaguely and implicitly, by the plain consciousness itself. Thus, by paying closer attention to those "significations" the philosopher brings out and assesses the *kinds* of claims that condition our plain understanding of ourselves as thinking and existing; and from this examination the philosopher concludes that these claims are logically independent of any claims concerning the existence of the external world. And if the plain consciousness does not understand that, it's because it does not grasp all of the ramifications of its own claims and beliefs. In conformity with Descartes's general procedure as we discussed it in the preceding section, the demon hypothesis is only the ultimate device with the aid of which the philosopher brings out and examines those ramifications of our plain, ordinary knowledge, including our knowledge that we think and that we are.

We have already noted, while offering preliminary comments upon Descartes's main argument in the Second Mediation, that what takes Descartes to the conclusion that he exists is his own thinking that the demon may be deceiving him about the world or (even) about his own thinking. For if Descartes thinks that the demon may be deceiving him about his own thinking, then it is still the case that he is thinking. Thinking, therefore, is something that the deceiver *can't take away* from Descartes no matter what or come what may; and since Descartes "has" something that no deceiving power can take away from him, he "is" something—a real thing, a substance of some kind. Instead of "thinking" another mentalistic term is often used by Descartes as a way of getting to his *sum*: "doubting." The argument is then very similar. Due to the actions of a powerful deceiver, Descartes is thrown into the state of universal doubt. But if he doubts still further—that is, if he doubts that he is in the state of universal doubt—then it must still be the case that he finds himself in the state of doubting. Both thinking and doubting turn out to be self-verifying.

It may be asked immediately whether both of them are self-verifying in the same sense and in their own right. On this point, Descartes hesitates, but his argument from doubting in its present form carries the day only if doubting is viewed as a case of thinking. If I doubt, I think (since doubting is a case of thinking) and if I want to deny that I think I must engage again in actual thinking. In contrast, my denial that I doubt does not, by itself, imply that I doubt. In this sense thinking alone is self-verifying while doubting is self-verifying only as a case of thinking. In the *Search After Truth*, Descartes will give several helpful indications to clarify this issue.[58]

On the other hand, even if doubting is self-verifying only as a case of thinking, Descartes's knowledge that he doubts is sound in its own right. Descartes does know that he is supposing himself to be vulnerable to a powerful deceiver. He himself made that supposition and everything else he did thus far was done on its grounds. But if Descartes knows that he may be vulnerable to a powerful deceiver, he also knows that he may be deceived in his beliefs. And this is another way of saying that he is already engaged, quite knowingly, in doubting the soundness of these beliefs. Consequently, he knows himself as doubting. His knowledge that he is in the condition of doubt is logically entailed by his knowledge that he may be deceived by the demon. Since he himself, by a voluntary and conscious decision, established the demon hypothesis, and since he reasons on its basis, he cannot cast doubt on his knowledge that he doubts, for this knowledge is implied by that hypothesis; in fact, the demon hypothesis was put forward with the express aim of allowing Descartes to "deceive himself". Thus, whatever other knowledge of his mental condition may be rendered suspect under the demon hypothesis, Descartes's knowledge that he doubts withstands this test. In spite of the demon's activities—or rather thanks to them—Descartes does know his own condition as the condition of a doubter. And he is thereby committed to the thesis that even under the demon hypothesis he does know what it is to doubt and when to apply the concept of doubting to his own experiences. And, in effect, like the earlier cases of "thinking" and "existence" the concept of doubting is viewed by Descartes as one of those basic concepts which belong to the inalienable equipment of every knower and remain, in that capacity, immune to any sceptical menace.[59]

Having tested himself, in the Second Meditation, against the threat of an ultimate deception and having discovered, in the light of this threat, that he exists, Descartes shows himself willing to infer his existence from less severely tested premises as well. Thus, in replying to Gassendi's question (why couldn't Descartes infer his existence from *any* of his activities, not just from his thinking) Descartes will indicate that thinking alone has the required "metaphysical certitude" to serve as the premise for the discovery of his *sum*, but he will also define thinking so broadly as to make it synonyms with awareness in general.[60] Given this broad understanding of thinking, Descartes will be quite prepared to infer his existence even from his "thinking that he is walking," provided that that thought as a whole is taken merely as a piece of his awareness, with its truth logically independent of all propositions referring to the existence of his body. In a similar fashion, Descartes will explain elsewhere that taken merely as the content of his awareness the thought "I am breathing therefore I am" amounts to the same as "I am thinking therefore I am."[61] For whereas we may be wrong in thinking that we are actually breathing, we can't be wrong in thinking that we are having precisely that thought: the "thought of breathing is present to our mind"[62] and everything which has such a presence to our mind supplies us with certain and incorrigible knowledge. In the *Principles of Philosophy* Descartes holds that just about any mental experience can be taken as a stepping stone for discovering that we are. In the *Principles* a whole theory to that effect is being advanced. As long as I take my mental experiences as completely unaffected by the existence or non-existence of bodies (and especially of my own body), I can't go wrong; and this certain and incorrigible knowledge of my own mental experiences allows me to affirm my existence at least *qua* owner of those experiences.[63]

As Descartes tells me, then, I am in a position to discover that I exist from the proposition "I think that I walk" but not from the proposition "I walk," because this second proposition—involving as it does a reference to the existence and the actions of my body—lacks the required "metaphysical certitude." But this claim goes far beyond the limits of what can be allowed under the demon hypothesis. If the demon can mislead me in my beliefs about bodies, why can't he mislead me in my beliefs about the content of my mental experiences? When I think that the demon may be misleading me in my belief "I think that I walk" I do not find myself compelled to assent to its truth. I will still find myself compelled to assent to the truth of one *part* of that proposition (to the "I think" in the "I think that I walk"), but not to the truth of my entire report "I think that I walk." And yet this is what follows from Descartes's reply to Gassendi. Consequently, we can't circumvent the present difficulty by first dividing every thought into its form and its content and then going on to claim that the formal element alone (the Kantian "I think" accompanying all of our representations, the mere form of all our mental experiences) can take us to our *sum*. Descartes's reply to Gassendi leaves no room for ambiguity: what is metaphysically certain is the *whole* thought "I think that I walk"; this is why Descartes sets it in contrast with the thought "I walk," and this is why he uses the former as a premise from which to infer his existence. He infers his existence not simply from the experience of *thinking* that he is walking, but from the whole experience of thinking *that he is walking*. Apparently, as long as I focus on what is actually present in my mind I can't go wrong; and any knowledge of my present mental states is sufficient to take me to my *sum*.

Descartes's view that our knowledge of our own mental states or at least of those of them that are given to us in the present and need not depend upon the workings of our memory—is certain and incorrigible stems from his conviction that mind is, as it were, "transparent" to itself in its experiences. This transparency thesis is much broader than the theory of the prereflective knowledge as we have seen it used by Descartes thus far. For the latter was called upon to account only for our immediate grasp of *some* notions or contents of our mental life (of our existence, thought, etc.), while the present thesis is meant to apply to our mental life as a whole. In fact, Descartes did not hesitate to formulate this thesis as if justified by the very *definition* of what a mental experience is. Since mind is a thinking thing, all mental experiences must be viewed as modes of thought (in the general sense of *cogitatio, pensée*). Now, "thought is a word that covers everything that exists in us in such a way that we are immediately *conscious* of it. Thus all the operations of will, intellect, imagination, and of the senses are thoughts."[64] To make this definition of thought less arbitrary, Descartes applied his standard procedure of appealing to what we can and cannot "conceive": "The fact *that nothing can exist in the mind, in so far as it is a thinking thing, of which it is not conscious*, seems to me self-evident, because we can conceive nothing to exist in it, viewed in this light, that is not thought, and something dependent on thought; for otherwise it would not belong to the mind, in so far as it is a thinking thing."[65] Thus, insofar as a thought is to *belong* to me *qua* thinking, conscious self, it must be part and parcel of my conscious life. Otherwise, that thought would be something like a piece of unthinking thinking, or unconscious consciousness, and this is absurd. Echoes of this argument can be heard even among contemporary Cartesians,[66] but, tested against Descartes's own hypothesis of the demon, the argument fails to convince. For even if we restrict Descartes's claim, as he himself does,[67] to our *present* thoughts, and even if we grand Descartes that all of our present mental life must be accompanied by some degree of awareness we are still very far from making that awareness certain and incorrigible, given the demon's activities of deception directed at our experience.

Perhaps Descartes's insistence that we can't go wrong in our knowledge of the present "acts" and "operations" of our mind[68] should be seen as a hint at his real argument. Descartes might be taken as claiming that my mental actions and operations *alone* are open to a knowledge free of any menace of deception or error. I would possess this sort of knowledge about whatever it is that I am (mentally) doing, since *I* would be doing it, calling it into being, as it were. Thus, I would have the "author's knowledge" of my mental actions—they would be transparent to me since they would be authored by me. Hobbes appealed to this type of knowledge in building his system of political philosophy. But then the concepts of "force and fraud" as Hobbes used them were not meant to undercut our capacity to have reliable knowledge but (only) our capacity to have a reliable mode of action. In contrast, the threat of Descartes's demon is, above all, epistemic. In the light of this threat we can grant Descartes the author's knowledge of *some* of his actions (of the action of "deceiving himself" with the aid of the demon hypothesis, of the action of "suspending" his assent to some beliefs etc.), but certainly not of all of his actions, or even of most of them. For why couldn't the demon mislead me in my knowledge of my mental activities just as he misleads me in my knowledge of my bodily activities? I can't rule this out simply because I can save, from the demon's menace, my knowledge of being engaged in that one special activity called "doubting"; and there is certainly no hope of finding the self-verifying status in all thoughts of the form "I am (mentally) doing *X*, or *Y*, or *Z*."

The transparency thesis supplies a rather shaky basis for Descartes's discovery of his *sum*, but it cannot be ignored and passed over, for it represents an important source of support for all kinds of claims put forward by Descartes. As Descartes continues his inquiry in the *Meditations* he often shows an amazing trust in the reliability of his introspective grasp of this or that idea or faculty of the mind; and the source from which this trust springs is precisely Descartes's conception of mental life as accessible to our immediate knowledge. This does not mean, of course, that Descartes had nothing else to go on while pushing ahead with his meditative inquiry. As we shall see, the main source of support for his claims lies elsewhere. He thinks that his grasp of himself as being in the condition of doubt presupposes certain further theses about himself and his condition. He adopts those further theses not because he simply inspects his ideas and his mental faculties but because not adopting those theses would deprive him of the right to advance even his very modest claims that he is thinking, doubting, suspending his judgments, and so on. To what extent Descartes is successful in this strategy can only be evaluated on a case-by-case basis.

So far, we have not even hinted at another important difficulty associated with the problem of the Cartesian doubt. When I say, "I think" or "I am thinking", I refer not only to a thinking process or activity but also, and even above all, to a *particular* self; and the same holds for the expression "I exist." And yet neither the ontological context of the Cartesian doubt nor the self-verifying status of thinking seem to warrant such a reference to a *particular* self. In fact, quite the contrary seems to be the case. Let us start with the context of the doubt. As I apprehend the collapse of the world I, qua witness of that collapse, emerge as its survivor: in apprehending the nonbeing of the world I am thrown back upon the being of my apprehending. But isn't my "I" going to be lost with the loss of the world? After all, my "I" too seems to be a part of the world: the personal pronoun that I use when I speak of myself refers to my ordinary, everyday self, identifiable by my body, my character traits, habits, preferences and so on. If I cease to take for granted the reality of what makes up the content of my everyday, ordinary self, what right do I have to continue to use the personal pronoun "I"? Furthermore, the use of this personal pronoun seems meaningful only if I view myself as a member of a community. For me to apply to myself the concept of a particular self—and I

do at least that when I call myself "I"—I must be willing to grant that there
are other such selves in the world I live in, the selves I refer to by such expressions as "You", "He", "They" and so on. But then how can I go on describing
myself as an "I" at the (present) stage of methodical solipsism generated by the
universal doubt?

Perhaps we could try to bypass such considerations of ordinary usage by
attributing the self-verifying status to the entire proposition "I am thinking",
But to do this would be to beg the question. If the thinking I am aware of
when I am in the state of universal doubt is necessarily *my* thinking, then the
whole proposition is indeed self-verifying. But the implied necessity of that
connection between the "thinking" and the "I" has, so far, eluded us. If our
ordinary understanding of the "I" is suspended—and it must be, at the stage
of methodical doubt— then it seems that we should grant the self-verifying
status only to propositions such as "there is thinking going on here" or "there
is a thought here", propositions which imply no necessary connection between
the thinking and the I. Or is the connection definitional? If our definition is
not to be an arbitrary stipulation we must find it validated by our grasp of the
relevant connection between the idea of thinking and the idea of a particular
self. But where do we look for such a necessary connection between these
two ideas?

One possible answer to this question has already been given. In the first-
person present-tense case, at least, thinking can't fail to be experienced as a
real, actual attribute. But no such attribute can exist by itself. A real, actual
attribute must belong to a substance,[69] and so the thinking that we discover in
the *cogito* experience refers us to its underlying bearer; the bearer is thus *inferred* from the apprehended presence of the attribute of thinking. And what
candidate could better fill the slot of this bearer than our own thinking self,
our "I"?

Some obvious difficulties involved in this inference can be quickly brushed
aside. Is it really possible, one may ask, to observe first an actual, real attribute
and only then infer from it its underlying substance? If a real attribute must
always be an attribute of something, then for me to grasp my own thinking as
a real attribute I must already know that it belongs to a substance; consequently,
I must be acquainted with the substance underlying my thinking prior to my
grasping the latter as a real attribute. There seems to be no room here for the
suggested inference; or rather, if there is to be an inference at all in the present
case, it ought to go in the opposite direction—I ought to ascribe reality and
actuality to my own thinking only due to my prior knowledge that I, as a
bearer of thoughts, enjoy actual and real existence.

This difficulty should not be considered a serious stumbling block in our
way. Whereas, from the ontological point of view, no attribute can exist without being anchored in a substance, in the order of discovery this need not be

so. There is nothing inherently wrong in the suggestion that the evidence of the reality of an attribute could be the basis for my coming to know the underlying substance; in fact, in the order of discovery the step *could* not be from substance to attribute, since it is Descartes's consistently held view that we can't know substance otherwise than through its attributes. The actual path of discovery outlined in the Second Meditation conforms fully to that general rule. Thrown into the state of universal doubt by the demon I first hit upon my own thinking as upon the only property the demon can't take away from me; and it is on this basis that I discover myself as a "something", a "real thing", i.e. as a substance.

But do I thereby discover myself as a *particular* substance? I can't know that, if the step from thinking to its underlying bearer is taken on the basis of an inference. For it may very well be the case that what is having all these thoughts which I now apprehend in what I call "myself" is, in fact, some general and impersonal substance underlying all the other thoughts occurring in the universe. I do know that I have cognitive access only to a limited subset of thoughts (to those I call "my own" present thoughts), but I cannot rule out the possibility that the same substance may support all the other thoughts occurring in the universe. To be sure, I can not know, as yet, if there *are* any thoughts other than those I call my own. But this is besides the point. For if I want to justify my claim that the substance behind what I call "my thoughts" is indeed particular, I need to be in a position to show already at this stage, that the substance at issue is different from the substance that would underlie the thoughts I would normally call "his" or "hers" were they to occur in the universe or were I to become aware of them. But I can't rule out this possibility if I simply infer the substance from the thoughts that I am aware of at the stage of methodical doubt.

Will we fare any better in this respect by starting out with (mental) *actions*? It seems indisputable that actions are, in some sense, performed by an agent; even if we could form a conception of a quality unattached to a bearer, it would be much more difficult to speak of a freefloating action. Action seems to be the action of someone. And even if we refuse to share Descartes's view that mental actions are always "transparent" to the agent who performs them, we could still depend upon the appearance of any of them to infer the presence of the agent behind them. For this reason the acts of thinking or doubting we are acquainted with even at the stage of methodical doubt could very well be used as stepping stones for our inference of an active substance behind them.

Would such an inference discover the substance in question as a *particular* being? There is no reason to think so. The many different actions, whenever and wherever they might occur, could well be viewed as the doings of a general active substance, of some force spread throughout the universe etc. In this respect, at least, mental actions are in no way different from mental states.

Since the particular character of the "real thing" that supports my thoughts cannot be discovered by an inference, might it not be viewed as an original givenness of our mental life? To say this would not amount to saying—since Descartes would not allow us to say it—that we are capable of grasping a "bare particular" without any attributes. Rather, the claim would be that thinking is *immediately* grasped as an activity of a particular self.[70] Let us spell out in more detail what would be involved in such a claim. In some sense, thinking itself can be considered as something given to us; for, as we recall, we do have an original *experience* of our own thinking which we can't fail to identify with the aid of the appropriate concept. But Descartes committed himself to this view only after he has subjected that givenness of our thinking to the test of self-verification. As it turned out, our denial that we think implied the actual presence of our thinking; and only in the light of this circumstance did Descartes conclude that thinking has an irremovable actuality for us. Now while he was performing this test he was speaking in the first person, and so it is possible to conclude that the connection of "thinking" with an "I" maintains itself even in the moment of supreme doubt as an immediate, intuitive datum. Couldn't it be the case that I am simply denying *my own* thinking only to find out that *I* am still doing this denying? Like the ideas of thinking and existing the idea of myself is innate in me. Why couldn't it maintain itself, like those other ideas, even within the context of the methodical doubt? Descartes himself seems to be suggesting something along these lines in the *Principles of Philosophy*: "because each one of us is conscious that he thinks, and that in thinking he can shut off from himself all other substance, either thinking or extended, we may conclude that each of us, similarly regarded, is really distinct from every other thinking substance, and from every corporeal substance".[71] But it is not clear why the self so apprehended should still be viewed as a *particular* existent. The difficulties we have mentioned earlier reemerge. By "shutting off" from himself the external world—including other selves and his own body—Descartes has shut off from himself his own ordinary worldly self (determined by a body, by the relations with other selves etc.). In what sense, then, is he still a particular self if, as we noted before, his ordinary ways of thinking and speaking of himself as a particular "I" have by now lost the very context allowing them to be meaningful? Even if we were to grant him that his mind as he discovers it in the moment of doubt does have a truly indivisible *unity*, this would still be a far cry from having to think of that unified mental field as anchored in a particular "I";[72] and there would be every incentive not to apply a grammatical category to a context within which it is not ordinarily applied and where it seems to lose its very meaning.

Faced with these failures to justify the use of the personal pronoun "I" at the stage of doubt, we could resign ourselves to view Descartes's "I think" as the prototype of the Kantian *Bewusstsein überhaupt*. The "I think" would be a mere logical function accompanying all our representations; it would refer not to any (numerical much less qualitative) differences among particular selves, but, rather, to their common intellectual nature in which the human knowledge finds its ultimate condition of possibility.[73] But this anonymous, formal "I" would fit badly the particular, indeed the highly personal, "I" speaking to us from the pages of the *Meditations*. There is no doubt that thinking is, or turns out to be, a universal characteristic—a characteristic of all human selves as merely rational. But the meditating self is also particular. The connection betweeen thinking and the (particular) self survives even the most severe test— the operation of the methodical doubt—through which we purify our thought from its links with the ordinary, everyday self. The task of tracking down that connection must be faced up to.

Let us review our steps. If the presence of an "I" in the *cogito* experience is not to be explained away as an illusion or—at the very best—as a misguided usage of a concept or a word within a context that won't bear it, the "I" must be discovered either as an immediate datum of the *cogito*, or as the term of a valid inference. So far, however, we have had to reject both of these possibilities.

But the attempts we have made so far to find the "I" in the *cogito* experience had one thing in common: we concerned ourselves with the purely cognitive quality of the state the thinker finds himself in at the stage of doubt. And yet this stage is not reached, or sustained, with the aid of cognition alone. Our will, too, contributes to that venture. In positing the demon, Descartes voluntarily "deceives himself." His decision to abstain from assenting to doubtful or uncertain beliefs (and, even more so, his decision, in the Synopsis, to view as non-existent all things the existence of which is doubtful and uncertain) is also an act of will. Descartes's radical doubt does not befall man's inherently passive mind but represents a free, voluntary achievement of a self striving for total autonomy and independence. And might we not find the "I" of the "I am thinking" by scrutinizing more closely that free activity of a self striving to achieve its autonomy and independence with the aid of methodical doubt?

It is true, of course, that this striving of the self to purify its cognition of all untested and unexamined beliefs is, or may be, shared by many selves. If the will is active here, it is active only as the *will to truth*; and what could be less particular than this, at least within a community of rational selves? Unless the will to truth affirms itself through a struggle with that *other* will, with the *will to deceive*.

But this is precisely what Descartes holds both in the *Meditations* and in the *Principles* as well. In the *Principles* he will speak again of a "God" who deceives us (but we should keep in mind all the reasons, given in the First Meditation, why the concept of an evil or malicious "demon" does a better job at first producing the suspicion that we may be deceived in all of the beliefs we have been accepting so far). The freedom to abstain from assenting to doubtful or uncertain beliefs is first characterized as a fact of our *experience* as we measure ourselves against a powerful will bent at deceiving us.[74] But Descartes goes on to present this experience of opposing ourselves to the deceiver as a sufficient *proof* of the reality of our freedom and he then adds, in the same passage, that the concept of freedom must be counted amoung our most fundamental notions, with its objective validity tested by its endurance and its indispensability within the condition of even the most extreme doubting.[75]

This high standing of the concept of freedom puts it on the same level with the concepts of thinking, doubting and existing. All of these concepts are necessary for articulating the operation of methodical doubt. All of them are validated by the philosopher as he discovers their strength, and their indispensability, on the reflective, philosophical level. We recall what this validation implies for Descartes: it implies that the concepts at issue must be so basic to us that they ought to be viewed as always already shaping our plain, prereflective consciousness. The task of the philosopher is to take those basic concepts out of the plain ordinary consciousness and to test their worth within the context of the philosophical inquiry. The concept and the experience of freedom are also fundamental to our plain, prereflective consciousness: "We are so conscious of the liberty which exists in us, that there is nothing that we comprehend more clearly and perfectly . . . it would be absurd to doubt that of which we inwardly experience and perceive as existing within ourselves".[76] And to doubt freedom would be even more "absurd" given its (philosophically attested) indispensability for implementing even the most extreme form of doubt. The concept of freedom must be deemed sound, for I find it indispensable to articulate what is taking place when I oppose myself to a powerful will bent at deceiving me. For Descartes, the situation is quite simple. Either I can escape the net of deception, but then I must attribute to myself a certain kind of freedom (and this happens to be the same kind of freedom that I perceive in myself in the everyday, ordinary experience) or I refuse to grant myself such a freedom, but then I can not avoid falling under the dominion of some powerful deceiver and my philosophical search after truth cannot even begin.

The *cogito* is an achievement of the self's will to truth, but this will asserts itself through a struggle with *another will*. To will the truth means, among other things, to resolve oneself to uproot all of one's untested, taken-for-granted beliefs and habits of thought. But this uprooting takes place as one's response to the danger of falling under the dominion of a powerful deceiver. By finding myself vulnerable to such a deceiver, I begin to suspect that all of my certainties and beliefs may turn out to be unfounded, since the very cognitive powers I ordinarily rely upon to separate truths from errors must now be viewed as unreliable. Only by collecting myself, or trying to collect myself, against the deceiver can I regain any hope for discoverying the truth.

The reference to that elusive "I" in the *cogito* experience ceases to be puzzling now. The *thinking* from the "I am thinking" has already established its reality through the self-verification test conducted under the conditions of universal deception. We can see now how the establishment of these conditions and of that test implies that the "I" from the "I am thinking" does indeed refer to a self made *particular* by its will to overcome another will, the will of the deceiver. To be sure, that will to deceive is also, and even in the first place, Descartes's own will. Descartes decided to "deceive himself," thereby confessing, and demonstrating, that the will to deceive operates within him. But to set himself against that will he had to posit it outside him, in the other. To actualize the will to deceive and to actively oppose himself to that will, he had to view it as the will of another self set in opposition to him. Elsewhere, I have tried to show[77] how this idea of Descartes, abandoned by his immediate successors, will emerge again in the philosophy of Hegel who will give us a systematic conceptualization of that duplication of a self positing itself in another self and asserting its own separate identity through a struggle with that other self.[78] In the opening moves of the *Meditations* Descartes's struggle with the deceiving "demon" has the same structure and the same function.

As a matter of fact, without that struggle Descartes could not have established himself even as the universal self that he is *qua* merely thinking. For to establish himself as merely thinking—that is, as liberated from all taken-for-granted, untested beliefs and habits of thought—he had to pass through the same crucible that established his will as the will of a particular self: he had to oppose his cognition to a "demonic" power of deception. The operation of such a power against him was indispensable for probing his cognition to its utmost limits; and thus we should not be surprised at Descartes's confession[79] that the "fire and steel" with which he probed human knowledge in the *Meditations* were not yet applied to it in the *Discourse*, where our cognitive faculties were not yet tested against the power of the demon. The latter is instrumental both in driving the self's cognition to the *universal* level of pure thinking and in establishing to will to truth as the will of a *particular* self.

Descartes's struggle to establish himself against a deceiving will is at the root of his ability to discover and to clarify his identity: "what am I, now, that I suppose there is a certain genius which is extremely powerful and if I may say so, malicious, who employs all his powers in deceiving me?".[80] Descartes already knows that he thinks and that, as long as he thinks, he exists. He still does not know his nature or his essence. Ordinarily, he refers to himself as a man and he is familiar with the definition of man as a rational animal. But the extreme doubt he has been forced to adopt will not allow him to fall back upon these, easily available, concepts and definitions. He will be in no position to do this for at least two reasons. First, even if he accepts the current ordinary meanings of these concepts, he can not know, as yet, whether he has the right to apply them to himself. Whatever else an animal may be, it is certainly a corporeal being and, so far, Descartes does not know whether he has a body. It may still be suggested to him that he can securely fall back at least upon his own ordinary understanding of himself qua rational. But Descartes already knows he can't take for granted the ordinary conception of rationality. He has been forced to cast doubt even upon his ability to perform elementary operations of arithmetic; and if he doubts this much, he may find that the very concept of "reason" as he has been using it both in everyday life and in theoretical investigations must be profoundly reformulated. Like Husserl after him, Descartes carries out a genuine philosophical *epoche* meant to suspend the everyday usage of certain terms and to recover their original significations, coverd up by the habits, the prejudices and the commonplaces of ordinary life.

On the other hand—and as I have already pointed out— Descartes's suspension of his ordinary beliefs and meanings is not meant to leave him in a conceptual vacuum. Descartes does engage in improving upon and clarifying the ordinary understanding of many concepts, and he is quite open and unapologetic about it.[81] A special, philosophical, effort is needed in order to come face to face with the significations of our ideas and to adapt our concepts and our vocabulary accordingly. But these significations are not invented by the philosopher, and they are not entirely alien to the understanding embedded in the ordinary consciousness. Rather, they constitute the deepest layers of that ordinary consciousness itself; and it is Descartes's hope to be able to wrest the ordinary consciousness away from its habits and prejudices and to allow it to come face to face with those original significations of our ideas.

The present issue—the issue of Descartes's question "what am I?"—can be taken as a case study for Descartes's procedure. Under the threat of the deceiver—for we must constantly keep in mind that this is how Descartes proceeds to discover his identity—Descartes will come to know himself as a "mind" in the sense of a "thinking thing," a *res cogitans*. The demonic threat is used, in the Second Meditation, as the ultimate lever with the aid of which Descartes extracts an understanding of himself from the treasury of ideas deposited in the ordinary consciousness itself. Replying to an objection raised against him by the authors of the Sixth Objections, Descartes says : "Nor can it occur that, when one perceives that he thinks, understanding at the same time what it is to move, he should think *that he is deceived, and that he does not think but only moves.* For since plainly the idea or notion he has of thought is quite different from that of corporeal movement, he must necessarily understand the one as quite different from the other. Yet on account of his habit of ascribing many diverse properties, between which he discerns no connection, to one and the same subject, he may doubt, he may even affirm that he is one and the same thing which thinks and moves in space."[82] This passage comes on the footsteps of the passage I have commented on earlier, in which Descartes has explained how the plain, prereflective self is perfectly capable of recognizing that he thinks and (on this basis) that he exists. As we recall, the concepts of thinking and existing and their application in the first-person present-tense case are so basic and so fundamental to us that they survive even our very attempt to cast doubt upon them by the hypothesis of a demonic menace to the integrity of our cognition. Thus, the philosophical, meditative test is used to validate a certain area of the prereflective, ordinary knowledge. We know that we think, we know that we are, and in this respect, the plain man and the philosopher will find themselves in complete agreement. But even in the case of our thinking and being—and still more in the case of our identity qua "mind"—the ordinary man may find himself caught up within all kinds of prejudices and habits which will cloud his otherwise "necessary" understanding of the significations involved. In this respect there is, at the very least, a difference of degree between our knowledge that we are and our knowledge that we are minds. The degree of confusion ordinarily surrounding that first piece of knowledge is much less than the degree of confusion surrouding the second. No ordinary man will fail to acknowledge immediately that he thinks and that he exists. Many ordinary persons will fail to conceive of themselves as minds and will continue to think of their identity in corporeal terms. This is why, from the point of view of the philospher, it was much easier to test the worth of the prereflective knowledge of our thinking and being and to come to a quick agreement, on this issue, with the ordinary consciousness. The force of habits and prejudices is much greater in the case of our knowledge of our identity, or of our "essence," to use again the technical philosophical term.

The difference in the degree of confusion surrounding our knowledge *that* we are and our knowledge *who* we are is not a matter of accident. The difference itself can be validated from the philosophical point of view. The truth that, if we think, we are, is very simple and it validates itself immediately. The truth about our essence can only be discovered by a more complex operation and, as we shall see, it will need to be validated by God. This is why the ordinary consciousness will find it easier to succumb to its habitual distortions of the second truth. But the purpose and the procedure of the philosopher remain the same in both cases. Reminding himself that he is still under the threat of the deceiver and reflecting upon what he has achieved so far Descartes aims at discovering who he is. But his forthcoming discovery will also be a rediscovery of what is already present (under those layers of habits and prejudices) in the ordinary consciousness.

But how does Descartes know that? How does he know that in discovering himself as a "mind" he is not putting across a defintion which will be unacceptable to the ordinary consciousness itself? It is here that the relatively smooth road to a quick agreement with the ordinary consciousness becomes quite rocky. Any ordinary person will assent immediately to the proposition that he thinks and that he exists—or this, at least, is Descartes's claim. Many ordinary persons will refuse to assent immediately to Descartes's definition of the self as a thinking thing. To these persons Descartes can ony give one answer, but it is an answer as good as any that could be given under the circumstances. Descartes will remind his opponents that he himself began his meditative journey as a reflective but ordinary individual. This is why he chose the analytic method of philosophizing. He reflected upon simple, ordinary cases and he made every effort to make his moves acceptable to himself qua ordinary consciousness. His hope is that if the ordinary consciousness, his own or anyone else's, has followed him thus far in his journey, it will follow him to the next station as well, provided that it carefully considers the steps already taken and what these steps imply for the issue of the self's identity.

Descartes has already learned a number of things by measuring himself against the threat of the demon. He has learned that he is thinking, that he exists, and even that he is a particular substance (although he still does not know what kind of a substance he is). He has learned all of this by realizing that there is one thing the demon can not take away from him: his own thinking. He continues to think in spite of the demon and (as a will to truth opposed to a will to deceive) against the demon. This was the basis of all of his discoveries and this continues to be the stepping stone for his next discovery as well. We just heard him reaffirm that he continues to view himself as being under the menace of a powerful deceiver. In the same passage of the Second Meditation he goes on to report to us on his new discovery: "I find here that thought is an attribute that belongs to me; it alone cannot be separated from me."[83] There are two elements in this new discovery of Descartes: (a) no demon can mislead him about the belief that he, Descartes, "has" the attribute of thinking—thinking belongs to him as the one possession he can be certain of, and (b) for all he knows, were he to be deprived of the attribute of thinking, he would cease to exist;[84] in this sense thinking is essential to him at the stage of doubt.

But this discovery as a whole is only the first part in Descartes's mind/body argument—for this is indeed what he is about to offer us. He goes on to argue, that he can exist with thinking *alone* (i.e., without any corporeal properties): and it is in this sense that he identifies himself, in the Second Mediation, as a "mind" or a "thing which thinks," a *res cogitans*. As he will explain later to Arnauld, what he perceives in himself at the stage of doubt—his mere thinking—is "quite adequate to allow of [his] existence with it as [his] sole possession."[85]

There are thus two steps in Descartes's argument to the effect that his "essence" or "nature" (these two expressions can be used interchangeably in the present context) is to be a "mind," a "thing that thinks." Both steps are indicated in the Second Meditation and in that brief declaration with which Descartes begins to counter Arnauld's objections.

First of all, given the knowledge we have achieved thus far, it makes perfect sense to think of ourselves as endowed with thinking as our only certain and essential property. We do not know, so far, if we have a body— and a host of other things as well—for our body remains part and parcel of the material world which is now dominated by the power of a deceiver. But even while I entertain the possibility that I may not have a body, I can not cease to attribute to myself the property of thinking; indeed, my very doubt in the reality of my body is itself nothing else than "thinking in a certain way," to recall one of Descartes's characterizations of doubting. And I am also warranted in claiming that, for all I know, if thinking were to be separated from me I may cease to exist: thinking is thus essential for me *qua* doubter. It does not follow, from this, that my doubt concerning the reality of my body, joined with my inability to doubt the reality of my thinking and its essential role to me at the stage of doubt, is *sufficient* to decide the issue whether my body (or corporeal nature in general) does or does not belong to my essence. To draw such an overhasty conclusion would be to overlook the possibility that my knowledge of a necessary connection (between my nature and bodily properties) may not itself be necessary. Descartes is fully aware of the danger of confusing these two different issues, he gives a repeated warning to the reader not to confuse them, and he takes all the necessary precautions to avoid the confusion.

The inevitability of the second step in Descartes's argument becomes clear now. Having considered himself again as being under the threat of the demon, having reaffirmed that thinking is the one sure thing the demon can't take away from him (while, perhaps, he has been misled by the demon in his uncritical belief that he has a body) Descartes will proceed to show that thinking is *sufficient* to allow him to exist *per se*: he will proceed to show that he can exist with thinking as his only attribute. An attribute of this type bears the technical name of "principal" or "essential" attribute and it allows its owner to be considered a genuine substance, identifiable by that attribute alone; indeed, the principal attribute *is* the substance insofar as it is known to us.[86] Descartes is now in a position to claim that he is a thinking substance.

I have outlined the main thrust of Descartes's argument, but this outline must still be filled with more detail. Our task demands that we pay closer attention to the structure and the disposition of this important argument.

It is not by accident that even such an acute and sympathetic critic as Arnauld was confused by the presentation of the argument in the Second Meditation. The two steps of the argument are not clearly separated; and it often seems as if Descartes was relying upon the first step alone to produce the conclusion that his essence consists only in thinking. What makes matters even worse is the reemergence of the issue in the Sixth Meditation; the impression is thereby created that something is lacking in the proof as presented in the Second Meditation and that Descartes himself is trying, in the Sixth Meditation, to fill some gaps left open by the Second Meditation.

Now, in *some* sense this impression is quite justified and well grounded in the substance of Descartes's views. For in the Second Meditation we can not yet know whether our conception of ourselves as thinking things, however sound, corresponds to the order of being. We cannot conclude from knowledge to being prior to the Third Meditation, where we are given the proof of the existence of God and, consequently, the right to consider all of our clear and distinct ideas as indications of some features of the external world. In this sense, the proof that our essence consists only in thinking will have to wait for its final validation until after we have supplied ourselves with compelling proofs of the existence of God. There is no doubt that Descartes does address himself, in the Sixth Meditation, to that aspect of the problem.

But he seems to do much more than that in the Sixth Meditation. Only then[87] does he begin to give proper weight to the second step of his overall mind/body argument; conversely, the first part of the argument is trimmed down if not ignored altogether. That is, in arguing again for the proposition that mind and body are "really distinct" Descartes ceases to be interested in the circumstance that when we doubt the existence of bodies we do not doubt the existence of ourselves qua thinking; his entire interest, in the Sixth Meditation, seems to be to show how various features present in our concept of the body are incompatible with the features we detect in our concept of the mind. The change is somewhat puzzling. For if, in the Sixth Meditation, we can come to know ourselves as ("really") distinct from the body without relying upon the Second Meditation's doubt in the reality of our body, then that part of Descartes's overall argument—the part where the contribution of doubt is crucial—seems to be unnecessary to give us the knowledge that we are only thinking beings. But then why did Descartes put such a great emphasis upon that part in the Second Meditation? And if it's the second part of the argument—the part fully developed in the Sixth Meditation—that really does the job for him, why did he say so little about it in the Second Meditation thereby exposing himself so easily to the objections of his critics?

The answer to these questions can be gathered from Decartes's own attempts to dispel the confusion surrounding the issue. In his reply to Arnauld, Descartes is categorical: the proof that his essence consists only in thinking is to be found in the Second Meditation.[88] This means that both parts of the argument are supplied to us already in the Second Meditation. The Second Meditation can not be read as teaching us only that we can doubt whether the body belongs to our nature while we can not doubt whether thinking belongs to our nature (since we can doubt the existence of bodies even while we can't doubt that we, as thinking, exist). It must be read as teaching us that nothing *but* thinking belongs to our nature; and this means that we can't wait for the Sixth Meditation to impress upon us that part of Descartes's position on the mind/body issue. Descartes gives us another helpful indication as well. In the Synopsis he says that much of what he can teach us about the nature of the body will be supplied by the Fifth and the Sixth Meditations. Now, when Descartes claims that his essence consists only in thinking he supports his claim with an insight into the incompatibility between our concepts of mind and body. Our concepts of mind and body exclude each other: nothing that belongs to our concept of the mind belongs to our concept of the body (and vice versa); and this allows Descartes to conclude that there exists a real (substantial) distinction between mind and body.[89] We will have to take a closer look at what this means for Descartes, but some grasp of this conceptual conflict between our ideas of mind and body is an indispensable piece in Descartes's argument to the effect that his essence consists in thinking. It becomes clearer now both why the argument as given in the Second Meditation needs some completion and why the work still outstanding will have to be done in the Sixth Meditation. The establishment of the real distinction between mind and body presupposes our knowledge of the conceptual incompatibility between our ideas of mind and body. But to *fully* grasp this conceptual incompatibility we need to know more about the nature of the body than we know at the beginning of the Second Meditation. To be sure, already in the Second Meditation we must know *enough* about both mind and body to be able to achieve that minimum conceptual understanding of their natures which will allow us to conclude that they are different substances. Otherwise, Descartes would be in no position to claim that he has "sufficiently shown in the Second Meditation" why mind and body must be viewed as two different substances.[90] But we should not forget that the *Meditations* follow the order of discovery; and so, as we learn more and more detail about the nature of the body and, accordingly, achieve an ever-growing awareness that no characteristics found in the concept of the body can belong to the concept of the mind, we get more and more indications of the real difference between mind and body.

How can we achieve *any* understanding of that difference prior to at least some analysis of our concept of the body? If even the (very provisional) analysis of corporeal substance conducted with the famous piece of wax example is situated toward the end of the Second Meditation, that is, *after* our characterization of ourselves as "mind" has already been worked out, then where do we get even that minimum understanding of corporeal nature needed to establish, be it even in the order of knowledge, the proposition that mind and body are two different substances?

It is here that Descartes's own presentation of his discovery of himself as a "thinking thing" is especially likely to produce the confusion between the two parts of his mind/body argument in the Second Meditation. For it clearly seems that Descartes is drawing upon his lack of knowledge of the *existence* of bodies in order to establish the required (however modest) contrast between the *natures* of mind and body:

I know that I exist, and I inquire what I am, I whom I know to exist. But it is very certain that the knowledge of my existence taken in its precise significance does not depend on things whose existence is not yet known to me; consequently it does not depend on those which I can feign in imagination. And indeed the very term *feign* in imagination proves to me my error, for I really do this if I imagine myself a something, since to imagine is nothing else than to contemplate the figure or image of a corporeal thing. But I already know for certain that I am, and it may be that all these images, and, speaking generally, all things that relate to the nature of body are nothing but dreams [and chimeras] . . . And, thus, I know for certain that nothing of all that I can understand by means of my imagination belongs to this knowledge which I have of myself, and that it is necessary to recall the mind from this mode of thought with the utmost diligence in order that it may be able to know its own nature with perfect distinctness.[91]

This passage concludes Descartes's attempt to "imagine" what he *could* be, given his condition at the stage of doubt. And his reasoning seems clear: since imagination can "contemplate" only corporeal natures and since no corporeal nature can be known to exist at the present stage, whereas Descartes can know and does know that he exists, nothing that can be entertained in imagination can belong to his essence. For this reason, it is enough to inspect objects entertained in imagination to learn something about the nature of the body as contrasted with the nature of the meditating self.

Unfortunately, this entire piece of reasoning can only be given a very limited function in Descartes's argument. Its function can only be to supply a more detailed version of the first step of Descartes's argument on the mind/body issue. We do learn, from this experiment with imagination, that at the stage of doubt we have no right to attribute to ourselves any properties of such entities (namely: bodies) as we entertain in imagination. We do not learn that such properties do not in fact belong to our essence. This still remains an open question. Can we at least hope that the imagination will perform the more limited function of allowing us to acquire some modest information concerning the nature of the body, information which we will then use, in the argument's second step, to separate our nature from the nature of the body? Even this claim cannot be sustained. For when Descartes says that imagination can feign only corporeal nature he must *already* know something about corporeal nature in general; and it would be very strange indeed if he did not have such knowledge independently of what his imagination can and can not do for him, since the concept of the body is an innate idea of the intellect. The question remains: to build the second step of his argument Descartes needs to fall back upon some knowledge of corporeal nature required to draw the contrast, even at this stage, with the nature of the mind.

If it weren't for Descartes's theory of the prereflective knowledge, the question could not be answered. But we have already heard Descartes saying that some degree of understanding of the difference between the concepts of mind and body—and hence also, eo ipso, some degree of understanding of what a body is—belongs to the prereflective equipment of every knower. And so when Descartes, before proceeding to argue that he is a mind, describes to us his plain understanding of the body as, essentially, a thing endowed with extension, figure, and motion[92] and uses *that* understanding to give him the much-needed indications concerning the nature of the body, he is drawing upon his own prereflective knowledge of the concept of the body.

Doesn't he thereby uncritically presuppose this knowledge? His desire to rule out such a possibility may be one reason why he returns again and again, in the course of the *Meditations,* to the issue of the nature of the body, and why he keeps supplying us with more and more detail about that nature and, consequently, about the mind/body difference. In the Synopsis he tells us that the distinct conception of corporeal nature is at least partly achieved only in the Fifth and Sixth Meditations.[93] And even though Descartes thinks that his knowledge of bodily nature in the Second Meditation is not only clear but has a sufficient degree of distinctness to allow him to identify his nature as mental and not material, he keeps pressing on for more and more of that distinctness, and the details he gradually supplies corroborate his initial grasp of himself as a mind "really distinct" from the body.

We can see again that his discovery of his identity as a "thing which thinks" is not derived merely from his doubt in the existence of bodies. Descartes draws upon his knowledge of the nature of the body and of the nature of the mind and this knowledge—however modest it is, and must remain, at the present stage of his inquiry—allows him to establish his distinctness from the body at least as far as the order of knowledge is concerned.

But this does not mean that Descartes can discover that his essence is to be a *res cogitans* without considering what he can know about the existence of bodies and of himself at the stage of doubt. The stage of doubt too is instrumental here, so much so that in Descartes's assessment the Augustinian *dubito* fell short of his own "I doubt, I exist" precisely in this particular respect: St. Augustine's *dubito* allowed him only to affirm that he exists, Descartes's doubt led him to discover not only that he exists, but also that his soul is not corporeal.[94]

Let us look again at the entire mind/body argument in the Second Meditation. Descartes first reminds himself that he continues to be exposed to the power of the demon. He then spells out the negative effects of this predicament upon his ordinary understanding of his identity: as of now, he is not sure whether he can attribute to himself any bodily properties, since all bodies, including his own, may turn out to be the illusions created by the demon. By the same token, Descartes must refrain from attributing to himself such functions—he gives the examples of walking, nutrition and sensing—which are clearly dependent upon the possession of his body. This list is not exhaustive, and it will have to be amended and qualified (for one thing, sensing will reappear again as a mere mode of thought), but it gives a sense of the direction in which Descartes intends to move us. He wants us to acknowledge that with one exception—that of thinking—all these properties that we usually attribute to ourselves may be attributed falsely, on account of the net of deception spread around us by the deceiver. That is, Descartes can envision certain circumstances—and these happen to be the very same circumstances he finds himself in right now—under which these properties might not belong to him even while he would be thinking about them and pondering whether they do or do not belong to him. But he can envision no circumstances under which his thinking itself might not belong to him while he would be thinking. Here, we recall, Descartes finds something that the demon can't take away from him and without which he, Descartes, might not exist.

Thus, the consideration of the most extreme form of doubt Descartes could find himself in was necessary to allow him to grasp just *what* it is that he must have no matter how far he pushes his doubt concerning his identity. He discovered that thinking is his certain and essential property. He can now focus on that privileged posession he has just found in his own thinking, he can attempt to grasp at least some of its features, and he can then move on to the second step of the argument, where he will assert that thinking would be entirely *sufficient* to allow him to exist as an independent entity. If Descartes had not considered himself as being under the menace of the ultimate, "demonic" deception, he would have no way of knowing whether some of the properties he attributes to himself may not turn out to be attributed falsely. To find out the real worth of his "possessions" he must have them probed by the power of the demon. If he can hold onto them in spite of the demonic threat, he can be sure that they must "belong" to him under all possible circumstances—at least as long as he is around to consider what does and does not belong to him—since he has just tested their link with him under the worst-case scenario. We need not point out again that no *lesser* test would satisfy Descartes. He does not return to this test in the mind/body arguments in the Sixth Meditation, for the results of the test are, by then, known to him and he can take them for granted. But the test had to be performed and, without it, the supporting arguments from the Sixth Meditation would lack their ultimate grounding.

Descartes does know that thinking "belongs" to him, but he does not yet know if he can exist with thinking alone. He does not know if the body belongs to him; but the body may still belong to him. But Descartes also has a clear and distinct idea of this "thinking" he has just discovered to be his inalienable possession. By inspecting this idea he comes to realize that it is, in some sense, incompatible with and exclusive of the idea of the body, and that he could exist with thinking alone, that is, merely as a "thinking thing."

This second step of Descartes's main argument is presented so sketchily in the Second Meditation, and so much is taken for granted, that Descartes's explanations offered to Arnauld become almost indispensable for grasping not just the meaning but the very existence of the many claims that go into producing Descartes's final conclusion concerning his identity.

His first claim is that "there is nothing included in the concept of the body that belongs to the mind; and nothing in that of mind that belongs to the body."[95] We recall the difficulty with formulating this claim: at the opening stages of the Second Meditation (prior even to the analysis of the piece of wax example) our concept of the body is still quite poor and undetermined, and we have very little to go on to support the proposition that "nothing" in the concept of the body belongs to the concept of the mind and vice versa. But at least we can draw here an important distinction. While we must still be given an explanation as to how we can know that no property *at all* can be shared by mind and body alike (might there not be some still outstanding, and unknown to us, properties *X, Y, Z* which belong to both mind and body?), our claim is sound, Descartes thinks, if we limit ourselves to the properties we have already inspected at the beginning of the mind/body argument in the Second Meditation. For we already know that our concept of the body includes such features as extension, figure, and motion, and we already know that these features are incompatible with the features of that privileged possession of ours we have just identified as our thinking. The properties of extension, figure, and motion can't be attributed to a "thinking thing" while thinking can't be attributed to a bearer of those properties. Our understanding of *this* difference between mind and body is, we recall, so basic and fundamental to us that it must be counted as belonging to the prereflective knowledge of everybody. The task of the philosopher is to dig out that understanding from underneath the layers of ordinary habits and prejudices and to validate it again by a careful philosophical analysis.

I will return later to the issue whether there may not be some *unknown*, or even *unknowable*, properties that mind and body may still share. This is the issue Descartes will address by trying to convince Arnauld that our knowledge of minds and bodies is "sufficiently" adequate to allow us to rule out the possibility of there being those unknown and unknowable properties that minds and bodies may still have in common. The answer to that question will depend, above all, upon the lessons we will soon derive from our apprehension of those properties of mind and body which are already known to us and which make up the basic features of our present concepts of mind and body.

Our concepts are what we mean when we use our linguistic expressions, and they are, at least in that capacity, the same as our ideas.[96] Thus, our clear and distinct perception of what does and does not belong to our idea of the mind and to our idea of the body allows us to characterize mind and body as they are apprehended in our present concepts. We apprehend them conceptually as "complete" without each other. Not only is it the case that I perceive that nothing that belongs to the concept of the body can belong to the concept of the mind (and vice versa), but on the grounds of this perception of mine I can formulate the claim that mind and body are thereby apprehended by me as complete entities. Descartes has already explained this in his earlier reply to Caterus,[97] and he draws upon these earlier explanations in meeting the objections of Arnauld. Thus he says that "mind can be perceived clearly and distinctly, or sufficiently to let it be considered to be a complete thing without any of those forms or attributes by which we recognize that body is a substance . . . and body is understood distinctly and as a complete thing apart from the attributes attaching to the mind."[98] The two claims I have just mentioned are clearly separated in this passage: we have, first, a clear and distinct perception of mind and body as endowed with different attributes and then also, second, the accompanying perception of mind and body as "complete" without each other, that is, as not needing one another in order to exist. And this amounts to saying that we apprehend mind and body as really distinct.[99]

One item on Descartes's agenda remains still outstanding. So far, he has proved only that *we* can't fail to apprehend mind and body as really distinct. But, he reminds us here again, as long as we remain within the parameters of the methodical doubt, we can't know if "things are in their true nature exactly as we perceive them to be."[100] For this reason, our apprehension of the real distinction between mind and body does not represent the proof that mind and body *are* really distinct unless that apprehension of ours is joined with our (further and independent) knowledge of the divine origin of our clear and distinct ideas. Our knowledge of this origin of our ideas in God allows us to assert not only that mind and body can coexist in us as two different substances, but that minds could actually have been created as existent without bodies. We could not have known that prior to the knowledge of the existence and the essence of God, and this is why "the conclusion as to the real distinction between *mind* and *body* is finally completed in Meditation VI."[101] And, in effect, the presentation of the mind/body argument in the Sixth Meditation will begin with Descartes restating the implications, for the argument, of his earlier discoveries concerning the existence and the essence of God; and only then, after having reassured himself that God can create whatever it is that he, Descartes, perceives with clarity and distinctness, Descartes will proceed to show us how he can clearly and distinctly apprehend mind and body as two different substances. Only from these premises taken jointly will he be able to arrive at the conclusion that his mind could exist without his body.[102]

But this fallback upon the power and the veracity of God reopens for us another issue—the issue of Descartes's ignorance when he draws his mind/body distinction. In replying to Arnauld Descartes days: "Since that which I do perceive [in me] is adequate to allow of my existing with it as my sole possession, I am certain that God could have created me without putting me in possession of those other attributes of which I am unaware."[103] How does he know that his perception of what is "adequate" for him to exist per se is *itself* adequate? These do seem to be two different questions and Arnauld's comments brought the issue to the surface. The issue remains outstanding not only after the Second Meditation, but after the Sixth Meditation as well. Descartes does know *some* properties of the mind and of the body. He does know that these properties of mind and body are incompatible; and from this basic insight he goes on to draw the real distinction between mind and body. But how does he know that some further inquiries may not discover certain other properties of mind and body, properties which may prove to be compatible? Or how can he know if some property *X,* still unknown to him, is not the stuff out of which both mind and body are made? These are not merely empirical possibilities to be ruled out on conceptual grounds alone. To be sure, such would have been Descartes's immediate reply to us: he would have said that the (real) distinction between mind and body is indeed conceptual and thus all futher information concerning the mental and the material will be accommodated within a conceptual scheme where mind and body are understood as really distinct. But Arnauld's criticisms were meant to question the very conceptual distinction Descartes has drawn. How does Descartes know that his understanding of the *concepts* of mind and body is adequate to the task of establishing a real distinction between mind and body? If our grasp of the ideas of mind and body has improved so much as we moved from the Second to the Sixth Meditation, how can we know that a still further intuition and analysis of these ideas will not, in the end, abolish the conceptual difference we have drawn? *If* we are certain that our ideas of mind and body are beyond revision at least *qua* ideas, *then* we can fall back upon the power and the veracity of God to secure the correspondence of our concepts of mind and body with the objective order of things. But we can't know if our present ideas of mind and body will not be revised by further inquiries. We must rule out this possibility first.

Commenting on his earlier reply to Caterus, Descartes explains to Arnauld that he "took 'to understand in a complete manner' and 'to understand that a thing is something complete' in one and the same sense."[104] As it stands, this is not a very satisfying answer. Descartes says he has the complete knowledge of *A* because he knows *A* to be complete; but the thrust of Arnauld's line of questioning was to bring out the circularity of Descartes's answer. How can Descartes know *A* as complete if his knowledge of *A* is not independently known to be complete or adequate? Descartes removes the circularity by explaining further the explanation he already gave to Caterus: by saying that his knowledge of *A* is adequate he meant to say that it has "sufficient adequacy" for the purpose of allowing him to grasp *A* as capable of existing per se. By the same token, his knowledge of *A* is complete only in the sense of allowing him the sufficient grasp of A as complete. But his knowledge of A is neither complete nor adequate in the sense of allowing him to grasp *all* of the properties of A; to achieve *such* knowledge man's capacity to know would have to reach the level of the cognitive power of God, and this is an absurd supposition.[105]

But how does Descartes know that his grasp of the idea of the mind has (even) the required "sufficient adequacy"? He must know *this* much in order to be able to assert that those features of the mind as are already available to him in his present concepts are sufficient to allow mind to exist per se, at least in relation to bodies. But how can he know even this much without inspecting *all* of the properties of minds and bodies? Or how can he know that from some higher-than-human point of view the entire mind/body distinction may not be altogether illusory? Kant seems to be much more on target here: he grants the mind/body distinction within our own finite cognition, but he leaves open the possibility that the difference between the mental and the material may not exist in the (incomprehensible to us) ultimate nature of things.[106]

However, in spite of holding firm to his doctrine of the incomprehensibility of God, Descartes attempted to rule out the very same possibility that Kant was to accept later (not to mention the lesser menace that the progress of our own knowledge may yet discover some property shared by mind and bodies). He did this with full awareness of the difficulty of the task—his unusually subdued comments to Burman are a testimony to that[107]—and by falling back upon his usual device for overcoming the uncertainties and limitations of human knowledge. He appealed to the congruence between our own clear and distinct ideas and the ideas in the mind of God. That is, God is not only the guarantor of the truth of our clear and distinct ideas of X or Y or Z, but his own ideas of X or Y or Z are commensurable with our own. For example, "it is . . . manifest that the idea we possess of the infinite does not represent merely a part of it, but really the whole infinite, in that fashion in which it has to be represented through the instrumentality of a human idea, although doubtless another much more perfect, i.e. more accurate and more distinct idea can be framed by God, or by any other intelligent nature more perfect than a human being . . . Thus, just as it suffices to understand a figure bounded by three lines in order to have an idea of a complete triangle, so also it is enough to understand a thing bounded by no limits in order to have a true and complete idea of the whole of infinity."[108] Our idea of the infinite, then, may be represented as an element in an entire series of such ideas—framed by other intelligences and by God himself—arranged in an ordered sequence according to their degree of perfection and accuracy. In this series, the more perfect and accurate ideas do not invalidate their less perfect and less accurate predecessors but, instead, enrich and improve upon the content of the latter. All the ideas on the series are commensurable and anyone's clear and distinct perception of any of these ideas gives him the assurance that all further inquiries could only deepen and corroborate his own, however limited, understanding of that idea. And if even our idea of the infinite is commensurable with God's own idea of it, then the same can be said, even more emphatically, about our other ideas. For this reason, we can be sure that our own clear and distinct ideas of mind and body as "complete" without each other can never be invalidated by any further inquiries; in fact, we can be sure that the mind/body distinction remains valid from God's point of view.

Can Descartes adopt this solution while holding onto his theory of the incomprehensibility of God? Doesn't the theory imply a complete lack of convergence between our own conceptions—no matter how clear and distinct they may be—and the ultimate reality, accessible only to God's cognition? For the moment, these questions must be left unanswered; in order to deal with them we need to know more about Descartes's account of our knowledge of the existence and the nature of God. But if God's incomprehensibility need not render all of human ideas incommensurable with the divine ideas, then Descartes's problems with establishing the "real distinction" between mind and body are not any greater than the other problems imposed upon him by the circumstance that human knowledge is inherently limited.

So far, we have defined mind only by its principal (or essential) attribute of "thinking." This was not illegitimate on our part, since Descartes holds that the distinction between a substance and its principal attribute is a mere "distinction of reason" (*distinctio rationis*) drawn within our knowledge as we apprehend that substance.[109] But even at the stage of methodical doubt our apprehension of the mind is much richer than the mere knowledge of mind's essential attribute. "But what then am I? A thing which thinks. What is a thing which thinks? It is a thing which doubts, understands [conceives], affirms, denies, wills, refuses, which also imagines and feels."[110] This statement is not made in the *Principles,* in which Descartes confidently proceeds to develop a "synthetic" presentation of his system. The statement is drawn from the Second Meditation. And it may then be asked by what right can Descartes make this statement at the present stage of his "analytic" path of the order of discovery. He has just attributed a large number of properties to his mind. These are the very same properties which he will later classify in the *Principles* as the various particular modes of the two "general modes" of the mind: the perceptions of the understanding and the actions of the will.[111] But how can he know—how can he know *now,* when he still considers himself as being under the menace of the deceiver—that he is in a position to offer us such a rich inventory of his own mind? Or is this just another example of Descartes's dogmatic reliance upon the transparency thesis? Does he know the properties of his mind simply because his mind is, by definition, open to his cognitive inspection?

There is some truth to this, perhaps even a good deal of truth, but to reduce Descartes's entire move to a simple fallback upon some form of introspective evidence would be a mistake. In fact, it would be a mistake to suppose that the mental goodies Descartes has just attributed to his mind were simply "found" by him as mere givens of his experience. As if anticipating that such a mistake is about to be committed by careles readers Descartes proceeds to offer us important clarifications meant not simply to explain but indeed to justify his most recent move and the way the move was carried out. Having told us what a mind is, and having offered us, in the process, an important list of the mind's properties, Descartes begins to wonder how he can know all this at the present stage of his inquiry. He realizes that "it is no small matter if all these things pertain to my nature."[112] The very fact that he raises the issue shows his awareness of the much needed support for the claims he has just made. This fact alone ought to be enough to warn us not to consider Descartes as being here naïve and uncritical. Even if he were to fall back, in the end, upon mind's transparent presence to itself, he would not be doing this while unaware of the severity of his epistemic predicament and of the restrictions under which he is operating.

How, then, does he know that his grasp of all those various properties of his mind is not based on an illusion? He goes on to answer the question and to explain why the various items he just listed as partaining to mind's nature are indeed the mind's actual properties: "Why should they not so pertain? Am I not that being who now doubts nearly everything, who nevertheless understands certain things, who affirms that one only is true, who denies all the others, who desires to know more, is averse from being deceived, who imagines many things, sometimes indeed despite his will, and who perceives many likewise, as by the intervention of the bodily organs? Is there nothing in all this which is as true as it is certain that I exist . . . ?"[113] To our question Descartes opposes his question, but this does not mean that he is simply shifting the *onus probandi* upon the shoulders of his readers. His questioning of our question is done from within the vistas opened up by the journey we have made with him so far. He thinks that if we have agreed to take the steps he has taken, we ought to agree to his present step as well. We began our meditative journey by formulating the hypothesis of the demon and by deriving from it certain consequences for our epistemic condition. In doing both of these things we had to take for granted certain conceptual minimum with which to articulate our situation. Thus, we took for granted some knowledge of the ideas of thinking and doubting; and we took for granted our ability, and our right, to apply the concepts of thinking and doubting at least in the first-person present-tense case. This fact alone gives us the right to say, as Descartes now does, that we already "understand certain things." We have also discovered that in order to articulate and characterize our condition it was necessary to take for granted some knowledge of our will, since without this will or freedom of ours we could neither "deny" entire areas of belief nor "affirm that only one [that we exist] is true." And could we have done all of this denying and affirming if we did not want to avoid deception? And how could we be so averse from being deceived if we didn't "desire" to know more? There is much in this that can represent no more than a hint at the present stage of Descartes's inquiry. Only later will Descartes supply more detail on, say, the aversions and the desires of our mind even when they concern only the pursuit of knowledge and the avoidance of deception. But it does seem unlikely that he could articulate even to himself—much less to his readers—whatever it is that he is doing right now, and has been doing recently, without attributing to his mind at least some of the properties he has listed. In doing this, he simply characterizes what is implied in his very grasp of his present epistemic condition.

How can he tell that he does have (even that very modest) grasp of his condition? This question itself can be understood in only two ways. Either we mean to suggest to Descartes that he could be misled by the demon in his very grasp of the condition he is in under the demon hypothesis. To this suggestion Descartes would reply that our very entertaining of the possibility of such a second-order deception implies our knowledge of some features of our condition (for we must then grant ourselves at least the capacity to know that we doubt whether we know our condition, and the capacity to withdraw our assent to the first-order beliefs concerning that condition of ours, etc.). Or we want to undercut Descartes's right to claim that he knows something about his condition by using against him what is, in effect, a version of the traditional sceptical *regressus* argument (how does Descartes know that he knows, etc.). But Descartes is unmoved by this argument and he rejects the very principle behind it.[114] By understanding himself as being in the condition of doubt he does know something about himself: he does know that he thinks, that he gives or withdraws his assent to some beliefs, and so on.

At the same time, it is clear that not everything Descartes has attributed to his mind is implied by what he must attribute to himself in order to articulate his epistemic condition of the doubter. For Descartes also tells us that he imagines and feels (or perceives); and he even goes on to attribute to himself the power of imagining.[115] He does not and cannot offer any reasons as to how these attributions could be implied by his mere grasp of himself as doubting, and the reasons he does give do show his trust in the evidence of introspection. He attributes to himself the powers of imagining and sensing because he finds that he can entertain images and feelings; and even while he knows that he must refrain from believing that his images and sensations tell him something about the external world, he sees no reason for casting doubt upon his ownership of the faculties of imagination and feeling or upon his ability to know his images and feelings qua purely mental.[116]

Even so these two cognitive faculties are granted a lower status—both in our knowledge of them as belonging to the nature of the mind and in their actual belonging to the nature of the mind—than the other properties mentioned on Descartes's list in the Second Meditation. It is not just that both imagination and feeling seem to be connected, in some way, with the body,[117] but, above all, "without [them] I can easily conceive myself clearly and distinctly as a complete being"[118] while, of course, I cannot conceive myself, even under the most severe threat of deception, as being stripped of my capacity to understand, to affirm, to withdraw my assent and so on. There are, to be sure some differences even here. For even if Descartes knows that he preserves the faculty of will (involved in doubting, affirming, etc.) even under the most extreme deception, might it not be possible for him to think of himself as a "thinking thing" deprived of will? Perhaps it might, since thought alone (in the general sense of *cogitatio, pensée*) is his principal attribute—although it would be very hard to conceive what it would be like to think without having any capacity to withdraw one's assent from some beliefs, to affirm others, and so forth. In contrast, the faculties of imagination and feeling can be removed from our conception of ourselves and still leave us with a clear and distinct idea of ourselves as complete beings. Descartes is thus aware of the circumstance that neither imagination nor feeling (*even* as purely mental) can be attributed to mind as what is implied by, and implicated in, his own condition at the stage of doubt. If he is satisfied with his right to attribute them to himself, he is not unaware that he is stepping over an important line; but he still thinks that the evidence he has for the presence of imagination and feeling in our mental lives is *otherwise* so strong that he can accept their existence at least as modes of thought.

3

Self and God: Powerlessness and Power

Measuring myself against the will of a powerful deceiver, I have discovered that thinking alone is the one sure possession no one can take away from me—at least not as long as I continue to assess my epistemic condition and the damages inflicted upon me by the deceiver. No matter how far I push my doubt, I can not fail to be aware that I am still thinking; and, in addition, it is Descartes's consistently held thesis that some degree of awareness of our mental processes is always present in our experience. Thus, not only in the exceptional moments of a test—much less of that supreme test imposed upon me by the threat of a deceiving "demon"—but in the course of the everyday life I am, on the strength of a principle, aware of my own thinking.

Now, if thinking—not this or that piece of thinking, but thinking as such—is the essential attribute of mind, could I be aware of my own thinking as stripped of any concrete determinations? Could I actually produce an awareness of "mere thinking," without any other feature or characteristic? This would seem to be a very difficult task to accomplish. When, in reply to the question "What are you thinking of?" I answer that I am thinking of "nothing particular," I mean to say that I am not mentally focused upon any particular topic; but this certainly does not mean that I am not aware of all kinds of items—thoughts, images, feelings and so on—present in my thinking at the very moment when I give my answer. The essential features of thinking—its lack of extension or its indivisibility—can be apprehended in an abstract conception, but my *experience* of thinking qua unextended and indivisible consists in grasping the indivisibility and the unextendedness of this or that piece of thinking. To apprehend my thinking as stripped of any determinations could only mean, if it means anything at all, that the very lack of determinateness apprehended in such an empty and vacuous "thinking" becomes *itself* a determination of sorts.[119]

Thus, for me to be aware of my thinking, the latter must be endowed with some minimum of determinateness, with a certain *form*. And this element of form present in all instances of thinking is nothing other than an "idea": "*Idea* is a word by which I understand the form of any thought, that form by the immediate awareness of which I am conscious of that said thought."[120] This is

Descartes's most general definition of idea and the definition is put forward not only to clarify what an idea is, but to bring out its function as a *necessary* component of our mental lives. We don't simply happen to have ideas in our capacity of conscious beings. For if the life of mind involves some degree of self-awareness—that is, some degree of awareness of one's own thinking in the broadest sense of that term—and if we couldn't have *any* self-awareness without some element of idea informing our thought in this or that manner, then the presence of ideas in our thinking is indeed the indispensable component of our mental experience.

But this identification of every form of thinking with an idea creates a host of problems. To begin with, the formal element with the aid of which I grasp the thought T and distinguish it from the thought T^1 need not involve something that we would *ordinarily* consider an "idea." For example, I can distinguish between T and T^1 insofar as T is a volition while T^1 is a feeling of fear. Are we going to say that this volition and this fear are indeed two different ideas? In some passages Descartes says just that,[121] but this usage is odd in its own right and it is difficult to square with other uses of the term idea. For if volition and fear are themselves ideas, then why do we often *contrast* one's having a volition or fear with one's having an idea *of* that volition or fear one is having? If my perception that I understand something involves my having the form or idea of mental action,[122] then the mental action itself (i.e., my "action" of mentally perceiving this or that) ought to be viewed as different from my idea of it even if it could otherwise be granted that I could not be aware of my mental actions without grasping them through the appropriate ideas. How can Descartes employ the ordinary usages of the term idea—and he does this constantly in his writings—and then tell Mersenne that he does not view the action of the will as different from his idea of that action?[123] For he does not simply say that by having the idea of a mental action he achieves an indubitable cognitive grasp of that mental action (of perceiving, of willing, etc.). He says that the action *itself* is not different from his idea of it; and it is very difficult to accept such an unusual way of speaking about ideas.

Even more severe problems are here created by Descartes's claim that all our ideas are apprehended as endowed with a representative function; indeed, we are told that we grasp this function of our ideas by the light of nature.[124] Thus, every idea qua idea purports to represent (although it may fail to represent) something external to it. But in this case we ought to restrict the term idea to our *representations* of volition or fear and refrain from applying this term to volition or fear *themselves,* since the latter are not, quite clearly, representations. To be sure, both volition and fear are joined with representations—for I can't will without representing to myself, however vaguely, just what it is that I will, and I can't fear without having some representation of what I fear—but this is not to say that volition and fear are themselves representations.

Perhaps Descartes himself felt uneasy about the way he has drawn these distinctions. Perhaps this is why he draws them differently in the Third Meditation. In any case, the argument of the Third Meditation is carried out with the aid of a more restricted, and a more plausible, usage of the term "idea." Only those of our thoughts that are, as it were, "images of things" are now called ideas;[125] and by those "images of things" Descartes understands, in *this* context, any representations of objects.[126] Apart from ideas, the forms of thoughts include also "the actions of the mind" ("*action[s] de mon esprit,*" as the French version has it; our earlier cases of volition and fear belong under this heading, together with such other items as acts of affirmation, denial, and so on), which, although not separable from ideas, are nonetheless distinct from the latter: "Though I always perceive something as the subject of the action of my mind yet by this action I always add something else to the idea which I have of that thing; and of the thoughts of this kind some are called volitions or affections, and other judgements."[127] Every action of the mind—every volition, affection, or judgment—is "about" something or other given to the self in a representation. When I judge by joining a subject with a predicate I assert a certain state of affairs entertained in a representation; when I will, my will aims at achieving a certain goal of which I must have some conception or other and so on. Thus every action of the mind finds its representative component in an idea of the mind; and every idea of the mind refers, qua representation, to an object that it purports to represent.

The important concept of "objective reality" is used by Descartes to capture that inherently representative quality of every idea. Apart from being different episodes in my mental life, ideas differ by their representative content—the idea X differs from the idea Y since the first is the representation of a house, the second the representation of a tree, and so on—and this representative content of theirs is nothing other than the *object itself* insofar as it has an existence in the mind. In the First Replies, Descartes explains at some length how it is that the objective reality of an idea is not only a representation of an object but, in effect, the existence of the *object itself* in the mind. Thus (this is Descartes's own example) the sun viewed as a physical entity is certainly unaffected by its being represented or nonrepresented in a mind. But the physical, extramental existence is only one possible mode of existence. Taken as a physical entity, the sun exists "formally," but the sun can also be viewed as existing "objectively" in our idea of it. In general, then, the extramental existence of an X is termed its "formal" existence, while the intramental existence of the same X is called its "objective" existence. The order of ideas in the mind and the order of things outside the mind are linked together by the identity of their content.

Now, as long as there is no reason to question that identity, the problem of scepticism does not arise. The order of ideas and the order of things are linked up by the same common element present "objectively" in our ideas and "formally" (or "eminently," i.e., in a superior fashion) in the entities external to our ideas. There are various ways of undercutting our immediate, unthinking confidence in the correspondence of our ideas with the entities outside them. In the Third Meditation, Descartes will try to show that our confidence in this respect would be misguided even independently of the reasons to doubt produced by the hyperbolical doubt of the First Meditation. There exist, he will now argue anew, no sound reasons for thinking that our representations are caused by external objects; and there is even less reason to believe that such representations, even if caused by external objects, would have to resemble the latter. We hold such beliefs only by a "blind impulse,"[128] although, perhaps, we could not have discovered its "blindness" if we had not gone through the procedure of hyperbolical doubting, allowing us to adopt a proper distance towards *all* of our natural impulses. In any case, the methodical scepticism generated in the First Mediation is fully adequate to the task of breaking up the immediate link between what exists "objectively" and "formally."

Even so, the collapse of this link has its limits in our knowledge of both what causes the sceptical predicament and what what causes its dissolution. The cause of our sceptical predicament was the menace of the demon; and in order to identify that cause we had to depend upon *its* similitude to our representations: we had to take for granted our representations' capacity to capture some features and actions of the demon and some of their possible effects upon our condition. In considering the possibility of being vulnerable to a deceiver, we described him with such terms as "powerful," "malicious," and so on; and even though we did not claim that we are *in fact* in the power of such a deceiver, the very thought that we *may* be in this condition could be viewed as a sufficient reason for philosophical scepticism only if joined with the thought that our ways of representing the demon have at least some connection with what the demon would be like if he were operating against us. The same observation can be made about the cause of the dissolution of our sceptical viewpoint. For how could we see scepticism dissolved by our discovery of our origins in the perfect, and hence veracious Being, if we did not think that our idea of perfection (which we take to be incompatible with a will to deceive) bears some resemblance to what that Being is *qua* independent of our ideas? The problem of scepticism arises on account of Descartes's discovery of the ontological vulnerability of his condition: his ideas may be illusions and traps planted by a demon against whom he, Descartes, has initially very little with which to defend the integrity of his cognition. The solution to the problem of scepticism is found with Descartes's discovery that he himself—and hence also his faculties and his ideas—is created and sustained in existence by God. Thus, what allows Descartes to pass from scepticism to knowledge lies, in the last analysis, in the *kind* of being that he, Descartes, depends upon. What decides the issue is not the mere content, or the "what" of our ideas, but, rather, just "who" it is that we find behind them—who is their "author," to use Descartes's own expression. But to characterize the issue in this way Descartes must assume that at least *some* of his ideas of those potential "authors" are in correspondance with what these authors are, or would be; for if Descartes thought that his own inability to conceive perfection as compatible with a will to deceive could itself be nothing more than a "blind impulse," he would be in no position to validate his knowledge by the discovery that his author is the perfect being.

It is important to Descartes's antisceptical strategy that the concept of "objective reality" be given an *evaluative* function as well. According to Descartes, objects are arranged on a scale of perfection; and since our ideas just are the objects qua existent in the mind, the degree of perfection of a given object is mirrored in the degree of perfection of the corresponding idea. The objective realities of ideas can thus be graded and arranged on a scale where we can compare them according to the degree of perfection they embody. Indeed, in one of Descartes's uses, reality *means* perfection and, consequently, Descartes's frequent talk about some idea or other having "more" or "less" objective reality comes quite naturally to him, just as naturally as talking about this or that (extramental) object having more or less formal reality. As we noted, the degree of perfection embodied in an idea mirrors the degree of perfection characterizing the object represented by that idea. By identifying the representative content of an idea with the mental existence of the object itself we have, eo ipso, applied an evaluative yardstick to our ideas.

The yardstick itself is nothing other than our idea of the perfect being—that is, our idea of God: "[All] that I conceive clearly and distinctly of the real and of the true, and of what conveys some perfection, is in its entirety contained in this idea."[129] Our idea of the divine perfection supplies the standard with which we can arrange all other ideas on the scale of perfection. It is not just that God as the infinite substance is more perfect than finite substances, or that finite substances are more perfect than accidents and modes, but, above all, the various items within these general categories can also be arranged on a scale of perfection. For example, Descartes will talk about the perfection of a stone or of a highly intricate machine—and he will then consider them not merely as two finite material substances but as two such substances endowed with a certain degree of complexity, or sophistication, and so on. It is not clear whether Descartes can supply us with some consistent and reliable rules for grading in this way the perfections of objects and ideas. But, perhaps, we need less than that to satisfy ourselves with Descartes's use of the concept of degrees of reality in the only place where it really matters—in Descartes's proofs of God.

A much more important difficulty must be confronted. We are at the stage of the methodical doubt. Given this circumstance we ought to doubt not only whether our measurements of the perfection of our ideas come out correctly, but whether the very standard that we are employing—the idea of God—is sound. Where do we find this standard? And how can we justify its use at the stage of doubt? Or, to put these two questions together, can we find our standard in such a way as to justify its use even at the stage of doubt?

Descartes thinks we can, and he thinks the two questions we have just asked have one and the same answer. I already know that my present epistemic condition—the condition of the doubter—is the one of imperfection and finitude. But I can not know myself as imperfect and finite without comparing myself with a standard of perfection and infinity which I can find only in my idea of God. And so even that very modest understanding of myself which I am allowed, or even forced, to adopt at the stage of doubt presupposes my acquaintance with the idea of God. Moreover, given the features of the divine being present in my idea of Him, that idea is even prior to the idea I have of myself. I should not imagine "that I do not perceive the infinite by a true idea, but only by the negation of the finite . . . for, on the contrary, I see that there is manifestly more reality in infinite substance than in finite, and therefore that in some way I have in me the notion of the infinite earlier than the finite—to wit, the notion of God before that of myself. For how could it be possible that I should know that I doubt and desire, that is to say, that something is lacking to me, and that I am not quite perfect, unless I had within me some idea of a Being more perfect than myself, in comparison with which I should recognize the deficiencies of my nature?"[130]

This is the most complete statement of Descartes's argument and it opens up a number of issues. It seems to run together two independent lines of thought. It may be that I cannot understand myself as finite without employing some conception of the infinite; and we may even grant Descartes—although this will need more argument than what he has supplied us with so far—that our grasp of the infinite is in some sense *prior* to the grasp of the finite. But why should we think that the imperfections we have discovered in ourselves at the stage of doubt imply the idea of the perfect being? If I doubt A or B, and if I grasp myself as doubting A or B and desiring to know A or B, I need not compare myself with the idea of a being who is omniscient. It is quite enough for me to entertain the idea of a being who does know A and B—but such a being need not be thought of as omniscient. Even Descartes's later suggestion, in the *Meditations*, that the idea of God "presents itself" (*occurrit*) to my mind when I consider that *qua* doubting I am an "incomplete and dependent being"[131] is still insufficient. Once again: if my incompleteness and dependency mean only that I fail to know A or B, then I need not evaluate this failing of mine in terms of the standard represented by the divine perfections—a far lesser standard would do just as well in this respect. It may still be the case that that lesser standard, in turn, would have to be evaluated as lacking perfection and

I would thus be led, step by step, to posit the idea of an omniscient knower as the ultimate standard in this series. But this is not to say that merely by pondering my failure to know *A* or *B* I must compare myself with the idea of an omniscient being. Neither can I expect that when I think of that failure of mine to know *A* or *B* the idea of God will simply "present itself" to my mind. If the link of these two ideas—of myself *qua* doubting *A* or *B* or failing to know *A* or *B* and of God *qua* standard of perfection—is to be a necessary one, then it must be explained to us why the first idea cannot be fully grasped without implying the second idea. But if the link is merely contingent, it is hard to see how Descartes's talk about the idea of God occurring to him when he thinks of his imperfections could be anything more than a report on his own introspective findings; and these findings can then be questioned, and repudiated, by anyone who does not find that his idea of himself qua doubting this or that is accompanied, in his mind, by the idea of a being free of any doubt and of any other imperfection.

But this is precisely what explains the pivotal role, in Descartes's argument, of my awareness that I am finite over against the infinite (as represented in the idea of God) and that the infinite is *prior* to the finite. The idea of God presents itself to my mind not merely on account of my awareness of my imperfections, but due to the circumstance that my grasp of those imperfections is such that I discover myself as lacking the infinite perfections of an infinite being. When I say that I doubt and that, insofar as I doubt, I compare myself with a standard represented by a being free of any doubts, I do not mean to suggest that the mere fact of my doubting *A* or *B* is of itself sufficient to impose upon me (by implication, contrast, or in any other way) the idea of such an omniscient being. But the "doubting" that I attribute to myself at the stage of methodical scepticism is not an ordinary doubting. It is seen in a certain context and it is characterized in a certain way: it is the sort of doubting from which I can't be free unless I know what is the metaphysical *origin* of my ideas and my faculties;[132] the sort of doubting from which an atheist can never liberate himself.[133] This "supreme doubt"[134] that Descartes must attribute to himself at the stage of his scepticism expresses the vulnerability of his condition to the menace of the supreme deception represented by a powerful deceiver. But to entertain the possibility of such supreme doubt and supreme deception Descartes must aspire to an equally supreme certainty; and it is this aspiration of his that will disclose to him the idea of an infinite and infinitely perfect God as "prior" to his own finitude.

Let us pay closer attention to this point. Hegel already has shown that just as our grasp of the finite presupposes our grasp of the infinite, so too our grasp of the infinite presupposes our grasp of the finite. The finite and the infinite are polar concepts, and we cannot understand one of them without understanding the other. In addition, at a certain level of reflexion this conceptual

contrast between the finite and the infinite takes the form of a mutual exclusion, or negation, of the one by the other. Consequently, Descartes's claim
that the finite is understood as the negation of the infinite whereas the infinite
is not understood as the negation of the finite may easily be seen as lacking
any support in the nature of the concepts involved; and an objection to this
effect can easily be advanced against Descartes, even from some surprisingly
unHegelian quarters.[135] From a purely formal point of view, the positive and
the negative concepts are on the same footing; Descartes's own examples[136] of
darkness and light or movement and repose not only fail to shed light on the
priority of the infinite over the finite, but, if anything, help to abolish it. For
if I can be said to perceive repose as the negation of movement, or darkness as
the negation of light, I can also be said to perceive movement as the negation
of repose and light as the negation of darkness; and there is no reason why, on
the strength of this analogy, a similar observation could not be made about
the relationship between the finite and infinite.

But if Hegel has shown how the infinite presupposes the finite just as much
as the finite presupposes the infinite he has also shown why, and in what
sense, the infinite remains *prior* to the finite. The infinite is prior to the finite,
for whereas the infinite actualizes itself in the finite only in order to affirm
itself, the merging with the infinite is the ultimate vocation or calling of the
finite; the infinite is that towards which the finite strives and aspires as to its
own final completion. The entire idea is in Descartes: "When I reflect on
myself I not only know that I am something [imperfect], incomplete and
dependent on another, which incessantly aspires after something which is better
and greater than myself, but I also know that He on whom I depend possesses
in Himself all the great things towards which I aspire."[137] Thus, while it is
true that some appeal to the meditating self's propensities (or "aspirations")
must be made to justify the priority of the infinite over the finite, it is also
true that these propensities are the very same ones that we have already discovered
in the *cogito* experience. For the discovery of the *cogito* was sustained by the
will to reach absolute certainty over against the absolute menace to our knowledge;
and that will, in turn, expresses the self's aspiration to absolute perfection in
every respect.[138] The existence, in me, of such an aspiration will be instrumental
in the proof of God; Descartes's argument will be that man aspires to possess
the perfections of God, and since he cannot possess them, he cannot be (given
some further premises) the author of his being. It is on account of *this* aspiration
in me that I come to know myself—when I think of all my doubts and
limitations—in the light of an ideal embodied in the idea of God; indeed, my
perception of myself *qua* aspiring and failing to reach that ideal allows me to
grasp myself as the image and the similitude of God.[139]

To sum up the two points made so far: (1) when I think of my imperfections
the idea of God can be said to present itself to me only if the perfections to

which I aspire are indeed infinite, and (2) only in the light of my aspiration to reach this idea of an infinite perfection can I view the latter as prior to the former. Descartes's explanations given subsequently to Burman must also be read in this sense.[140]

The dependence of my apprehension of my own finitude and imperfection upon my apprehension of the infinite perfection represented in the idea of God gives rise to one more difficulty which must be removed before that idea of mine can become the starting point of the proofs of God's actual existence. If I am finite, then just *how* can I be in a position of having the idea of an infinitely perfect being? It is not enough to say that I do have it (or even that I must have it) merely on account of my ability to describe myself as finite and imperfect by reference to the standard of the infinite perfection. For even if my idea of God is not—as it was for many mystics—a mere limit and negation of every finite determination but is a positive concept endowed with such determinations as omniscience, omnipotence, and so on, I must still account for the condition of possibility of my capacity to apprehend God through this concept of mine in spite of the inherent finitude of my intellect.

Descartes escapes this difficulty by drawing the distinction between what we can conceive or understand (*intelligo*) and what we can comprehend (*comprehendo*) about the divine being;[141] indeed, this distinction must be drawn on the basis of our very concept of infinity.[142] It is in terms of that concept, supplied by our reason, that God *qua* infinite being is apprehended as incomprehensible to us in much of what he is and what he does. If we deemed our idea of God unsound on the grounds of the inherent finitude of our reason, then our very thought of God as being beyond our comprehension would cease to be a *rational* thought—if it could still be a thought of *any* kind—and would thereby disqualify itself from having any relevance to our knowledge. So even if we do not "comprehend" God's infinity, we at least "understand" it. How *far* this understanding of ours extends and, even more important, how *coherent* it is, is another matter.[143] But it is sufficiently adequate and sufficiently coherent to allow us to assert that God's infinite perfection is incompatible with a will to deceive; and this, in turn, allows us to put our knowledge upon a secure foundation.

If Descartes is to have any chance to escape the trap of circularity in his proof, the proof must be simple enough to allow him to apprehend it in a single mental act relying only upon the same "light of nature" with the aid of which he has made his other important discoveries (that he exists, that his ideas are apprehended as representations of things, etc.). And, in effect, in spite of the many explanations, amendments and qualifications, the core of the proof is simple.

Descartes starts with the principle of causality which he takes to be identical with "the common truth *nothing comes from nothing*."[144] The principle of causality is known by the light of nature; and it is still the same light of nature which tells us that there must be at least as much reality in the "efficient and total cause as there is in the effect."[145] For if the effect was more perfect than the cause, then the surplus of (formal or objective) reality found in the effect would have to have emerged from nothing—and this would represent the violation of that "common truth" *ex nihilo nihil fit*. Thus, for every degree of reality in the effect there must exist the corresponding degree of reality in the cause. Of course, the cause may be *more* perfect than the effect—there may be (to take Descartes's example) more heat in the source from which this or that object we are considering has derived its high temperature than in the object itself. But to think that the cause may have had less heat (or, say, less of some chemical substance capable of generating heat) than found in the body heated by that cause would have amounted to admit the emergence of the heat out of nothing. This would be contrary to the light of nature and we would thus be forced to search for some still other causes contributing to the emergence of the heat. Taken together, these various causes would then supply the *total* efficient cause of the heat. Similarly, when asked to explain how animals and plants, so much "nobler" than inanimate bodies, could have been produced by "the sun, rain and the earth,"[146] Descartes will give a simple answer: either there is no perfection in the living beings over and above the perfections present in the physical elements said to produce life or those elements are not the total cause of life.[147]

The principle of causality applies not only to objects but to ideas as well and it applies to them not only *qua* episodes in my mental life, but *qua* representations of things. Now, if I took the view that my ideas are *merely* the episodes in my mental life, I would have no problem, even given the strictures of the causal principle as defined by Descartes, to account for the presence of these ideas in my mind. My formal reality is so much greater than the formal reality of my ideas (i.e., their perfection merely qua mental items) that I could very easily be that total and efficient cause of all of them. Caterus, in his objections, went so far as to suggest to Descartes that an idea, being only something in the mind, should be viewed as nothing actual, as a mere "non-entity" (*nihil*) for which no cause at all is needed.[148] But this was to forget that Descartes's causal principle applies also to the *objective* reality of our ideas. Even in their formal reality they do not deserve the label of "non-entities" glued upon them by Caterus, but Descartes does agree that their formal reality presents no great challenge to our search for causes. It is their objective reality that represents such a challenge, for we often run across an idea the objective reality of which is so great that a special effort is needed to find its cause. Take the idea of a sophisticated machine conceived by someone.[149] We find it natural to wonder at once how he got that idea or where it comes from. Did he copy it from some place? Did he learn it from someone else? Unless we can trace back that idea to some such sources, we will be forced to consider the possibility that the individual might have come up with the idea all by himself. We will then want to know whether his technical knowledge, skill and ingenuity were adequate to the task—and in searching for an answer to these questions we will take for granted that if he, as the originator of that idea, is to be its cause, then the formal reality of his cognitive powers must be adequate to the task of producing the objective reality of that idea. In the end, we must always confront the task of finding a *non*-ideal cause at least for the first element (or elements) in a causal series of ideas. And this task will be imposed upon us by the very principle (known by the light of nature) that ideas are representations of things. On account of this principle, ideas are endowed with objective reality, and the degree of the latter is measured by the degree of formal reality of the entities represented in the ideas. For this reason, even if an idea might have originated from other ideas and even if those ideas might also have originated from other ideas, that series as a whole must have had its original cause (or causes) in something that is not an idea but an actual entity: "Although it may be the case that one idea gives birth to another idea, that cannot continue to be so indefinitely; for in the end we must reach an idea whose cause shall be so to speak an archetype, in which the whole reality /or perfection/ which is so to speak objectively /or by representation/ in these ideas is contained formally /and really/."[150]

It is Descartes's claim that only our idea of God exhibits such a high degree of objective reality, that the human mind could not have contained formally (much less eminently) the perfection needed to produce that idea. Furthermore, as the idea of the perfect being, the idea of God has such a degree of objective reality that only a being endowed at least with the perfections contained objectively in this idea could have been its author. There can only be one such being—and that is God.

Isn't there some other idea of ours which might have had a cause other than ourselves? Descartes must deal with this question, for if there were to be such an idea, then we could reconstruct our knowledge of the external world without relying upon the idea of God and *its* author. But it is Descartes's claim that we can't.

But how do we test that proposition? It would certainly not be enough to conclude that we don't have the power to produce this or that idea merely on the grounds that we are not *conscious* of having such a power (although, most unfortunately, Descartes will suggest, now and then, precisely such an introspective test). For it was Descartes himself who admitted the possibility of there being some unconscious productive powers operating in us—and he took that possibility seriously enough to dismiss, on its grounds, the claim that the involuntary character of sensory ideas represents a sufficient indication of their origin in the external objects' causal impact upon us.[151] And if Descartes could use the concept of such a faculty capable of producing his sensory ideas even

while remaining unknown to him, we can't rule out the possibility that all of
Descartes's ideas might have originated in the workings of some such faculty
or faculties. To be sure, Descartes does say that we become conscious of any
faculty we dispose ourselves to exercise.[152] But there is no reason to accept this
thesis other than Descartes's view that every mental action must be accessible
to the immediate knowledge of the agent. If we find this view unfounded,
Descartes will have to come up with other arguments to convince us that all of
our ideas could not have been produced by the operation of some powers of
ours of which we were not, and are not, aware. To rule out this possibility, we
need more than the lack of an introspective evidence of the existence and
activity of such a power.

We do get more from Descartes when we focus upon the degrees of objective reality of our ideas and compare these degrees with the degree of formal
reality possessed by ourselves qua real existents. This is the main route Descartes
will pursue, and what he finds there will be used to accept or reject the possibility that he himself could have had the power to produce this or that idea.
Thus, the actual existence of such a power in him is not accepted or rejected
on the basis of an introspective evidence but on the grounds of an assessment
conducted with the aid of his concept of a scale of perfection which he applies
both to himself and to his ideas. If the degree of objective reality of this or
that idea exceeds the degree of formal reality present in him, then he is warranted in concluding that he could not have been even the unconscious author
of that idea.

Put in this form—as more or less dogmatic reliance upon the idea of a
hierarchy of perfections—Descartes's procedure can easily be dismissed as en-
tangled in the very same scholasticism Descartes wanted so badly to escape
from.[153] But Descartes's actual uses of this procedure are, if anything, distinctly modern. He attempts to reconstruct what is in effect the transcendental
origin of our fundamental concepts: he tries to show how the concepts of
substance, or duration, or number are formed within the human cognition as
the latter is conditioned merely by the structure of the self. Perhaps Fichte's
early *Wissenschaftslehre* represents the most radical and complete attempt at
such a reconstruction. But Descartes has laid the basis for it in the Third
Meditation. He *will* tell us beforehand that such and such intellectual idea
(sensory ideas are dismissed from the very beginning: they are so unclear and
confused that they either represent nothing at all or, if they do represent something, their representative component is so insignificant that we can easily view
them as dependent upon our own cognitive constitution) has a lesser degree of
objective reality than the degree of formal reality he finds in his own self as
apprehended within the strict limits of the methodical doubt. But he does not
stop at this assertion. He procedes to show how the idea at issue was generated
out of the materials found within himself *qua* thinking being; and only then,

after supplying this kind of account, does he conclude that it was in his power to produce the intellectual idea he has already identified as "objectively" less perfect than he himself is "formally."

Is Descartes giving us a reconstruction of what might have taken place, or is he talking about what actually did take place? Even the first claim would have been enough for his present purposes (for the claim would have meant that when he studies those intellectual ideas he is not forced to view them as having their origin in some causes other than his own mind; and this, in turn, would have meant that he has found no argument thus far for believing that something other than his own mind actually exists) but, in the end, Descartes seems to be leaning toward that second and stronger possibility. He seems to think that our intellectual ideas are actually developed through our grasp of certain all-pervasive features of our subjectivity. For example, he will first reconstruct the origin of the idea of substance and he will then tell us that "the idea of substance is within me owing to the fact that I am a substance."[154]

But what does this mean, especially in the light of Descartes's view that the idea of substance (or of number, duration, etc.) is in me simply as an innate idea of my intellect? Let us note, to begin with, that there is no incompatibility between Descartes's view of the innateness of those ideas and his derivation of them, in the Third Meditation, from the self's apprehension of its own features. If the innate *disposition*[155] to develop the ideas of substance or number, or duration were not a part of our mental makeup then, as Descartes sees it, there would be *no* process through which we could have formed these idea. Given such a disposition, however, Descartes can show how the materials found in the self's apprehension of its own features are sufficient to allow it to form those ideas. Moreover, Descartes need not be concerned with this disposition at the present stage of his argument. The disposition is an implicit condition of the process of concept formation as reconstructed in the Third Meditation; but we need not concern ourselves with mind's innate dispositions right now, and in order to show how our awareness of such and such features of our self was instrumental in allowing us to form such and such ideas.

A quick glance at Descartes's examples will make all of this much clearer. He beings with the ideas of substance, duration, and number—these are, to him, the most universal components of our conceptual scheme, since they apply to minds and bodies alike. Nevertheless, my awareness of these ideas is formed only on the basis of an acquaintance with my own thinking self and "I can afterwards transfer /them/ to any object that I please."[156] We have already followed Descartes in his attempt to show how I discover myself as a thinking substance, a "thing that thinks." His demonstration was offered on the reflective, meditative level: insofar as he, as a philosophical doubter, suspended all kinds of beliefs under the threat of supreme deception, he also discovered himself as endowed with that sole unshakable "possession" no deceiver was, or could have been, powerful enough to take away from him—and that was the "possession" he found in his own thinking. By discovering this possession of his, he realized that he himself must be a "something" if only as the owner of that possession. He was thus led to think of himself as a substance. But this meditative, reflective validation of himself qua substance was in conformity with the implicit and prereflective knowledge that he already had. He knew all along that he existed and that he was a thinking thing; in fact—such was the general thrust of Descartes's solution of the Meno paradox—if he had not known this all along, he would not have discovered it reflectively during the philosophical meditation. Now, his prereflective grasp of himself as bearer of thoughts, images, recollections and so on, allows him (given the appropriate "innate" disposition of his mind to think in certain determinate ways) to form the idea of finite substance. Once the idea is formed, it will be applied to areas other than his own mind. For even though such properties as extension, figure, and motion are not, even on the prereflective level, attributable to his mind, there is no reason why the bearers of those properties could not also be viewed as (finite) substances. A stone—this is the example with which Descartes conducts his present analysis[157]—is altogether different from myself qua thinking being; but the very same stone from which I distinguish myself as a mind from a body is still a bearer of properties, and thus the understanding of substance achieved on the basis of my acquaintance with myself can be applied to the stone as well. This is not to say that the difference between these two types of finite substances, mental and material, is being glossed over. Descartes's teaching from the Synopsis and the Sixth Meditation remains in force: as we recall, a body is a substance only in a relative sense while a mind is a "pure" substance; and this is due to the difference between the essential attributes of minds and bodies—while thinking cannot be divided and split up in parts, extension can be so divided and, consequently, this or that body can always lose its status of a particular substance by being divided and split into parts. With this qualification, however, the concept of substance can be applied to minds and bodies alike even though it originates in the self's prereflective grasp of itself.

The account of the origin of the idea of duration procedes along the same lines. We think that a stone endures, but the original source from which we draw the very idea of duration is, once again, our own self. I exist now, but I remember that I also existed earlier than at the present moment, and this recollection of my past existence gives me the idea of duration. There is, to be sure, a difficulty with this account of duration—a difficulty which we did not need to confront in our earlier case of the idea of substance. For the latter, although present in the self's prereflective experience, can also be detected, and validated, on the meditative level in the very instant of methodical doubt; and it seems that the idea of duration is much less fortunate in this respect. How do I know that my recollection of my past existence is anything more than an illusion? Couldn't some evil demon deceive me in my very recollection (which Descartes says I need to form the idea of duration) that "I have in former times existed"?[158] After having entertained the possibility of being deceived by the demon, "I persuade/ed/ myself that nothing has ever existed of all that my fallacious memory represents to me";[159] and there seems to be nothing self-verifying about my statements concerning my past existence.

But this would not affect the purpose, and the point, of Descartes's present analyses. Within the same paragraph he will attempt to give an account of the origin of his ideas of extension, figure, and motion. It will not occur to him to suggest to us that he now knows that there exist in fact, outside of his mind, entities endowed with those properties. He will be interested in showing how he himself could have formed the conception of these properties, but he will not claim that he is in a position to prove, at this stage, their external existence in bodies.

Similarly, it is not his task, right now, to prove that his recollections can be trusted. But whether they can be trusted or not—whether he actually does or does not have a past—he *is* having them right now, and he understands them as referring to his past experiences. Thus, even on the meditative level, he does have the concept or the idea of the past; and his having this concept is implied in the mere grasp of some of his thoughts as recollections (be they veridical or not). Couldn't he be misled even in this? Couldn't the demon mislead him in his very belief that some of his thoughts refer (correctly or not) to his past? It is very difficult to see how Descartes could find himself in the position he is in at the stage of doubt without having at least *this* idea of the past. For his doubt is joined with an aspiration to overcome it, and since what Descartes doubts is the content of his ordinary, everyday beliefs, he remains aware of his ordinary, everyday self as of something he must *leave behind* or, at the very least, prevent from having any influence upon his cognition. This ordinary, everyday self is now his old self, but it remains within his attention to the extent that he is trying to distinguish himself from his ordinary, everyday beliefs. The careful examination of his ideas and beliefs he is now engaged in represents a constant reminder not to lapse back into his past ways when he would accept all kinds of beliefs without sufficient examination. For this reason, even if he now pushes his criticism so far as to suspend faith in his memory, he cannot deprive himself of the very idea of his past. And, perhaps, at least *that* idea of his past deserves to be called a genuine recollection; Descartes himself comes close to suggesting this much.[160] No demon can mislead him about his having *that* idea, for he can only oppose himself to the demon by opposing himself to what he thinks he was as an ordinary, everyday knower. The demon makes Descartes suspend his reliance upon his ordinary cognitive faculties and, in responding to the menace of this deception, Descartes is constantly forcing himself *not* to succomb to the ordinary impulses and inclinations of his cognition. The demon injects discontinuity into Descartes's life; but in apprehending this position of the demon Descartes cannot fail to have the idea of the past—for the ordinary self he is mentally separating himself from in the moment of the doubt continues to be understood by him as the self he leaves behind while entering upon the path of his search for unshakable certainty. The suspension of his reliance upon the ordinary data of memory is *itself* performed in the context of that search. To sum up: Descartes doubts because the integrity of his cognition is threatened; but his desire to achieve certainty can have any chance of fulfillment only if the unreliable domains and areas of his cognition are put behind him. For this reason, his meditative position cannot be articulated without his thinking of himself as having a past even if he can't know, right now, whether he did in fact have such a past.

His derivation of the idea of number runs in no similar difficulties. He not only has the concept of number, but he is in a position to validate his right to apply this concept to various items in the experience he is having even right now, at the stage of doubt. Even under the menace of the most severe deception he can't fail to have several thoughts: the thought of the demon, the thought of himself as struggling against deception, the thought of doubting, of existing, of desiring to know, and so on. The multiplicity of these thoughts of his is more than enough to give him the idea of number (at least when that multiplicity is taken jointly with what Descartes will later identify as the innate dispositions of the human mind). The derivation of the idea of extension, figure, situation, and motion procedes along the same general lines, although Descartes is on less secure grounds here and he now seems to be less sure than in the earlier cases.[161]

The idea of God is subjected to the very same test Descartes has applied to all of his other ideas. He cannot be accused of asserting dogmatically that since the perfections contained "objectively" in our idea of God are so much higher than the perfections contained in us "formally," we could not have been the cause of that idea (with the next step being that its cause could only have been God himself). He tries to demonstrate why we could not have had the *capacity* to construct such an idea with the aid of our own cognitive powers and relying only upon the materials we could have found in ourselves. And only after *that* demonstration is carried out, Descartes thinks he is in a position to complete his argument concerning the divine origin of our idea of God.

Strangely enough, the crucial question, Could I have the capacity to produce the idea of God? receives both a no and a yes for an answer. But the yes amounts here to what is really a no in a disguised form; for, as Descartes will argue, if I *could* have the capacity to produce the idea of God, then that capacity itself would have to be viewed as given to me by God.

In point of fact, there is nothing strange about Descartes considering here these two possibilities and giving us his two answers. As we recall, I am not only different from, but similar to the ideal of perfection represented in my idea of God. The difference is obvious and it needs no elaboration. But the similarity is of equal importance to Descartes. I am similar to what is represented in my idea of God, for that idea represents what is in effect the highest potential which I myself want to realize. As an *ideal* toward which I aspire, the idea of God remains beyond my reach; but as the ideal of *my* aspiration, the idea of God contains, in a perfect form, the very same qualities (knowledge, will, etc.) which I also apprehend in myself. Thus, when I think of myself as *different* from God, it is immediately obvious to me that the objective reality of the idea of God could not have been contained in me "formally." But when I view myself as *similar* to God, it is not immediately obvious that I could not have formed my idea of Him merely by amplifying in thought the qualities that I find in myself. This second possibility is the main danger that Descartes must counter.

In the *Meditations,* Descartes concentrates on the first, the flatly negative answer to his question.[162] There is an unbridgeable gap between the infinite perfections of God as represented in our idea of Him, and the faculties we find in ourselves. For this reason, we could not have formed this idea by any (conscious or unconscious) process of reflecting upon our own faculties and representing them as gradually gaining in perfection. For example, I could not form in this way my conception of a knowledge free of any doubt, ignorance, and all other forms of cognitive limitation; that is, I could not envision *my* condition as actually reaching the stage where there would be literally "nothing more to know." Such a stage would either express some self-satisfaction with, or resignation to, the still-limited knowledge that I would have or it would become the condition in which I would cease to recognize myself and my faculties: the condition of an omniscient knower. Being a creature of limits, I cannot think of myself otherwise than as having the kind of knowledge which could always be expanded; and the idea of myself as an omniscient knower is irreconcilable with that. Moreover, I do not, as a matter of fact, form the idea of the infinitely perfect being by a process of reflecting upon my faculties and amplifying their perfections bit by bit. That idea is given all at once as soon as I am capable of thinking of myself as finite and imperfect. When I do apprehend myself in that finite and imperfect condition, the idea of God, we recall, "presents itself" as the polar concept and the term of my aspiration. In that capacity, *"the idea of God is not formed by amplifying the perfections of created beings,* but is constituted as a whole at one time by the fact that mentally we apprehend an infinite being that is incapable of any amplification."[163] There can be no process of working up to that idea by increasing in thought the perfection of my finite and imperfect faculties, for I could not even think of them as imperfect and finite without already having the idea of God with which to compare them.

But—to move on to the second possibility Descartes must explore—what if I suppose that I *could* have the capacity to form the idea of God by "amplifying" the perfection of the faculties I find in myself? This could only mean that my very capacity to increase in thought my faculties would have to be guided by an implicit idea of God. That is, I cannot envision my faculties as increasing in perfection until they reach the level of perfection contained in the idea of God unless that idea is *already* in me: "What can account for the power of amplifying all created perfections, i.e. of conceiving something greater and more ample than they, unless the fact that the idea of something greater viz. of God exists in us?"[164] The faculties of God are not only "greater and more ample" than my *present* faculties, but they are greater and more ample than anything that could be constructed by the process of reflecting upon my faculties and attributing to them an ever greater degree of perfection.

An analogy used by Descartes sheds some light upon this argument. The analogy is drawn from mathematics.[165] When I consider the sequence of natural numbers I know that there is always a number higher than any number I can actually think of. This capacity to form the concept of a number higher than any number I can actually think of must have been given to me by a being higher than myself. Similarly, even if we had the capacity to amplify in thought our own faculties until they reach the level of infinite perfection, we would first have to have the concept of such an infinite perfection and (this will be the next step in Descartes's demonstration) the cause of such an idea in us could only have been God himself. And so our very capacity to reach the idea of God by "amplification" would have to be viewed as having its origin in God.

As Descartes fully realized,[166] this analogy has nor force of argument, and it will convince no one who is not already prepared on *other* grounds to accept the view that our capacity to entertain the idea of an infinitely perfect being must have been caused by an actual being endowed with the infinite perfections. Descartes will try to supply these grounds by reducing to absurdity any supposition contrary to his hypothesis. He will try to show that his very *existence* as a finite being capable of entertaining (and aspiring to) the idea of an infinitely perfect being proves that (1) he himself could not have been the author of his existence, and (2) God alone could have created him as existing with the capacity to form the idea of God.

In Descartes's own opinion, this new attempt does not really represent a new proof, but "a more thorough-going explanation" of the proof already offered.[167] To be sure, in his new attempt Descartes will be concerned with demonstrating that he himself (and not just his idea of God) must have been created by God; and this does represent a new element in comparison with what Descartes has offered us so far. But Descartes will be able to demonstrate that he has been created by God by considering himself only insofar as he is capable of forming the idea of God.[168] To that extent, at least, his new attempt does not proceed from any features of our condition other than those already explored for the purpose of proving the existence of God.

Once again, the core of the proof is quite simple and, once again, the proof involves the attribution, to the self, of an *aspiration* to reach the infinite perfections embodied in our idea of God. It is the matter of explaining the discrepancy between desire and reality, between what we wish to achieve and what we can achieve. We aspire to all the perfections contained in our idea of God; and so if we had been the authors of our being we would have given ourselves all of the perfections we aspire to. This seems to be intuitively correct— for if my whole identity could be created by me then why would I deprive myself of anything I desire?—but there is also a rational basis behind it. For "it is quite evident that it was a matter of much greater difficultly to bring it to pass that I, that is to say, a thing or a substance that thinks, should emerge out of nothing, than it would be to attain to the knowledge of many things of which I am ignorant . . . nor should I have deprived myself of any of the things contained in the idea which I form of God."[169] In other words, if I had been the cause of my being I would have created a substance out of nothing, and this would have been much more difficult to accomplish than the creation of even the most perfect attributes a mind is capable of. Given my aspiration to acquire such perfect attributes, I would have had every incentive to produce them in my own self. With such a capacity and such a desire being present, I would have created myself as the perfect being I aspire to be.

But why should I view the capacity to create out of nothing this finite substance that I am as a sufficient sign of the power to give myself the infinite perfections I aspire to? Descartes will argue,[170] that the power to conserve a being in existence is the same as the power to actually create that being in every single moment of its life-history. Now, "the cause which has power sufficient to conserve a thing external to it must with all the more reason conserve itself by its own proper power, and so exist *per se*."[171] But Descartes has already explained that a cause which "possesses the virtue of self-existence . . . must also without doubt have the power of actually possessing all the perfections of which it has the idea."[172] Taken together, these two claims are sufficient to support his views: (1) if I could create (or conserve in being, which will soon turn out to be the same thing) this finite substance that I am, I would have the power to exist per se, and (2) this power of existing per se is so great that it would have given me the capacity to endow myself with all the perfections that I aspire to (for, as we just heard Descartes explaining to us, the power to exist per se is sufficient to allow its owner to endow himself with all the other perfections). The capacity to exist per se—which I would have to possess qua author of my being—demands "such a great and inexhaustible power," [173] such an "immense and incomprehensible power," [174] that my possession of such a power would have been quite adequate to instantaneously give me every perfection I ever wished for. Of course, it is absurd to suppose that *I* could ever have had such a power. But this is precisely what Descartes wants us to acknowledge; this is his way of reducing to absurdity the supposition that I could have been the author of my being.

Three more possibilities remain: (1) I could have always existed as I am now, with the idea of God in me, (2) I could have been created by some less than perfect being, and (3) I could have been created by several "authors" each of them perfect in his kind. These three possibilities (for there are no others) must still be ruled out before I can conclude that God alone could have created me in my capacity of a finite and imperfect being endowed with the idea of an infinitely perfect being.

First, then, the possibility that we might have "always" existed in precisely that capacity of finite and imperfect beings endowed with the idea of an infinitely perfect God. We do not know, of course, if we have had any actual existence in the past. Still, Descartes has already explained to us that our idea of time maintains itself (or even originates) within the strict boundaries of the *cogito,* and so we can legitimately explore the possibility that perhaps we had always existed as we exist now, with our capacity to entertain the idea of God and to aspire to the perfection contained in this idea. But this possibility must be ruled out given the lack of causal dependence of any slice of time upon the time that preceded it at least where "it is not a question of abstract time, but of the time or duration of something which endures."[175] Thus, the circumstance that an entity X exists at the moment t can not be viewed as the cause of X's existence at the succeeding moment t^1. Some cause other than the mere existence of X in t was needed to secure X's existence in t^1. This is why the continued existence of X amounts to X's being continually conserved in existence, that is, continually recreated. The power of conserving, or recreating in being, is the same as the power of creating being.[176]. Consequently, if I had "always" existed as I am now, this would have meant that *some* cause would have been needed to create me continually in every single slice of that past life of mine. Could *I* have been that cause?

It is most unfortunate that Descartes's immediate reply to this question represents what is in effect another fallback upon the alleged transparency of our mental lives. It is enough, he suggests, to look into ourselves and to see if we are conscious of having the power to produce ourselves, at least qua thinking beings, in the moment ahead of us.[177] For if we are not conscious of having such a power, then we do not in fact have it, and, consequently, a cause other than ourselves would be required to conserve our being throughout the different, causally independent, slices of time. Fortunately, Descartes's question here was more rhetorical than real, given what he has already argued for. If I had always existed the way I am now, without there having been any *external* cause of that continued existence of mine, I *would* have been (given the equivalence between the power to conserve X in existence and the power to create X) the author of my being. And this amounts to saying that I would have had the power to give myself, in any given part of time, all of the perfections to which I aspire. Descartes's talk about my lack of awareness of having the power sufficient to secure my being in time ought to be taken within that more general context of his argument. I am not "conscious" of having such a power, since I *am* conscious of having my aspiration to perfection frustrated by the realities of my existence; and there would be no such discrepancy between desire and reality in my existence if the power to conserve myself throughout time were in fact at my disposal.

My status of a creature capable of entertaining the idea of God and aspiring to the perfections contained in this idea allows me to rule out the second possibility under consideration: that the cause which sustains me in being might be imperfect.[178] There must be at least as much reality in the cause as there is in its effect. Therefore the cause of my existence must contain formally or eminently the reality that exists in me formally. But my formal reality is very high due to the presence, in me, of the idea of God with its very high objective reality. The cause of my continued existence must be adequate to the task of producing me as having that particular idea; and this means that the perfections of God must exist in the cause of my being at least objectively (i.e., in the idea of God present in the cause of my being). Whoever causes me to be must have the idea of divine perfections within himself. The question about *his* cause must now be asked. The cause of my being will either need another appropriate cause to be created as endowed with the idea of God (but then the question of this next cause's origin would arise and so on), or it must have enough power to create itself (but then the cause of my continued existence must be God, since the power to create oneself is sufficient to give oneself the perfections contained in the idea of God).

This looks very much like a version of the traditional cosmological argument (demonstrating the existence of God from the inadmissibility of an infinite series of causes), and it is not surprising that the author of the First Objections, Caterus, understood Descartes in precisely that sense. But Descartes soon corrected that impression. His argument, he explained, does not start from the observation of sequences of causes and effects occurring in the world, for he has suspended his right to accept the very existence of a world independent of his representations.[179] More important, Descartes searches for a cause capable of creating him, or sustaining him in being right now, when he is thinking and he does not arrive at the conclusion that his cause *in esse* is God on the strength of the supposition that he could not comprehend how there could be an infinite sequence of causes from which he would derive his being. He thinks that his inability to conceive such an infinite sequence of causes is no proof of the impossibility of their existence. He argues that the cause of his being can't be imperfect since the awesomeness of power needed to sustain him in being is such that whoever can do that must have within himself not just the idea of God (for we have already agreed that the cause of Descartes's existence must have the idea of God within it), but also the actual possession of all the perfections contained in this idea.

The third and last possibility—I might have received my ideas of divine perfections (and my very existence of a self endowed with these ideas) from several perfect causes contributing to produce such an effect—is in fact based on a conceptual confusion and cannot withstand a closer analysis. It simply makes no sense to think that there might have been several "perfect" causes. Every perfection—omniscience, omnipotence, eternity, and so forth—is necessarily connected with all the other perfections, whether taken in their objective reality (in our idea of them) or in their formal reality (as existent outside of our ideas). The unity of these perfections is itself a perfection, and this is why Descartes will argue, in the Second Replies, that we ought not to conceive the relation between divine intellect and will (where these faculties are fully united) on the model of the relation between human will and intellect (where such an unity of faculties is lacking). This, too, is an additional reason why no reflection upon *our* faculties could have generated the idea of God by the process of a gradual "amplification" of their perfection: by such a process we could not have reconstructed the unity and the interdependence of these faculties as contained in our idea of God.[180]

To sum up. I cannot be the cause of my own existence. The cause of my existence can't be imperfect. The perfections needed to produce me cannot be distributed among several allegedly "perfect" causes; they must be the attributes of one and the same cause. The cause endowed with such attributes is precisely what I understand by God.

Throughout his entire proof Descartes relies upon a certain conception of *power and powerlessness*. If I am not the cause of my being it's because I don't possess all the perfections to which I aspire; and this lack is incompatible with possession of the power to cause my own existence and to sustain it throughout time. Conversely, if God can be the cause of his being, he must also have all the other perfections, since the power to exist per se is so immense that it will give its owner whatever perfection he can aspire to—if indeed the word aspiration (implying as it does some gap between reality and ideal) could still have some meaning when applied to such a being.

If it can be charged that this conception of power and powerlessness is taken for granted by Descartes and should have been subjected by the philosopher to a prior, properly epistemological investigation, it must be realized that the latter is, in the *Meditations,* dependent upon the former. The epistemological inquiry was supported by an assumption that we may be exposed to a will to deceive powerful enough to generate that supreme doubt in the soundness of our ordinary cognitive faculties. We found no adequate power of our own to shelter our ordinary cognitive faculties from the operations of such a deceiver, and so we decided to suspend the beliefs which we found dependent upon those faculties. The solution to the sceptical predicament is the discovery of the veracious God as the author or our cognition. God can't have the will to deceive, for the will to deceive is an imperfection, and God's "immense" and "inexhaustible" power is sufficient to give him all the perfections. Thus the presuppositions concerning my own powerlessness and the immensity of the power of God are at work both in my formulation of the problem of scepticism and in the solution adopted to overcome it. If, in the Second Replies, Descartes pursues as a working hypothesis the possibility that our very conception of God may be unsound, he ends up by rejecting this possibility as irrelevant at least to our *cognitive* concerns, including our concern with scepticism and its overcoming.

Descartes's rejection of this possibility will be discussed below. Perhaps Descartes can defend it and, perhaps, his proof of God can't be attacked from this angle. Perhaps, too, Descartes's repeated claims that he is not guilty of what has come to be known as the Cartesian Circle are justified: perhaps the core of the proof *is* so simple that we could grasp it with a certainty equal to that of the *cogito* itself. Where the proof definitely breaks down is in its reliance upon the principle of causality. Hume was soon to expose the basic flaw: When I say that X has no cause, I need not mean that X's cause is "nothing," unless I already take for granted, quite arbitrarily, that everything must have a cause. The concept of uncaused occurrences or events cannot be deemed unintelligible or self-contradictory on *these* grounds, and since Descartes supplies no other grounds for the principle of causality and for that further corollary that there must be at least as much perfection in the cause as there is in the effect, his proof collapses. It may be that once we are assured of the existence of God and of the divine Providence, the notion of uncaused occurrences will indeed become close to being unintelligible. In this case, like in the case of the Hobbesian sovereign, the reality of a supreme power, once posited, will translate itself into a certain new way of determining what is and what is not rational. But the reality of such a supreme power must first be proved by an independent route. Consequently, only if I had reasons to believe on independent grounds (independent of the principle of causality) that *this particular* item called the "idea of God" in me originates in God, something could be salvaged from Descartes's attempt.

There does exist such a possibility even in the Third Meditation: "And one ought not to find it strange that God, in creating me, placed this idea within me to be like the mark of the workman imprinted on his work; and it is likewise not essential that the mark shall be different from the work itself."[181] Thus, the idea of God is a sign, or a manifestation, in me, of the power of my

maker. This sign, says Descartes, need not be viewed as different from myself—at least not inasmuch as I consider myself as an image and a similitude
of God—and so my own existence may well be viewed as a manifestation of
God. A systematic interpretation along these lines has been worked out by one
of the leading Descartes scholars of our century.[182] In terms of this interpretation, Descartes's attempt to discover God by proceeding from the *cogito* can
bear fruit only if the relation between God and his idea in us (or between God
and ourselves as endowed with the idea of him) ceases to be viewed as an
external relation to be reconstructed with the aid of the principle of causality.
Whereas, in a causal inference, we can identify and characterize the effect independently of the cause, the idea of God may come to be viewed not as a
representation of something merely external to it (which would also be this
idea's cause), but as the direct, although incomplete, "presence" of God.[183]

We can arrive at strictly parallel results by considering the a priori proof of
God from the Fifth Meditation, the famous "ontological argument," as it came
to be called subsequently. The relation between the two proofs is a difficult
issue, and it has generated much discussion and controversy in Descartes schol-
arship. Descartes's official view is to be found in the Fifth Meditation. He
there tells us that the proof he is about to offer will have at least as much
certainty as the demonstrations of mathematicians.[184] He can, by now, make
two assumptions to back up this confident assessment. First, he has already
proved, in the Third Meditation, that he is created and sustained in being by
a veracious God, and so he is assured at least of the truth of his clear and
distinct cognitions. Second, he has a clear and distinct knowledge of the eternal "essences" or "natures" of things. Such is precisely his mathematical knowledge
and such, too, is his knowledge of the essence of God. Like St. Anselm before
him, he thinks that his grasp of that divine essence will allow him to conclude
that God must be an actual existent.

Many questions remain open. The disposition of the two proofs in the
Meditations and Descartes's own comments suggest strongly that the causal
proof from the Third Meditation is more compelling at least within the order
of discovery (in the *Principles* the ontological argument comes first and, apparently, it is considered more simple and more compelling in the "synthetic"
order followed by that work). If the causal proof could not be taken for granted
as we approach the Fifth Meditation and our knowledge of the "essences," we
would be in no position to validate this knowledge as a whole, and hence also
our knowledge of the essence of God. But it is not clear why, even in the
order of discovery, the causal proof should be deemed more convincing than
the ontological one, especially in the light of Descartes's subsequent explanations[185] that the ontological argument can be reduced to a single act of intuition, not unlike the *cogito* itself. Neither is it clear how we could avoid taking
for granted already in the causal proof the very same knowledge of the divine

essence that goes into the making of the ontological proof. It is true that the first proof is a posteriori in the sense that the existence of God is inferred from the contingent fact of my own existence. But God is inferred as the cause of my own existence in his capacity as the all-powerful, and hence the perfect, being—and these are the very same features of his essence which will be used, in the ontological argument, to attribute to him not simply actual, but eternal and necessary, existence. It seems, then, that both proofs presuppose some reliable knowledge of God's essence; and it also seems that this knowledge is pretty much the same in both proofs.

There remains the one basic difference between the two proofs. In the causal proof we found an actual existent with which to start the entire demonstration—and that actual existent was simply ourselves *qua* finite beings endowed with an aspiration to reach the infinite perfections. Given this actual existence of ours it at least made sense to try to demonstrate the actual existence of the appropriate cause of our being. But the case of the ontological argument is different. Our own actual existence—or the existence of anything else, for that matter—is entirely irrelevant in the proof. Of course, we formulate the proof by inspecting our "idea" of God. But the fact of our own existence as we ponder and reason from the idea of God to his actual existence is not itself an element in the demonstration. Since we thus lack an actual existent from which to infer another actual existent, there is an obvious danger that God will be made into a real entity by a pure decree of our thought.

Descartes is not unaware of this danger, and he takes the steps to avoid it already in the Fifth Meditation. He does this by drawing a distinction between fictitious ideas (or "fictions of the mind," as he calls them elsewhere) and the genuine "natures" or "essences" of things, such as the essence of a triangle. Since the idea of God is not one of the fictions of the mind and since the property of existence is contained in that idea, the proposition "God exists" cannot be lumped together with such propositions as "a winged horse exists." Whereas the truth of the first of these propositions, and the method of its justification, are open for discussion, the second proposition fails to qualify for such purposes, since the subject to which it attributes existence is merely a figment of our own imagination. And this would be one reason why we could not define into existence such familiar entities as Santa Claus, Superman, and so on.

However, to establish this distinction between fictions of the mind and genuine essences of things, Descartes needs some dependable criterion. In the First Meditation, when he was pursuing his analysis of dreams, he formed the suspicion that all of his composite ideas may be fictitious; and he then told us that there was still some hope of saving from doubt certain "simple and universal" ideas present in the dream images. For even such obviously fictitious ideas as the ideas of "sirens" and "satyrs" (these were the examples he gave in the First

Meditation) are composed of certain simple elements that need not themselves be fictitious. Only at the next stage of his doubt—at the stage of thinking of himself as being in the grip of a powerful deceiver—will Descartes be forced to apply his doubt even to those simple and universal elements of his representations. Since, in the Fifth Meditation, the doubt is behind him, he can be sure that at least those elements themselves are not fictions of his mind.

Descartes can be sure of that, but this won't be enough to allow him to draw a general distinction between fictions of the mind and essences of things. Not all essences are simple ideas; most essences are composites. Descartes needs a criterion allowing him to discriminate between those composite ideas which are (or may turn out to be, on a closer analysis) fictions and those that represent the essences of things. The criterion he offers in the Fifth Meditation is his ability to demonstrate certain properties about essences: this, he says, is the best indication that the idea which lends itself to such a treatment has a "true and immutable" nature, independent of his own mental operations. For example, the fact that we can demonstrate that the three angles of a triangle add up to 180 degrees gives us sufficient reason to think that we are dealing with the true essence of a triangle and not with the product of our own fancy. But this does not go far enough, for it does not allow us to stamp out as "fictions" the very same examples Descartes was offering us for consideration in the First Meditation. There is no reason to refuse an "essence" of sorts even to a siren. To think of an X as failing to be a female would, it seems, amount to depriving X of one of the essential properties of what counts as a siren. Given this understanding of the essential properties of a siren, we could proceed to demonstrate all kinds of propositions that must be true about any siren.

Descartes tries to dispel such an obvious worry. He says, in the First Replies, that a fictitious idea is put together only by our mind and "can be by that same mind analysed . . . by a clear and distinct mental operation."[186] Thus, our mind has the power to separate the idea of wings from the idea of a horse and this gives us sufficient reason to think that the idea of a winged horse has been manufactured by the mind as one of its "fictions." In this respect, the case of a triangle is entirely different: we can't separate the idea of triangle from the idea of a figure with three angles adding up to two right angles. Here the idea imposes itself upon our mind as being fully independent of mind's power to put together and split apart its various contents; and this independence of the idea suffices to recognize it as representing a "true and immutable" nature.

Once again, Descartes's own examples undercut the effectiveness of his criterion. In the First Replies, he considers a composite idea of a triangle inscribed in a square and he himself seems to be of two minds on how to deal with this example.[187] On the one hand, this particular composite idea can certainly be analyzed in our minds into its basic components, the triangle and the square, and so Descartes denies the status of a true and immutable nature to what is represented in that idea. Viewed from this angle, the idea of a triangle in a square finds itself relegated to the category of fictitious ideas. But, on the other hand, since we can demonstrate certain properties about the figure of a triangle inscribed in a square ("it will be right to affirm that the square cannot be less than double the inscribed triangle, together with the similar properties which belong to the nature of this composite figure"), Descartes concludes that the figure as a whole has a nature that is by no means less real than the nature of a triangle or of a square taken separately.

However, the difficulty of defining a criterion allowing us to separate mental fictions from essences can be circumvented at least in the case of our idea of God. For if some composite ideas are, or may turn out to be on a closer analysis, entirely fictitious, the simple ideas can't be fictitious, at least not in the sense that they might have been put together in some arbitrary ways by the workings of our fancy. But the idea of God, we had learned in the Third Meditation, is by all means a simple idea. The diversity contained in the idea of God, Descartes told us (the diversity of the various divine faculties) represents such a perfect unity and simplicity, that the latter is itself one of the main perfections of God as we conceive him. There is no danger, then, that this particular idea might have been concocted by the imagination employing, to that purpose, some elements found elsewhere in our mental experience. Even the First Meditation would have granted this much, for it taught us that the truth of our "simple and universal" ideas is unaffected by the truth or falsity of our composite ideas. Moreover, the Third Meditation soon put the simple idea of God beyond the scope of doubt at least qua idea. As Descartes explained it to us, our very grasp of ourselves as being in the condition of doubt presupposed (be it even implicitly) our grasp of the idea of God. Were we to doubt the soundness of that idea at least qua idea we would have to doubt that we find ourselves in the condition of doubt—and this, for Descartes, was not a serious possibility. In any case, after the Third Meditation's proof of God, the doubt is behind us at least as far as our "clear and distinct" ideas are concerned; and it is enough for the idea of God to have the clarity and the distinctness of mathematical ideas to allow us to employ it in an argument meant to have at least the same degree of persuasiveness as the propositions of pure mathematics. It is enough to give Descartes his essences (and however difficult it may be to formulate a general criterion for separating them from fictions of the mind we do not want, on these grounds alone, to deprive ourselves of mathematical knowledge if it is otherwise true, as Descartes argues it must be, that such knowledge commits us to the acceptance of his essences), and to give him the right to make true predications about these essences,[188] and he will have all the elements he needs to proceed with the ontological argument.

It remains to be seen whether existence is a property that we can truly predicate about the essence of God. And to decide this issue we must also decide whether existence can be viewed as a property at all. Let us first offer a brief outline of the proof from the Fifth Meditation. Just as it is a property of the essence of a triangle that its three angles are equal to two right angles, so, too, the property of existence is inseparable from the essence of God. There exists a "repugnance to our conceiving a God (that is, a Being supremely perfect) to whom existence is lacking (that is to say, to whom a certain perfection is lacking)."[189] The entire proof is compressed in this single sentence. When we think of God, we think of the supremely perfect being: that is what makes up God's essence. But existence is a perfection. Hence the essence of the supremely perfect being includes the property of existence—were we to conceive this being as lacking actual reality we would be, by definition, conceiving something less than supremely perfect.

Even before Kant set out to refute the ontological argument by attacking the premise that existence is a property, a similar criticism was advanced against the Fifth Meditation by Gassendi.[190] Existence, Gassendi argued, is neither a perfection nor an imperfection for it is that which allows something to either have or not have such and such perfections or imperfections. Being thus the condition of something's having any properties—be they perfections or imperfections—existence is not a property at all and it should not be counted among properties. But Descartes was unmoved by this objection: "I do not see, he replied, to what class or reality you wish to assign existence, nor do I see why it may not be said to be a property as well as omnipotence, taking the word property as equivalent to any attribute or anything which can be predicated of a thing."[191] And in the *Principles*,[192] existence is considered as an attribute of a thing in precisely the same sense as the thing's duration; there is no more difficulty in "predicating" existence of an *X* than there is in predicating duration of it.

Descartes did not give us much to go on in order to understand just *how* existence can be a property, but his view can be extracted from various hints and comments scattered throughout his writings, including the *Meditations*. For example, when offering us his main arguments as to why we could not have produced the idea of God, he explains why we should not think that the perfections contained in this idea might have existed in us potentially. He tells us that the objective reality of an idea "cannot be produced by a being that exists potentially only, which properly speaking is nothing."[193] Some characteristics of what Descartes understands by the property of existence are clearly indicated in this passage. In the first place, only an actual existent is said to be capable of having a causal impact upon the properties (or "perfections") of other existents. This is still in line with the traditional, medieval understanding of existence, where the causal powers of something are the expressions of its actuality, of its own power of being.[194] Thus, whatever has being, has the power to have a causal impact upon other beings. It follows from this, that the being of an *X* can never be established in isolation: we can establish it only by viewing *X* in its various relations and interactions with other beings. From a purely abstract, isolated viewpoint (as when I mentally extract *X* from the web of its interactions with *Y*, *Z*, etc.), there may not be any apprehendable difference between an existent *X* and an imaginary *X*. But this changes altogether when I move on to determine whether the *X* I am aware of does or does not impose changes upon *Y*, *Z*, and so on. Suppose I suffer from a painful illness and someone begins to describe to me a wonder drug for it. When he has me dreaming, he tells me suddenly that the drug "really exists." This does seem to add a new property to the drug as he has been describing it to me thus far; and the new element is represented precisely by the drug's power to have a genuine impact upon my health and my condition. In this sense, contrary to Kant's later famous analysis of the existence and non-existence of a hundred thalers—but quite in line with Hegel's criticism of this analysis in the *Science of Logic*—existence does turn out to be a "real predicate" of the thing. There is a determinate difference between an existent and an imaginary *X*; this difference does express the presence or the absence, in the *X*, of a certain kind of property, and the possession, by the *X*, of such a property does increase *X*'s "perfection"—if only because it allows *X* to act and to have an impact in the many ways that remain closed to the imaginary, or the merely conceived *X*. For this reason alone a "supremely perfect being" deprived of the property of existence would not be supremely perfect.

But the transformation of existence into a property and a perfection allows us to go still further. We learn not only that the concept of the supremely perfect being implies that such a being be thought of as existent but, by the very same reasoning, we learn that the supremely perfect being must be thought of as existent in a certain way. When we think of all other essences, we apprehend them as endowed with only the possible (or, at the very best, with the actual but purely contingent) existence; whereas the essence of God contains within itself the property of eternal and necessary existence.[195] If a being had only a finite and contingent existence, then such a being would not be the *supremely* perfect being even if it had all the other perfections. Moreover, for such a being the ontological argument would not work in any case. If I conceive an *X* endowed with only a contingent and finite existence, I cannot learn that such an *X* does in fact exist unless I have some factual (perceptual or other) evidence of this. Since it is not logically impossible that such an *X* be non-existent, I must go beyond the concepts and must consult the actual data to learn of *X*'s existence.

So far, however, even this very difference can be understood as applying only to the different ways in which we conceive beings. It is true that our concept of the supremely perfect being is logically connected with the concept of eternal and necessary existence; and it may even be granted that if there were to exist a supremely perfect being, then such a being would have to be endowed with the necessary and the eternal existence. But, as Caterus was soon to point out to Descartes,[196] even if it is granted that the concept of the supremely perfect being is necessarily connected with the concept of existence, it still does not follow that there actually exists such a supremely perfect being. Nothing is changed if the existence at issue is thought of as eternal and necessary. While it may be logically contradictory to assert that a supremely perfect being could have a contingent existence, it is not logically contradictory to assert that such a being does not exist at all.

Descartes was not deaf to the objections of Caterus and in replying to him he tried to supply the ladder with which to step over from the (merely conceived) essence of God to His (actual) necessary and eternal existence. Descartes employed, to that purpose, one particular perfection contained in the idea of God: the perfection of omnipotence. In the *Meditations*, Descartes reasons directly from the concept of the supremely perfect being, and the idea of the divine omnipotence is not given any special role in the proof. In the *Principles* he goes even further, for he contrasts the divine omniscience and omnipotence with God's absolute perfection which, he says, is "far the most important of all" the ideas of the divine attributes, and which contains in itself the idea of necessary and eternal existence.[197] But this is not how he chooses to answer the very pertinent criticisms of Caterus.

He begins to formulate the new version of the ontological argument by considering the example of a body.[198] He shows us first why the eternal and necessary existence cannot belong to the essence of a body—be it even to the essence of the most perfect body conceivable. A body, if it were to exist, could only lead a finite and contingent existence, since it is of the essence of corporeal nature to lack the "force" (*vis*) of producing and sustaining itself in being. Since a body is, by its essence, deprived of such a force we may quite easily conceive the circumstances under which this or that, or any, body would go out of existence and cease to be. By the same token, we apprehend the necessary link between the essence of God and the property of eternal and necessary existence. The link is supplied by one particular property belonging to God's essence: by his power. This power, we recall, was characterized as unlimited and inexhaustible; and these terms were meant to capture the incommensurability between the divine power and the power of all finite substances. This gap between the (exhaustible and limited) powers ascribed to the essences of finite things, and the truly infinite power ascribed to the essence of God, leads Descartes to assert God's eternal and necessary existence.

In effect, just as it is inconceivable that an X the essence of which does not include the power adequate to the task of producing and sustaining this X in being might be endowed with anything other than a merely finite and contingent existence, so too an X the essence of which includes the inexhaustible and unlimited power can not be conceived otherwise than as leading a necessary and eternal existence. To think of such an X as losing existence and ceasing to be would be a contradiction in terms, since it would imply that such a being has no force to maintain itself—a supposition which is at odds with our ascription, to the essence of such a being, of an unlimited power. For the same reason, we can not conceive God as beginning to be, since this would mean that we impute to him a certain lack of power: an inability to posit himself in existence prior to some boundary line marking the "beginning" of his emergence. On this supposition, God's power would by all means deserve to be called exhaustible and limited, for even if we could not measure it by the stretch of time within which it would be capable of operating (given the circumstance that God's existence could not have a temporal beginning), we would certainly view it as ineffective "prior" to God's emergence as an actual being.

Might God not fail to *want* to exist even if we grant him the power to translate such a desire, should he have it, into the property of eternal and necessary existence? The question can have hardly any meaning once we are prepared to grant Descartes that existence is a perfection. God is conceived as the supremely perfect being. Since existence is a perfection, the eternal and the necessary existence is the supreme perfection as far as the property of existence is concerned. A supremely perfect being who would fail to desire to exist, and to exist necessarily and eternally, would deviate from his essence of the supremely perfect being; in refraining from desiring to be as much as he can, such a being would aim at diminishing and lessening himself, and, as we shall see in the next section, that is the one possibility that Descartes will repudiate again and again. Given this premise, and given the conception of God's power as truly inexhaustible and infinite, the (eternal and necessary) existence of God is known by the "light of nature": "For the light of nature makes it most plain that what can exist by its own power always exists. And thus we shall understand that necessary existence is comprised in the idea of a being of the highest power, not by any intellectual fiction, but because it belongs to the true and immutable nature of the being to exist. We shall at the same time easily perceive that that all-powerful being must comprise in himself all the other perfections that are contained in the idea of God".[199]

The last sentence of this passage connects God's omnipotence with his perfection, but the possibility of the crucial move from God's essence to his existence is secured by his omnipotence and by his omnipotence alone. Once we prove the existence of an omnipotent being we can "easily perceive" that such an all-powerful being must also be the supremely perfect being; but the proof itself employs only the concept of the divine omnipotence. Thus, the sheer power of the supremely perfect being comes to be given a very special and privileged place. It is both a necessary component of the essence of the supremely perfect being and the "intermediary" between his essence and his existence.[200] Nothing similar is to be found in Anselm's original formulations of the ontological argument; indeed, Descartes's new version of the argument may well be viewed as a break with the entire framework of the medieval philosophy and a radical transformation in the history of metaphysics.[201]

At the same time, the proof as formulated in the First Replies is quite in line with the distinctly modern orientation of the *Meditations* and even with the causal proof of God from the Third Meditation. Descartes's philosophical journey began with the hypothesis of a deceiving power he struggles to overcome; if he found his cognitions imperfect and unreliable, it is because he viewed himself as being vulnerable to such a "demonic" power bent at deceiving him to the highest degree possible. If he was led to discover that he does have some genuine knowledge after all—be it only the knowledge that he himself is a "something"—it was only after he had measured himself against the power of the deceiving demon. In the Third Meditation, he discovered that God exists by reflecting upon his own powerlessness to create and sustain himself in being. He first concluded that the cause of his being must have the power to create him *ex nihilo*. The *lumen naturale* then told him that a being capable of creating other beings out of nothing must possess such an awesome power that he would easily give himself all the other perfections were we to suppose that, *per impossibile*, such a being would lack those other perfections to begin with. In the causal proof, then, the sheer power of the cause of Descartes's existence allowed Descartes to conclude that that cause is indeed the supremely perfect being; in the (revised) ontological argument, the same sheer power (unlimited, inexhaustible, etc.) apprehended as part of the divine essence allows us to conclude, as we just did, that the all-powerful being to whom we have attributed the necessary and eternal existence "must comprise within himself all the other perfections." In one and the same passage Descartes gives us one and the same reason why God must have both the eternal and necessary existence *and* all the other perfections as well. The reason is to be found in the divine omnipotence.

Both of Descartes's proofs of God—the causal and the ontological—hinge upon a certain conception of the divine power, but they proceed in the opposite directions as far as the relation of that power to our own powerlessness is concerned. In the causal proof our powerlessness supplied the point of departure: I find myself as an existent unable to sustain myself in being and I reason from there to the existence of God as to the required causal support of my existence. In the ontological argument, I do not start with the existence of myself as powerless to sustain my being, but I reason directly from the essence of God as omnipotent to the eternal and necessary existence of the divine being. Still, once the argument is supplied I not only have the assurance that God exists, but I also come to understand that I am dependent upon him. In this sense, the ontological argument proceeds from a conception of the divine power to God's existence and it yields a conception of myself as depending on the power of God in the very powerlessness that characterizes my own existence.

But, of course, the basic difficulty with the ontological argument is still in place. It is one thing to ascribe to the essence of God the desire and the capacity to posit himself as necessarily and eternally existent, it is quite another thing to assert the actual existence of a being whose features correspond to such an essence. To put it differently, while there may be a necessary link between the perfection of omnipotence contained in the concept of God and the highest "perfection" of existence contained in the concept of the eternal and necessary existence, it still does not follow, from this alone, that there must be a being in whom these concepts (however necessarily they may be linked up as concepts) are instantiated.

Let us look again at Descartes's understanding of existence *qua* perfection. When someone describes to me a wonder drug for my illness and then tells me suddenly that such a drug "really exists," he adds a new property to the subject of his predications. There is a change in my apprehension of the drug, for its newly established reality is by all means a "real predicate" of the drug. And just as the existence of the drug boils down to its capacity to have an impact upon my condition, so too the existence of God allows him to have an impact—indeed, any impact he would want to have—upon anything and everything in the world. This is the "real predicate" that I attribute to the essence of God when I conceive him as existing, and as existing in the only way he could exist in conformity with his essence of an omnipotent being.

Now, it is true that to conceive God as existing in any *lesser* way would be incompatible with his omnipotence. But, we must remind ourselves, the divine omnipotence is here called for to accomplish two entirely different tasks. On the one hand, it is simply one particular component of the divine essence. On account of this component's presence in the divine essence, God's power, were he to exist in actual reality, would extend everywhere and would encounter no limits. But, on the other hand, the divine omnipotence is not just one particular component of the divine essence. In Descartes's reply to Caterus, the divine omnipotence turns out to be that one special component of God's essence due to which we can attribute to him an actual existence. Since God can't be conceived as failing to desire to exist and since he is undoubtedly conceived as having the power to implement all of his desires, it must be the case that God is an actual being leading an eternal and necessary existence.

It is this second function of the divine omnipotence that reopens the basic difficulty with the ontological argument. As Bernard Williams comments, the idea that if an essence "has power enough, its desire to exist can be effective, seems utterly mysterious";[202] unless, of course, the effectiveness of this power were to be understood from the very beginning as applying only to the world of essences. But this would not bridge the gap between essence and existence and it would bring us back to square one. If it were the case that an omnipotent being does actually exist, then it would have to be the case, on the grounds of logical necessity, that such an omnipotent being would have unlimited influence in the world of existents. But it is not the case that the essence of an omnipotent being logically entails his actual existence.

We have seen how the *causal* proof of God can be salvaged only if we cease to construe it as a straightforward causal inference with the principle of causality as its ground. The idea of God in us—and we ourselves qua finite creatures endowed with such an idea—may then be viewed as a direct manifestation or "presence" of God himself. The ontological argument lends itself to a similar interpretation. There may not be a purely *logical* necessity that will allow us to step over from God's essence to his existence, but the idea of God may come to be viewed as having a "weight"[203] which will "refer"[204] to the presence of God in it and behind it. Revealing itself in our idea of him, God's actual existence ceases to be a "predicate" that we can "attribute" to God[205] and it becomes the ultimate ground of all thinking. Malebranche, with his *vision en Dieu*, becomes the true heir of Descartes.[206]

One may want to conclude, as Bernard Williams does, that the road from the *cogito* to God "essentially goes over a religious bridge."[207] One may also want to see that road as the road of an existential experience sui generis, quite independent of (although not incompatible with) religious faith. One thing seems clear in any case: this road can't be built on the foundation of either the causal or the logical principles. Like the positing of the Hobbesian sovereign, the positing of God, in Descartes, is not an act of reason. Thrown back upon himself by an ultimate threat—the threat of the Hobbesian death at the hands of others or of Descartes's demon—the individual can only abandon his isolated viewpoint by what amounts to an irrational submission to a higher power.

This shift represents a shift in the self's temporal experience. We have seen earlier how, in Hobbes, the sovereign, once posited, acts in return upon the individuals and constitutes them within a stable and secure temporal framework. In the present section, we have witnessed the same shift taking place in Descartes. When Descartes views himself as being under the threat of the demon, he can know that he exists only as long as he thinks. Since he lacks the power of sustaining himself in being, his thinking, and his existence as he apprehends it in (and only) on the basis of his thinking, may come to an end at any moment; and, perhaps, this is one respect in which the notion of an "instant" becomes indispensable to Descartes.[208] He escapes the instantaneity imposed upon him by the threat of supreme deception only by recognizing that he depends upon a power assuring his continued existence.

4

Reason, Will, Power

Having discovered who is the author of his being, Descartes can proceed to validate his knowledge. Nothing short of that discovery could have helped him in this respect. The cloud of doubt that hung over the main body of his beliefs had its source in Descartes's uncertainty about his metaphysical condition; and as long as Descartes was in no position to dispel his suspicion that his entire condition might be a condition of vulnerability to "some deceiver or other," he could not be sure if his cognitive faculties and his ideas could be sheltered from error and illusion. If this danger has, by now, disappeared, it is not on account of any change in the nature of these faculties and ideas. They remain what they were before. Only they are now being viewed as created and sustained in being by a power which can not be endowed with a will to deceive. The change occurs only in Descartes's understanding of who it is that he, Descartes, depends upon; and this change is both necessary and sufficient to allow him to move from scepticism to knowledge.

But how does Descartes know that God can not be a deceiver? Granted, if we have allowed him to go this far, we can't anymore accuse him of remaining under the spell of the demon and being deceived for *this* reason about the nature of God. If Descartes *can* achieve knowledge of the existence and the nature of God in spite of the demon's threat to his cognition, then the demon-induced doubt can not be used to undercut Descartes's confidence that God is not a deceiver. But there are other grounds, supplied by Descartes himself, on which this confidence may be undercut. In concluding the Third Meditation, Descartes tells us in one and the same breath that we have only some idea of the divine perfections, and that our understanding of them is limited; but still we understand them well enough to realize that they are, qua perfections, incompatible with the will to engage in fraud and deception.[209] But if our grasp of them is so limited how can we know even this much? On what grounds can we claim, as Descartes now does, that fraud and deception must proceed from some defect?

Ever since the *Discourse*, Descartes was in a position to answer this question: "I had only to consider in reference to all these things of which I found some idea in myself, whether it was a perfection to possess them or not. And I was assured that none of those which indicated some imperfection were in Him, but that all else was present; and I saw that doubt, inconstancy, sadness, and such things, could not be in Him *considering that I myself should have been glad to be without them*".[210] The causal proof of God was built on the assumption that I desire to have all the perfections contained in the idea of God. God is the ideal of *my own* aspiration and I am, on that account, not only aware of what counts as the divine perfections, but I am also an image and a similitude of God. To be sure, I remain "different" from God to the extent that I *fall short* of that ideal of divine perfections. But it was precisely this conjunction of similarity and difference between man and God that allowed Descartes to supply us, in the *Discourse* passage, with grounds for achieving some knowledge of God. Within certain limits, our knowledge of our own selves will allow us to know something about God.

And this is precisely how we come to know that God is not a deceiver. All acts of fraud and deception express some form of imperfection, that is, a *lack*. To be sure, a distinction must be drawn between the power to deceive and the desire to do so. While God could not lack the power to deceive—for that would represent an unacceptable limitation upon his omnipotence inasmuch as the power to deceive may be viewed as a sign of subtlety—he can not possess the motivation actually to use that power in any form or shape, since any desire to do so would testify to his imperfection.[211] But why? Answer: "Although the capacity for deceit would seem to be a mark of subtlety of mind *amongst men* [apud homines], yet the will to deceive proceeds only from malice, or fear, or weakness, and it cannot consequently be attributed to God".[212] Thus, what allows Descartes to assert that God can not be motivated by a desire to deceive is Descartes's knowledge of what takes place "amongst men."

This statement is quite revealing. On the one hand, the *Discourse* passage tells us that if Descartes attributes or denies something to God, he does this on the grounds of his acquaintance with himself. Moreover, at the present stage he couldn't draw upon his observations of what takes place amongst men even if he wanted to. For even if he could find it helpful to support his claim that God is not a deceiver by observing men other than himself, he is as yet in no position to have such knowledge at his disposal. He can not have any such knowledge unless he already knows that God is not a deceiver and does not deceive him in his belief that there exist people other than himself and that they actually are what he takes them to be both in their motives and in their actions. So far, he has only his own self—his self as discovered in the *cogito*— to supply him with the resources to draw upon in his attempt to learn something about the nature of God. If he thinks that God can not deceive him because the motivation to do so is absent from God's nature, it is because he is familiar with such a motive from his own case. On the grounds of *this* knowledge he recognizes that such a motive is a sign of an imperfection, of a lack in the deceiver. But any lack can be attributed to a being only insofar as that being participates in nothingness.[213] Thus, if a motivation to deceive were to be found in God, God would have to incline to nothingness and this is incompatible with his perfection.[214]

What Descartes tells us he finds "amongst men"—the connection of the will to deceive with imperfection—is extracted from Descartes's knowledge of his own self. But, on the other hand, this knowledge does not concern some peculiarity of Descartes himself. The entire disposition of the First Meditation is a testimony to this. If Descartes has dismissed the claims of madmen as grounds for doubt and has adopted, instead, the hypothesis of the demon, it is because the "will to deceive" motivating the demon to act the way he does is clearly a universal human characteristic. If Descartes was hoping that the demon hypothesis would induce his readers to follow him onto the path of doubt it is because he thought that they too would be familiar with a will to deceive and they too will find in this will a persuasive reason to doubt if they thought they might be exposed to precisely such a will operating against them. In "deceiving himself" by imagining what would happen to his knowledge if a powerful deceiver was bent at misleading him in his beliefs, Descartes is putting himself in a condition which, he thinks, would be recognized by all men as their own condition. And he thinks he knows enough about this will to deceive as he finds it in himself to view it as a sign of imperfection in general. He suspected something to this effect already in the First Meditation—this is why he chose to speak of a deceiving "demon" rather than of a deceiving "God"—and he has gained additional clarity about this after familiarizing himself more closely with his own aspiration to perfection.

By the same token, we rediscover the *human* face of the demon. In the Third Meditation, Descartes has shown how a host of my ideas might have been produced by me out of the resources found within myself. This finding applies even to those ideas—of number, duration, and so on—which are not the ideas of a self, and it applies even more strongly to the idea of the self. If I can form those ideas (of number, duration, etc.) by observing some features of my self, I can certainly form the idea of the latter on the grounds of my own acquaintance with myself *qua* thinking, willing, desiring, and so on. There is no obstacle to my "amplifying" this idea to a great degree—in imagining a being who is, say, much more intelligent or powerful than I am. The process of amplification fails to produce only one particular idea of a self—and that is the idea of the self of God. Furthermore, the *Discourse* passage provides us with a rule for identifying such properties as can not be attributed to God. These are the very same properties (such as sadness or doubt, to use Descartes's own examples) which testify, in my own case, to my self's imperfection and finitude. All other properties found in me may be (if thought of as infinitely perfect) attributed to God on the grounds of my "similitude" to Him. Now, the will to deceive is the will to nothingness and it indicates a *lack* in the deceiver. Thus the motivations inducing one to deceive—weakness, fear, or malice—can not be attributed to God. They belong to me not *qua* similar to God but *qua* different from him. Since no other ideas but the ideas of divine perfections could not have been produced by me out of the materials found within myself, there is no reason why my idea of the demon's motivation should be viewed as anything more than the "amplified" image of my own malice as I find it in my own will to deceive. This, by itself, does not decide the issue whether some features of the idea of the demon *other* than his will might not have been beyond the limit of any "amplification" process beginning with our own features. For one thing, the demon *may* be thought of as omnipotent; and this seems to be one idea which remains beyond the limit of what we can arrive at by amplifying in thought the idea of our own power.

But if, in the First Meditation, it was at least possible to view the demon as omnipotent, this is no longer the case. As Descartes taught us while unfolding his proof of the existence of God, God's (immeasurable and inexhaustible) power would be sufficient to give Him all the other perfections should he lack them to begin with. Thus omnipotence implies perfection and, for this reason, omnipotence is incompatible with the will to deceive. In the final analysis, even deception done from malice is indicative of some lack of power (not just of perfection) in the agent.[215] If we thought, for a while, that the demon who deceives us may be omnipotent, this thought now dissolves itself due to our better grasp of the relation between one's power and one's will to deceive. If we find the latter in ourselves it is because we are not perfect; and since we know that perfection implies omnipotence, we know that the will to deceive can not be at work in an omnipotent being. And, as we recall, the demon *need* not be omnipotent to induce in us the sorts of doubts listed in the First Meditation. Far lesser powers (of accident, fate etc.) than the powers of an omnipotent agent are adequate to produce these doubts.

All of our recent conclusions were formulated on the grounds of a certain understanding of the concepts involved—concepts such as "perfection," "omnipotence," and so forth—and it was only given this understanding that we found it necessary to deny that the will to deceive could be attributed to God. But our understanding of God was, and must remain, limited and incomplete; and this seems to open the possibility that our conception of God as unwilling to engage in deception might not correspond to what God is in and by himself. Moreover, this thought is not just an arbitrary supposition. Even within our limited conception of God we conceive him as incomprehensible and unconditionally free. On both counts he could be a deceiver: for if he is incomprehensible to us, then our inability to conceive his perfection as going together with a will to deceive is no proof against his having these two attributes jointly; and if he is unconditionally free, then there is no reason why he would have to be limited by his own veracity. But even if God were to be veracious, there is no reason why (given God's incomprehensibility and absolute freedom) everything that *our* cognitive faculties recognize as the truth could not turn out to be an illusion: God may not want to mislead us about what is and is not the truth, but we may still fail to understand him in this respect. On both counts, we may be imposing upon God the limitations of our own concepts, and on both counts we not only lack support for doing this, but we seem to be violating our own understanding of God as incomprehensible and unconditionally free.

Descartes's first try at an answer to these questions may be construed as moving along two tracks. Remaining within the confines of *our* understanding Descartes will first come down decisively on the side of nondeceptiveness of God against whatever else we may conceive God as being. That is, Descartes will stress that God's veracity as *we* understand it must be attributed to God within any conception of him *we* are capable of entertaining. Descartes will then consider and dismiss the possibility that our *entire* understanding of the truth—and, above all, our understanding that God is not a deceiver—could be an illusion from some absolute, other-than-human point of view.

In the Second Replies, Descartes proceeds to give us his two track answer to our questions. In the first place, then, it is clear that *we* can not conceive God as being a deceiver.[216] Now, since our entire being, and hence also our "faculty of recognizing truth" must be viewed as given to us by a nondeceiving God, this faculty, when properly employed, can not be deceptive; to think that we are *in principle* unable to know the truth would amount to accusing God of being a deceiver.[217] Thus, *our* understanding dictates to us that God is nondeceiving and that we can't be deceived in all cases where we exercise properly our (God-given) faculty of recognizing truth.

We must still ask Descartes whether our *entire* understanding of what is true—of what is true about God and hence, indirectly, about everything else we claim to understand—is not illusory and deceptive. But what would this mean? "What is it to us though perchance some one feigns that that, of the truth of which we are so firmly persuaded, appears false to God or to an Angel, and hence is, absolutely speaking, false? What heed do we pay to that absolute falsity, *when we by no means believe that it exists or even suspect its existence?*"[218] We may safely dismiss this supposition. Our dismissal of it does not mean that there still *remains* the possibility that our entire understanding of truth may be illusory from the point of view of God or an Angel. Our dismissal of this supposition means that it is ruled out altogether.[219] While the supposition remains *logically* possible, it is not Descartes's purpose, in the *Meditations*, to concern himself with doubts that can be generated on such grounds alone. We learn this already in the First Meditation: the reasons to doubt ought not to be far-fetched and extravagant, since they must compete with the "highly probable" opinions of the everyday knower. The supposition that our *entire* understanding of what is true about God (and, indirectly, about everything else) may be false from some absolute, other-than-human, point of view, must be dismissed for precisely that reason. However limited and imperfect our understanding may be, it does capture some aspects of things as they really are and it does agree, at least to some extent, with the understanding available to an angel or even to God himself. If this were not Descartes's view he could not claim, as we recall he does, that our understanding of infinity is not at odds with God's (or some other "superior intelligence's") understanding of it.

But, once again, there is an obvious problem with this. For the supposition that our entire conceptual scheme could be "absolutely false" seems to be *more* than merely logically possible. This supposition seems to flow from our idea of God as omnipotent. Descartes will explain this very clearly in a letter to Mesland: while we find it difficult to conceive how God could have decreed that the three angles of a triangle be not equal to two right angles, or that contradictories could be true together, this difficulty of ours "is easy to dispel . . . by considering that the power of God cannot have any limits"[220] and that its *modus operandi* certainly remains beyond the grasp of our understanding. Thus, our supposition that from the point of view of some superior intelligence what we take to be the "eternal truths" (for Descartes speaks consistently of the "eternal" rather than the "necessary" truths) may well be illusions ceases to be based on a "fiction" and seems to be grounded, quite naturally, in our idea of the divine omnipotence. We now have a reasonable motive for entertaining this supposition and this seems to be quite enough, even by Descartes's own standards, to call into question the beneficial results we have just achieved by assuring ourselves that God is not a deceiver. Descartes must now supply us with a means for reconciling God's veracity—his veracity as *we* understand it—with his omnipotence. Descartes does supply us with such means in his doctrine of the creation of eternal truths.

The doctrine of the creation of eternal truths by an omnipotent God, while not advanced explicitly in the *Meditations*, fits in with the overall argument of that work, where the notion of the divine omnipotence plays the key role. As the being capable of producing other beings out of nothingness, God must have an inexhaustible and immeasurable power. But if God were constrained by the existence of some truths independent of his decrees, his power would be constrained by these truths. If, say, the mathematical truths were to be viewed as independent of God, this would be "to talk of Him as if He were Jupiter or Saturn, and to subject Him to the Styx and the Fates."[221] This comparison was drawn by Descartes, for Mersenne's benefit, as early as 1630. It was meant to bring out the conception of divine omnipotence Descartes was working with in the *Meditations* themselves, even if the doctrine of the creation of eternal truths by God remains in the background in the *Meditations*.

But why should the dependence of these truths upon God mean that they are actually *created* by him? Even if they are "true or possible only because God knows them as true or possible,"[222] this need not entail the stronger claim that they have actually been called into being by a decision of God. They may have their proper place in the divine intellect, but they need not be viewed as established by the free decrees of the divine will.

But this more restricted view of the dependence of eternal truths upon God, the view that was held before Descartes by scholastics and after Descartes by Leibniz, was found wanting by Descartes himself. In the Sixth Replies he gives his argument: the omnipotence of God involves the supreme indifference of his will (indeed, as Descartes puts it here, "the supreme indifference in God is the supreme proof of his omnipotence"), and *such* an indifference of God's will is incompatible with the existence, in the divine intellect, of any truths independent of his will.[223]

In point of fact, given what we do know about God's nature, the very idea that something may be dependent on his intellect but not on his will makes hardly any sense. Since in God knowing and willing are one,[224] our earlier saying that the eternal truths are true because God knows them as true means also that he wills them as true and that they would not be the eternal truths if he has not willed it so.[225] As for the idea of the unity of God's will with his intellect, this idea is part of our idea of him as a being endowed with all the perfection we can think of: for when we think of will and intellect as distinct from each other we think of them as less than perfect. This is how they are, and how they operate, in our own case, but this can not be how they are, and how they operate, in the case of God. Here, as elsewhere, our grasp of our own imperfection is tantamount to our grasp of what counts as perfect to us, even if, here as elsewhere, our grasp of the idea of perfection is prior only implicitly and not explicitly. We understand ourselves in the light of our aspiration to reach the perfections contained in the idea of God and we judge the relationship between *our* will and intellect in the light of a standard we aspire to reach. These judgments of ours are implicit, but if we attend to them more carefully we will quickly realize that we consider the separation of our will and our intellect as a sign of imperfection; and this fact alone indicates that the faculties of willing and thinking as we attribute them to God must be viewed as fully united. We must accept the formula that "He understands and wills— not indeed as we do, by operations which are in some way distinct one from another, but ever by one identical and very simple action, and that He understands and wills and effects everything: that is, everything that really exists,"[226] including the truths of mathematics and all other truths we consider as eternal, since such truths are always about the essences of things and such essences are undoubtedly real.[227]

As supremely indifferent, God's will can not be bound by some preexistent law or order, or by some truths and values constraining his will from outside. The divine will is prior to them all insofar as all of them are established by the free decrees of God. The will of God establishes them even as possible, since there is no realm of the possible independent of God's will.[228] Now, since God's will is at one with his intellect, his decrees ought not to be viewed as flowing from some blind impulses of his will. Although God's decision to decree that the truths of mathematics be such and such has no preexistent standards to justify itself, it must also be understood as a cognitive act. When we speak of God's creativity we must understand it as that "one identical and simple action" in which the will, although supremely indifferent, knows itself as intellectual as well. Thus God wills inasmuch as he acknowledges and he acknowledges inasmuch as he wills.

Let us focus again on the main line of explanation given by Descartes to Mesland. *We* can not conceive how God could have chosen that it should not be true that the three angles of a triangle are equal to two right angles, or that contradictories can not be together. Our inability to conceive such states of affairs has at least two components: We can not conceive what is logically impossible and, if only for this reason, we can not conceive how God could have brought it about that what is logically impossible, be actualized. But, Descartes points out to Mesland, our inability to conceive this can easily be removed when we consider that the power of God can not have any limits. That is, our supposition that what is logically impossible may still be possible for God becomes *itself* possible on the grounds of our concept of God as omnipotent. It is clear—and Descartes repeats this tirelessly—that we can not "comprehend" the divine power and its ways of working. Still, as Descartes always adds, we can at least "understand" God through our (however limited) concept of him; indeed, our assertion that his power is beyond our comprehension is itself contained in what we "understand" of him through our own concept of divine omnipotence. To be employed at all, this concept must have some minimum of determinateness; it must include certain marks and exclude others; it must convey to us some sense of what is and is not God's omnipotence. It "is absolutely impossible that He should lessen His own omnipotence."[229] But if God can not lessen his omnipotence—much less escape from it—then there is at least one essence which can not be freely chosen and created by God, and that is precisely the essence of the divine omnipotence. There may be no fate to which God is subjected except the fate thrust upon him by his own omnipotence. There is a sense in which we may be prepared to talk about something as being "condemned to greatness," and this makes it easier to understand Descartes's claim that God can not incline to nothingness. For if God were to will nothingness, he would have to will to diminish and lessen his power; he would have to will to endow himself with a lack, and this would be one route barred to God by his own essence.

But how do we define that essence of the divine omnipotence and what can we conclude from it, at least as far as Descartes's own test cases are concerned? Could God have created beings independent of himself? Could he have created atoms? Or the void? Unfortunately, Descartes's texts do not allow here for a clear answer.[230] On one extreme interpretation, our admission, on the grounds of divine omnipotence, of the possibility of what is logically impossible means that even such propositions as "God is a deceiver" or "God knows that he does not exist" could have been true.[231]

This seems too high a price to pay and there is no textual support for such claims in the works of Descartes. In spite of his hesitations and inconsistencies on many of his examples, on the issue of God's nondeceptiveness, Descartes is categorical and perfectly clear. Perhaps the line ought to be drawn here:[232] to ascribe to God the will to deceive would amount so clearly to ascribe to him the will to diminish himself and it would be, for this reason, so much at odds with our conception of divine omnipotence that it would not allow us to even "understand" (and not just to "comprehend") God as omnipotent.

At any rate, in Descartes's own formulation of his theory of eternal truths, the omnipotence and the nondeceptiveness of God are put on the same footing and they play equally important roles: the theory is constructed in such a way as to accommodate the claims of both of them. As dependent upon the divine omnipotence, the eternal truths are indeed established by God's free decrees; God is, in this respect, like a king who sets up laws in his kingdom, with this difference that the immense power of God allows him to implant these laws in the minds of his subjects, whereas a king has no power to do so.[233] If we can't conceive some, say, arithmetical truths other than the truths of the arithmetic as we know it, it is only because the God-established structure of our minds prevents us from forming any such alternative conception. Thus, it is useless for us to try to understand how God could have brought it about that twice four is not eight, but we should cease to view our own inability to understand this as a sign of the absolute impossibility of precisely such a state of affairs, since "it would have been easy for Him so to appoint that we human beings should not understand how these very things could be otherwise than they are."[234] Indeed, God not only "could have" created, but has in fact created man's mind as being incapable of conceiving any eternal truths other than those actually established by God.[235] This part of Descartes's position brings out the total dependence of eternal truths upon the creativity of an omnipotent God. But, at the same time, the God who established these truths by his own free decree, remains a nondeceptive God. For example, when we speak of geometrical essences and of the truths pertaining to them, we must remember that "they are . . . conformable certainly with the real nature of things, which has been established by the true God [*vero Deo*]."[236] It is not just that these truths are valid forever (since, as Descartes will argue, God's nature is immutable and so he won't change the truths he has decided to establish), but, above all, they must correspond with the "real nature" of things, since the maker of these truths is himself the "true God." The ultimate contingency of eternal truths (their dependence upon God's creativity) does not mean that we are deceived in considering them as corresponding with the ultimate nature of things. God is omnipotent in that he could have made these truths other than they actually are; but he remains nondeceptive insofar as he does not mislead us in our conviction that these truths, such as we know them, represent the (arithmetical, geometrical, etc.) essences as they really are.

In contrast with the will of God, the human will must conform to the preexistent standards of the true and the good and it must follow the truths and the goods *found* by the human intellect.[237] Otherwise, man can be led only into error and evil. Still, in several respects the human will resembles the divine will so closely that Descartes does not hesitate to call it infinite and to view it as that faculty of man due to which he can be said to be the image and the similitude of God.

We have already mentioned one aspect of this kinship between the will of man and the will of God. In the very depth of the Cartesian doubt man apprehends himself as finite and imperfect. But this apprehension presupposes, if only "implicitly," a certain ideal of infinite perfection contained in the idea of God. Now this idea is not given to man merely as an object of a disinterested contemplation. Man "aspires" to the perfections embodied in this idea; and this is why, we recall, the idea of the infinitely perfect being is "prior" to the idea of that finite and imperfect creature man discovers himself as being in the act of doubt. In aspiring to reach the ideal contained in his conception of the divine perfections man shows himself as endowed with an infinite will, and this is the first sense in which he can be said to be the image and the likeness of God.

Descartes formulated this claim very clearly in a letter to Mersenne written in 1639, but the Third Meditation itself gives all the elements needed to support such a view. The idea of God, Descartes tells us in the concluding part of the Third Meditation, is like a mark imprinted by our maker upon his work—upon ourselves. This mark, he tells us further, is not different from the work itself. That is, insofar as I am a creature aspiring to the perfections contained in my idea of God, I myself am the work of God, marked by its maker. Now the idea of God is not only the mark of God but, above all, the image and the similitude of God. Since this mark of God is not different from myself qua aspiring to the divine perfections, I myself am the image and the similitude of God: I am the image and the similitude of God insofar as my will strives to reach the infinite perfections contained in the idea of God. In the letter to Mersenne, Descartes leaves no room for doubt: "The desire, which everybody has, of having all the perfections he can conceive and, consequently, all of those which we think exist in God, comes from God having given us a will that has no bounds. And it is mainly because of this infinite will in us that one can say [God] has created us into his image."[238]

The will is infinite, for its calling, or vocation, is to strive toward the infinite perfections of God as to *its own end*. As endowed with such a will, man is the image of God. But, of course, man is *only* the image of his maker. Descartes does find his own qualities comparable to the qualities of God due to "the fact that he dared to aspire to them";[239] but, he hastens to add, this does not mean that he wished to make men equal with God.[240] The human will strives to reach, but does not and can not reach, the ideal of infinite perfections. These perfections are contained in God actually, but in man only potentially.[241] There is a tension, in man, between his ultimate calling and his actuality, between his exalted standing as the image of God and his finitude and imperfection. This gap between his vocation and his actuality is due to man's *lack of power*: if the human will "knows certain perfections that it lacks, it will immediately give them to itself if they are in its power."[242] This fits in with everything we have already learned from Descartes about the relation between power and perfection. In the causal proof of God, God was finally discovered as the author of our very existence as creatures endowed with the idea of God. God could discharge this function only as a being having the power to exist per se; and this means that he had to have all the other perfections as well since—such was Descartes's argument—a being capable of existing per se has enough power to give himself all the other perfections of which he has an idea. The very same view of the relationship between power and perfection was the basis of Descartes's conclusion that he is not the author of his being: for if he could exist per se, he would have such an immense and inexhaustible power that he would give himself all the perfections of which he has an idea. Since man's will aspires to these perfections and since man can't approximate them without increasing his power, man's pursuit of perfection is conditioned by his capacity to overcome, as much as possible, the limitations of his power.

The limitations that man strives to overcome are, above all, the limitations of his knowledge and of the practical efficacy of his actions. These are the two main respects in which the human will differs from the will of God.[243] The divine will does not *find* anything set over against it. The human will does. Man confronts an independent reality which he can make conformable to his will only be expanding successfully the reach of his knowledge and the practical effectiveness of his actions. The third aspect in which the human will is said to differ from the will of God is related to the first two but it has a special quality as well. Man's will differs from the will of God "inasmuch as in God it extends to a great many things."[244] But Descartes seems to involve himself in a contradiction on this issue. In the *Principles* he will tell us the exact opposite of what he just told us in the *Meditations*. He will tell us that no object of any will—even of the will of God—remains beyond the limit of our will;[245] and it would be very strange if Descartes did not, in the end, tell us just that, since our will can not be said to aspire to infinity while at the same time acknowledging its limitation in principle by some finite object. Descartes's final word is, and must be, that there is no object of any will to which our will can not also extend.[246] But while our will can extend to any object, it need not do so; and it is most unlikely that it will do so given the cognitive and practical parameters of the human condition. For example, man can always dream about imposing his will upon the whole universe and his will is, in this sense, free of any limitation by any object. But it is more than likely that man will focus this infinite striving of his will upon the segment of the universe that he can effectively explore with his cognitive and practical powers. This part of the universe will become a matter of concrete concern to human will;[247] it will become man's world, which he will set out to master with the aid of his science and technology.

The letter to Mersenne identifies the human will as infinite only by its proper end: by the ideal of perfections contained in our conception of God. Even in this sense—as a self striving for an infinite perfection—we are said to be the image of God; indeed, as Descartes points out to Mersenne, this is *precisely* the one clear sense in which man can be said to enjoy such a high status. But, of course, this infinity of the human will remains the infinity of a striving. Man can not actually reach the ideal of divine perfections since his powers—both cognitive and practical—remain finite and limited. We can succeed, and we do succeed, at expanding considerably these powers of ours. Encouraged by our scientific successes we can easily imagine, under the influence of our will's soaring ambition, how our knowledge could expand infinitely until it would finally reach the level of divine knowledge. But this ambitious impulse of man is profoundly misguided. As Descartes explains to Chanut, "Because our knowledge seems to be able to grow by degree to the infinity, and because God's knowledge is, as infinite, the goal of ours, we can, if we don't take into account anything else, come to the extravagance of wishing to be gods and thus, through a very great error, to love only the divinity instead of loving God."[248] Is Descartes taking away with one hand what he has just given us with the other? If our desire to be like the infinitely perfect being is extravagant and misguided, why was Descartes telling Mersenne that the very same desire makes man into the image of God?

There is enough room here for Descartes's hesitations and changes of emphasis, but he does not contradict himself. What he tells Mersenne is that our *will* (qua aspiration to reach the divine perfections) is infinite; what he explains to Chanut is that the growth of our *knowledge* should never be viewed as the proof of our ability to be like gods. He is trying to balance carefully both the similarity *and* the difference between man and man's ideal. Due to the limitations of his cognitive and practical powers man can only aspire or strive to reach his ideal. If the human will is infinite here, it is infinite only as such a striving or aspiration. And here lies the whole ambiguity Descartes struggles with: the aspiration to perfection exists *actually,* but it exists only *as an aspiration.* It is an actual sign of man's infinity, but it is also a sign of man's lack and imperfection.

There is no such ambiguity in the second sense in which Descartes speaks of the human will as infinite; and, perhaps, this is the reason why he concentrated on this sense alone in the *Meditations.* When we consider our will as the faculty of free choice, we find ourselves to be the *actual* possessors of something *just as perfect* as the will of God. Here, then, is the one quality of God toward which we do not have to aspire for we enjoy its ownership in spite of all the limitations and imperfections of our condition. And if we can consider ourselves the image of God on account of our mere aspiration to reach the divine perfections, we have even more reason to view ourselves as such an image of our maker due to our possession of "free will": "it is for the most part this will that causes me to know that in some manner I bear the image and the similitude of God."[249]

Our free will makes us resemble God, but only "in some manner," only when we consider it "formally and precisely in itself," that is, merely as the faculty of choosing.[250] All the other relevant differences remain in place: man's freedom of choosing plays itself out within the boundaries established by the limitations of his cognitive and practical faculties and by a rather limited range of issues and objects calling for his decisions. Even this qualification may not go far enough. The contrast between, say, human and divine knowledge is not simply that God knows "everything" while man knows very little. Whereas this is true, and whereas this circumstance alone limits the boundaries within which the human freedom of choice can be effective, the most important difference lies elsewhere. As we recently saw, there "is" no reality independent of the divine knowledge, to which the latter would have to adapt in order to allow God to act effectively. God's knowing that P is true is the same as his willing that P be true. If man has to collect sufficient information about the issues before he makes up his mind and acts, God faces no similar constraint: he is cognizant of all the conditions within which he chooses to act since he himself calls them into being. For the same reason, the practical effectiveness of his choices is not unlimited in the sense of being always victorious in overcoming the resistance of some independent reality. God's choices have an impact upon reality for they constitute the only reality there is. On all these counts human freedom is entirely different in that it operates under certain brute conditions which do not conform to, much less depend upon, human faculties.

Still, taken merely as the power of choosing, our freedom is not only as perfect as God's own, but it even "makes us in a certain manner equal to God and exempts us from being his subjects."[251] It is hard to see how these two claims could be separated. If man's freedom is in fact as perfect as God's own, then in *this* respect, at least, man is like God himself; and, as equal to God, man can't be God's subject. True, our own reason can not reconcile the divine omnipotence and omniscience with the reality of human freedom; but we should resign ourselves to live with this antinomy, since to "solve" it by denying the reality of our freedom would be an even greater offense to our reason.[252] We have seen earlier how important the concept of freedom was in making it possible to articulate the discovery of the *cogito*. To cast doubt upon the soundness of that concept, and upon our right to apply it to ourselves, would be to cast doubt upon the reality of the *cogito*. Descartes finds it impossible to suspend his assent to the *cogito*, and he is prepared to pay the price of this discovery by endorsing our unconditional right to employ such fundamental concepts as "thought," "doubt," "existence," and so on. The concept of freedom is one of those basic concepts and the experience to which we apply the concept of freedom— our own experience of choosing—is an incontrovertible fact of everyone's prereflective awareness.

Now, taken merely as the power "to affirm or deny, to pursue or to shun,"[253] the freedom of man is just as perfect as the freedom of God. In both freedoms, the human and the divine, there is an element of lack of constraint, of a certain "indifference" characterizing the choice of alternative judgments or courses of action. God was under no external constraint to create even such truths as (this is one of Descartes's favorite examples) the truth that there can be no mountain without a valley; and man is under no external constraint to affirm or deny this or that truth or to decide for this rather than for that course of action. Of course, there is a major difficulty with this analogy. Whereas the divine will is not constrained, in its choices, by any preexistent truths or values, man's will must, in the end, conform to precisely such truths and values. But this "must" is ambiguous. As we shall see in a moment, whereas human freedom is not only compatible with the existence of truths and values independent of it, but, in point of fact, turns out to be greater when man follows their lead, there is a sense in which even our inclination to follow the true and the good can still be said to express man's own free decision.

It needs to be stressed that in his practical philosophy—in his theory of human passions and actions—Descartes remains faithful to the results of his metaphysical discovery of human freedom. We are "masters of our actions" to the extent that our performing or not performing them results from our own decisions; and this capacity to be the free cause of our actions is *the* greatest perfection of man.[254] If, to some, this may not amount to much, Descartes will not hesitate to go further. What is the greatest human perfection is also the greatest perfection *conceivable*, since "in a certain measure [it] renders us like God in making us masters of ourselves."[255] Even the influence of passions upon the human will does not abolish its freedom. The will is "so free in its nature that it can never be constrained."[256] There is, to be sure, a difference between the will of a "strong" and a "feeble" soul. But even the feeblest souls can achieve "a very absolute dominion" over their passions by training and custom;[257] and, of course, the strong souls can raise to such a mastery over their passions by subjugating them with the "proper arms," that is, with a firm commitment to act only in conformity with the knowledge of the good.[258] The people who act that way display the virtue of *generosity*;[259] and, as possessors of that virtue, "they are entirely masters of their passions."[260]

The free will is not only the most perfect possession of man (indeed the most perfect possession man can conceive, since it characterizes God himself), but it can not be taken away from man under any circumstances. Even in the supreme test, when we view ourselves as vulnerable to some powerful deceiver, we can not doubt the reality of our freedom, since the very act of doubt—involving as it does a suspension of our belief—is itself an act of freedom. Thus, *qua* free beings we are not only made in the image and the similitude of God, but we can not abdicate that status as long as we enjoy the possession of the specifically human faculties and aspirations.

But this opens up a new problem. Human freedom is identical with human will.[261] But the human will is *both* a faculty and an aspiration. It is the faculty of choosing and it is the aspiration to reach the perfections contained in our idea of God. Furthermore, man's will is said to be infinite in *both* senses: as a faculty of choice and as an aspiration to perfection. In both senses, too, the infinity of the will is deemed sufficient to give man the status of the image and the similitude of God. We learn, in the Fourth Meditation, that the faculty of choice is "so great in me that I can conceive no other idea to be more great."[262] For this reason, the human faculty of choice is as infinite as God's own and it makes man similar to God. Descartes was also quite clear in his evaluation of our will qua aspiration to perfection. The calling or the vocation of our will is to transcend itself toward the perfections contained in the idea of God. And this is another reason we are warranted in calling our will infinite and in considering ourselves, on that account, the image and the similitude of God. Descartes explained this clearly in the letter to Mersenne, and his explanations there are quite in line with the description of the human will given towards the end of the Third Meditation. But then the difficulty is clear: If the will is said to be infinite in two different senses and for two different reasons, how are we to establish any connection between these two infinite aspects of the will? Since each of them taken separately gives us the right to view ourselves as an image and a similitude of God, could it not be that we are raised to such a high standing on account of two unrelated aspects of our will?

But the two infinite aspects of the will are not unrelated and their link comes out in Descartes's theory of error. I err when I do not restrain my will within the boundaries of what I clearly and distinctly apprehend: for when I

affirm or deny something in matters I do not clearly and distinctly apprehend
my will receives no firm guidance on whether it should affirm or deny in this
or that case and it thus "easily falls into error."[263] But why? How do we explain
this propensity of my will to "fall" into error by issuing hasty and unsupported
affirmations or denials? If the will is by its nature free, if all volitions are my
free acts for which I deserve praise and blame then my will can't "fall" into
error all by itself. If my will falls into error, it is because *I* let it fall into error.
And so Descartes soon corrects his diagnosis: it is I myself who do not restrain
my will within its proper bounds.[264] By doing this I do not use my free will as
I should and I can not escape the blame of misusing my freedom.[265] But if I
can thus use my free will either correctly or incorrectly, then, in the first place,
I must have the capacity or the power to do so. And, in effect, I do have the
"power of making use of [my] free will [*la puissance d'user de son libre arbitre*]."[266]
As it turns out, then, there are two powers or two capacities involved in my
cognitive and practical choices. There is the first-order capacity to affirm and
to deny, to pursue and to shun, and then there is also the second-order capacity
to make use of that first-order capacity. When I affirm or deny X, or when I
pursue or shun Y, I not only make the first-order decisions about X and Y but
also make a certain second-order decision which will affect the way in which I
exercise my capacity to decide about X and Y. It is easy to see what the first-
order decision is: it consists in the acts of affirmation, denial, pursuit, avoidance,
and so forth of X or Y. It is not immediately clear in what consists that second-
order decision of committing myself to use either correctly or incorrectly my
first-order capacity to decide about X or Y. It seems that I must be making
some fundamental choice about how to make various first-order choices. It is
clear that such a second-order fundamental choice of how to use my very
capacity for choosing about X or Y must be different from those (and similar)
specific and determinate choices, but it is not clear what kind of choice this
could be. In fact, it is not even clear whether the admission of such a choice
of how to exercise our capacity for choosing does not involve us in a *regressus*.

But there is no *regressus* here, and the two different "infinite" aspects of our
will—its infinity qua faculty of choosing and its infinity qua aspiration to
perfection—come together in Descartes's solution to the present difficulty.[267]
We fall into error when our faculty of choosing applies itself (by affirming or
denying, pursuing or avoiding) to matters which we do not clearly and distinctly
apprehend. But we apply our faculty of choosing to such matters because our
will is infinite qua aspiration. We overextend our faculty of choosing (about X,
or Y, etc.) by following up on our will's aspiration to decide about *all* issues,
including, those far beyond the grasp of our intellect. As Descartes said, we
"dare" to be like God; in acting that way we make choices about matters
which remain beyond the boundaries of what we clearly and distinctly apprehend
and it is then that we become deceived. When Descartes speaks of "the will

which we feel in ourselves to make good use of our free will,"[268] he is less paradoxical than it may seem. It is up to me to decide not to let my aspiration to be like God overstep the boundaries of what I clearly and distinctly perceive. When I make that fundamental decision, my specific and determinate choices about *X* or *Y* will be made differently than in the opposite case—in the case when I allow my aspiration to be like God to take me over the boundaries of what I clearly and distinctly perceive. What depends upon me on the deepest, second-order level, is the "free disposition of [my] will."[269] If I dispose my will not to judge beyond the domain of what I clearly and distinctly apprehend, then all my acts of affirming, denying, suspending my judgment, and so on will reflect that fundamental choice on how to dispose my will. Descartes's position is here exactly the same as Kant's. Kant too draws the distinction between our choices about this or that and our general disposition (also freely adopted) to engage in certain types of choices.[270] It is true that Kant spoke of our free adoption of the disposition to make choices about moral matters. But so, too, did Descartes, and although he was mainly interested in accounting for our choice of the false over the true, he stressed that our choice of the evil over the good has exactly the same source.[271]

The relation between will and intellect presents us with another challenge. There is no doubt that Descartes allowed for the autonomy of human choices vis-à-vis the mechanical causality governing the material universe, including man as a part of that universe. On this issue too Descartes's views anticipate the much more sophisticated account given later by Kant. Descartes speaks repeatedly of the human agents as "free causes";[272] he distinguishes the human actions which originate in our free volitions from those of our actions that are due to natural causes;[273] he restricts the language of moral blame and praise only to the first of those two classes of human actions, for, he argues, these are the only actions for which we can be held responsible. All of this is quite in line with Kant's theory of moral agency. But while both Descartes and Kant make the human will independent of *causes,* it is not quite clear whether the will can enjoy the same independence from *reasons.* As the will of *rational* agents, the human will may yet find itself confined within the parameters of some rational principles, so much so, that man's repudiation of those principles, while not inadmissible on the grounds of some natural necessity, would be incompatible with the very essence of human will qua rational. Hence the tension in Kant's position: the categorical imperative is adopted freely, but it is adopted as the rational principle realizing freedom itself, and so a rejection of the moral law can not be an act of will qua rational. But on the other hand, if our will has no option of repudiating its own law, the latter becomes a second nature to man: the human will is liberated from causal chains only to find itself locked up within the confines of the moral law. Ultimately, Kant will come down on the side of freedom even against the law—against freedom's *own* law—and he will make allowance for a notion of "radical evil" in which freedom, in full awareness of the rational principles of morality, turns against them. It is less clear whether Descartes too is willing to pay this price for saving freedom not only from the grip of causes, but from the compulsion of reasons as well.

This could seem to be an unfounded supposition given what we have already said about Descartes's views. For we have just heard him compare human freedom of choice to the freedom of God: both freedoms were said to be equally "perfect" and "infinite" when taken merely as the powers to affirm or deny, to pursue or shun. In deliberating upon and choosing the alternative options—in affirming or denying *X*, in choosing to do or not to do *Y*—man enjoyed the full mastery over his decisions; and it was precisely this mastery that put his free will on the level of equality with the will of God.

But what does this mastery consist in? At times Descartes defines it in terms of the agent's "indifference" toward the alternative options he envisions and deliberates upon. The agent may choose to do *X* rather than *Y*, but then he may also choose to do *Y* rather than *X*. This is certainly the case in situations where we don't grasp clearly and distinctly that one option is more justified than the competing option. But this is not the case in situations where we do have a clear apprehension of the true and the good. In those situations our will follows the lead of the intellect, and this seems to be another way of saying that our will does find itself under a compulsion of sorts. Moreover, Descartes does not put the will under the guidance of the intellect by making some arbitrary assumption about the nature of the will. He applies here his strongest test: he discovers the submission of the will to the intellect by studying the implications of the *cogito* discovery. He has tried to doubt his own existence. In carrying out that operation he has discovered that he exists even while he attempts to doubt his existence. He was forced to acknowledge his existence whether he wanted it or not. On the grounds of *this* experience he now knows that from a great clearness in his mind there follows a great inclination of his will.[274] He will repeat this principle in other contexts, he will note with satisfaction his agreement with the scholastics on this issue, but his own acceptance of the principle is achieved on the only basis he admits in the *Meditations*—on the basis of the *cogito*.

In conformity with the principle Descartes has just endorsed on the basis of his *cogito*, the indifference of the will toward the options deliberated upon by the agent seems to be both impossible and unnecessary at least in situations where our understanding of the true and the good is clear enough to provide a firm guidance to our choices. And so Descartes moves on to assert that freedom as indifference—the freedom we enjoy when our will lacks the firm guidance of the intellect—is only the lowest form of freedom. Freedom is now a matter of degree: the more clearly I recognize the reasons inducing me to act or to judge in one way rather than another, the more freely I act; and "if I always recognized clearly what was true and good, I should never have trouble in deliberating as to what judgment or choice I should make and then I should be entirely free without ever being indifferent."[275] If the will still preserves its independence from causes, it has lost any independence from reasons. Freedom and rational necessity are now one and the same thing, and we are now at the threshold of the rationalism of Spinoza and Leibniz; indeed, we may even be farther than Leibniz since there seems to be no place now for Leibniz's distinction, however shaky, between reasons "inclining" but not "necessitating" the motions of our will.

The indications given by Descartes in the Fourth Meditation allow us to at least put the problem in the proper terms. The will is free when we affirm or deny, pursue or shun while not being constrained by any *outside* force.[276] Apparently, then, freedom is not incompatible with being constrained by some forces operating "inside" us; although, of course, both the nature of these forces and the nature of their hold upon us still need to be brought out.

The nature of these forces is identified in unmistakable terms. I am drawn to the true and the good as they are imposed upon me either by my natural knowledge or by divine grace.[277] Thus, my will is not constrained by any outside forces when it assents not only to the data supplied by the intellect, but even to the truths of revelation. And this circumstance alone is sufficient to make us realize that the intellect is contrasted with various "outside" forces acting upon us not simply because it is the depository of our "innate" ideas or of those inner "germs of truth" from which our knowledge will develop.[278] For even divine grace is said not to belong to those "outside" forces in spite of the fact that such grace transcends the potential of our intellect.

Now, the reason why the intellect (or even divine grace) is not a force constraining our choices from "outside" should have become clear by now. There is no need to speak here, as some do, of a "mere coincidence" or an "almost occasionalistic correspondence" between the direction of the will and the clear and distinct ideas of the intellect.[279] Our will aspires to the perfections contained in the idea of God; and this aspiration has no chance of *any* self-realization if man turns away from the truth and the goodness established by God. In conforming to the good and the true man conforms, in the last analysis, to the "author" of all reality and he thereby moves closer to the realization of the striving of his own will. To turn away from the true and the good as established by God can only mean a lessening of man's knowledge and effectiveness. For this reason, the truths and the values discovered not just by the intellect but even by divine grace can not be viewed as outside influences upon the will. In following them, the will follows its own calling or vocation.

But, it turns out, this is only one part of Descartes's overall position on the issue of human freedom. In pursuing the good and the true, the will acts in conformity with its own vocation, but it still remains free to turn away, or even against, the true and the good. In an important letter to Mesland (dated February 9, 1645), Descartes goes a long way toward explaining the will's independence of the good and the true. Descartes first accepts a new sense of the term "indifference" as applied to the actions of the will. Whereas, he says, in the *Meditations* he spoke of the indifference of the will only in those cases where our assent or denial is not determined by the clear and distinct apprehension of some truth or goodness, he is quite prepared to grant that the will remains indifferent *even* in the cases where our understanding confronts it with precisely such a clear and distinct apprehension of some truth or goodness. Since Descartes mentions both senses of "indifference" in one breath, and since he accepts them both, it is clear that he sees no incompatibility between them and that he views his account from the *Meditations* as not only compatible with but indeed demanding those further clarifications he goes on to offer to Mesland.

But how could Descartes have it both ways? How—and in what sense— could the will enjoy the independence from the good and the true without losing its own vocation to strive for perfection? The will finds itself impelled to assent to clear and distinct propositions because in acting this way the will realizes its own aspiration to perfection. By suspending its assent even in such cases the will would, it seems, suspend its own striving to perfection, it would turn away from its own ultimate purpose; and this seems to be a paradox that needs to be clarified.

Aware of that need, Descartes begins to explain to Mesland just *how* the will can be indifferent "not only with respect to those actions to which it is not pushed by any evident reasons on one side rather than on the other, but also with respect to all other actions . . . [f]or it is always open to us to hold back from pursuing a clearly known good, or from admitting a clearly perceived truth, provided we consider it a good thing to demonstrate the freedom of our will by so doing."[280] This statement represents a strong and useful hint at Descartes's position, but, taken by itself, it can be misleading. Descartes does assert here that our will can turn away from clear and distinct cognitions displayed to it by the intellect. But we can perform this feat, Descartes adds, only if we think that some good will come out of this particular way of displaying our freedom; and so the good we thereby aim at achieving is the reason why we refrain from assenting to some clearly apprehended truths or from pursuing some clearly apprehended goods. In the last analysis, then, the show of freedom is here subordinated to our pursuit of the truth and the goodness. If our will refrains from assenting to *X* or from pursuing *Y*, it is because we know (or, at the very least, we think we know) that by being put to such an use our freedom will in the end bring us closer to the truth and to the goodness.

We need not look very far for an example of such an action of the will— Descartes's entire sceptical venture represents a good case in point. In preparing himself to embark upon the path of methodical scepticism, Descartes makes a "resolve" to empty his mind of all the beliefs he had been uncritically accepting thus far.[281] There is no doubt that his resolve stems from his own choice; and thus his readiness to enter upon the path of scepticism does represent an action of the will. But it is also clear that this action alone is not sufficient to make him adopt the sceptical viewpoint, much less endure in it. Both the purpose and the means of the will's sceptical commitment are rational through and through. Descartes decides to cut his ties with his uncritically accepted beliefs in order to achieve the purpose of knowing the truth (the possession of which is also a human good in its own right). He himself makes the distinction between doubt as an end and doubt as a means,[282] and it is clear that the doubts generated within his sceptical project fall into that second category: they are all means to the ultimate end of discovering the truth. If, in the process of carrying out these doubts, Descartes suspends his assent even to some very clear and very distinct ideas, it is precisely because such a demonstration of his freedom brings some rational benefits to him: it moves him closer to the discovery of the truth and hence also closer to the possession of an important human good. The action of the will is here guided by the intellect's clearly apprehended idea of an unshakable knowledge Descartes aims at achieving. Furthermore, not only this purpose of the will's action of suspending our beliefs, but the means to implement that action require the guidance of the intellect. Descartes's "resolve" to suspend his beliefs would evaporate immediately if he could not support it with some reasons to doubt. As we follow him through the First Meditation we notice how he examines all kinds of reasons—sensory illusions, dreams, hallucinations, and so on—and he finds them all wanting as a means with which to supply an unassailable support for his resolve to doubt. He finds the adequate instrument only in the demon hypothesis. He doubts and he endures in his doubt because he has a conception of the demon and of his own vulnerability to the demon's actions of deceiving him. He suspends his assent to clear and distinct cognitions only on the grounds of that entire conception of his epistemic predicament. To be sure, that conception itself could not have been achieved without an effort of Descartes's will. Descartes's will aspires to perfection, and so in order to test just how perfect his knowledge can be Descartes decided to "deceive himself"; and he did this by coming up with, and adopting, the demon hypothesis. But his decision to deceive himself was part and parcel of a rational inquiry and it required a rational support. If Descartes had not been able, in the First Meditation, to strengthen his resolve to doubt with the demon hypothesis then, he told us, his commitment to scepticism would not have been able to counterbalance the overwhelming pressure—and the probability—of the everyday beliefs and opinions. To sum up: in conceiving and implementing his sceptical strategy Descartes does exercise his freedom to suspend his assent to clear and distinct cognitions, but his resolve to do this is still subjected to the intellect's apprehension of the truth and the good to be achieved by this action of the will.

It can not be overemphasized that the *actual result* of the will's action to doubt is not thereby changed into a foregone conclusion. In opposing itself to the demon's will to deceive Descartes's own will to truth may still, in the end, prove to be the loser: Descartes may end up by being forced to conclude that he can't achieve any genuine knowledge. But even though such may be the actual result of his struggle against deception, that struggle itself is guided by his desire to move closer to the true and the good; and the demonstration of his freedom in the methodical doubt is a "good thing" only given that desire of his to apprehend the truth and to realize the good consisting in his apprehension of the truth.

The doctrine outlined in the letter to Mesland may be interpreted in this restricted way, but it need not be so interpreted, and there are strong indications that it should not be so interpreted. As Descartes explains it farther to Mesland, "a greater liberty consists either in a greater facility in determining oneself, or of a greater use of the positive power which we have of following the worse although we see the better. If we follow the course which appears to have the most reasons in its favour, we determine ourselves more easily; if we follow the opposite, we make more use of that positive power."[283] Now, this is very different from saying that the indifference our freedom may display toward the (clearly apprehended) truths and goods must itself serve as a means to achieve a good, or must be a good in its own right. When we follow the worse although we see the better we do make use of that "positive power" of turning away from the good (and the true), but we do not, thereby, achieve a good, or lay our hands on an instrument for achieving other goods. Quite the contrary: if our action were to be appraised in evaluative terms it would have to be labeled "evil." And it would have to be viewed as evil not on account of the agent's ignorance of the good, but on account of his conscious aim of turning away from the good for the sake of the worse. Such an action would be evil in the sense in which Kant speaks of the "radical evil" as a permanent possibility of human freedom. It is true that from Descartes's point of view such an exercise of freedom is the price to be paid for a world in which freedom is to exist at all—and a world in which freedom does exist is, in the last analysis, more perfect than a world in which all creatures would be deprived of free choices. This is the doctrine of the *Meditations* and it is on the grounds of this doctrine that Descartes can assert, in the *Principles,* that to freely choose the truth is far more valuable than to pursue it of necessity.[284] But this does not mean that the individual who follows the worse although he knows the better is in any sense worthy of praise.

The pursuit of the good and the true is the vocation of the human will. But, *qua* free, our will must be endowed with a capacity to turn away from the pursuit of its own vocation, and hence also with a capacity to withdraw its assent to clearly apprehended truths and to clearly known goods. For this reason, the letter to Mesland represents—both in fact and in Descartes's own opinion—a clarification of the doctrine Descartes was committed to all along.

This does not mean that the doctrine would have been sufficient to generate, all by itself, the methodical scepticism of the First Meditation. The freedom to withdraw one's assent to clear and distinct cognitions had to be backed up by a *reason* to do so in order to generate sufficient grounds for methodical scepticism. When Descartes decided to "deceive himself" he did this by postulating a will to deceive different and independent from his own; he did not produce his scepticism merely by asserting his ability not to assent to clear and distinct propositions. While such an ability remains an essential part of human freedom, and a necessary component in the methodical doubt, it is insufficient as a motive for undercutting our confidence in the truths and the goods apprehended with our intellect. It is one thing to follow the worse while seeing the better, and it is quite another thing to doubt whether what one sees as the better is in fact the better—and the same holds for the relation between the true and the false. To produce that kind of doubt, and to produce it in the moment of the most important test—on the path from the ordinary to the philosophical viewpoint in the First Meditation—Descartes had to go beyond the power of his own will to turn away from the good and the true. He had to view himself as vulnerable to some powerful deceiver operating independently of his, Descartes's, powers and faculties.

Conclusion

Conclusion

The project of modernity was to set man on the road of total mastery of the conditions of his existence. Descartes himself anticipated proudly, and prophetically, the days when the resistance of external nature, as well as of our own illnesses, would have succumbed to our science and technology; and the European imagination soon followed with the optimistic visions of a radiant future in which man will have become the true master of his world. To a large extent, these expectations of the modern man have already been realized, perhaps even surpassed, by the historical developments initiated by modernity's relentless drive to establish man's dominion over the conditions of his life.

The accomplishment of this project demanded, from a human individual, a total mobilization of his cognitive and practical powers. By liberating himself from the ties of tradition and external authority, the modern individual found himself in a world where nothing was to be taken for granted and everything had to be created anew. We have seen this idea at work in both Hobbes and Descartes. In the Hobbesian "state of nature," the individual finds no support in external institutions or in the internalized patterns of traditional evaluation and belief. Descartes's superscepticism undercuts just as radically the stability of man's epistemic condition. To cope with this new predicament of radical uncertainty the individual is forced to drive his powers and faculties to new heights of performance.

But in the end, this newly established total autonomy and independence of human individuals will prove an insurmountable obstacle to a *rational* reconstruction of the public realm. As we have seen again and again, once the individual finds himself thrown back upon only his own resources—be it in the Hobbesian state of nature or in the Cartesian doubt—the subsequent reconstruction of the public realm can only be described as an irrational act, at least given the standards of rationality such an individual is willing to accept within his predicament of uncertainty and isolation. Thus, in Descartes, the reconstruction of intersubjective knowledge depends upon the meditating self's ability to apprehend its ideas as authored by God; but the strictures of the Cartesian doubt will foreclose precisely this option to any consistent doubter. And neither will the Hobbesian individuals rebuild the shattered social world through a rational action. In both cases, what does the work for individuals is, in the last analysis, some form of an irrational commitment.

Judged by this outcome, and in conformity with its own standards, modernity

187

fails in at least one crucial respect. The total autonomy of individuals proves irreconcilable with their task of a rational reconstruction of the public realm within which they are to act and to know. And, by the same token, the predicament of violence within which these isolated individuals find themselves even while they assert their total autonomy proves beyond the grip of rational solutions.

Throughout the present study, we have spelled out the connection between the modern notion of the individual's autonomy and the predicament of violence. Whereas nature is apprehended as being no longer a significant limit upon man's power, such a limit is found in the powers of other men; indeed the only limit the autonomous individual will still encounter is precisely another individual similar to himself but set in opposition to him. The ensuing predicament of violence—the actions of the Cartesian deceiver or the all-pervasive violence in the Hobbesian state of nature—both result from the assertion of individuals' total autonomy and are also instrumental in bringing about an even deeper and more radical separation of individuals from one another and from the public world.

But in pushing this separation to its utmost limits, the modern self apprehends a new ground for some old categories of thought. As Fichte already saw while continuing to move along the modern trail of philosophizing, the ultimate ground of our notion of causality lies in the relation of the Ego to a "non-Ego" that limits it from outside. But in the fully humanized, man-made world of modernity man himself emerges as the only limit to reckon with. Thus, even while the modern individual asserts his autonomy vis-à-vis nature, he finds himself causally dependent upon other individuals like himself. And insofar as our notion of humanity continues to include an element of radical dependence and powerlessness, this element is now to be found in human relations, since the collapse of the everyday world—modernity's ultimate test of the self's predicament through the worst case scenario—still leaves individuals vulnerable to each other in an environment of force and fraud.

This inescapable dependence of individuals upon one another is also at the source of the modern self's conception of his own identity. In confronting the threat of force and fraud imposed upon him by another self, the individual is thrown back upon himself and upon his own, cognitive and practical, powers. This is what allows him to take the full measure of himself. With his ordinary world rendered inoperative by force and fraud, the individual's ordinary identity ceases to define him. Thus, in enduring against another self set in opposition to him in an environment of violence the individual establishes himself independently of the public world that ordinarily sustains him and defines him. In this radical isolation the individual discovers himself both as a particular self—for he still finds himself limited by the *other*—and as endowed with certain determinate powers he must bring to bear in order to respond to the threat he faces.

If it can be claimed, as many do, that man finds in *time* the ultimate framework of intelligibility, then modernity must be credited with discovering the two fundamental forms of man's experience of time. To the ordinary, everyday temporality within which man can securely take things for granted and plan for the future, modernity opposes the temporal experience of a self situated within an environment of force and deception. Under such conditions, the self's temporality becomes fractured, since the very real menace of violence radically undercuts the self's confidence in the reality of his future. Thus, in the Hobbesian state of nature man finds himself living in the "time of war," where his life is apprehended as doomed to be "short"; and the Cartesian knower discovers, while confronting the threat of the deceiver, what it is like to exist in an instant. This fractured temporality is private as well. There is no public, collective temporality for the self to participate in, since the collapse of the ordinary, everyday world has rendered all collective experience doubtful and uncertain, if not altogether unreal. The reemergence of collective temporality will require the reestablishment of the shared, public world; and only then, on the basis of such a world, will the individual's own experience of time rejoin the temporal experience of other individuals.

It would serve no purpose to review here the many criticisms of modernity advanced against it under the banners of our recent intellectual fads and fashions. Perhaps we are indeed at the threshold of the post-modern era. Perhaps some key ideas of modernity will soon disappear altogether from our ways of thinking. But even if such changes could be anticipated, the task of determining their meaning would lie beyond the limits of the present study.

Notes

Preface

1. R. Popkin, *The History of Scepticism from Erasmus to Descartes* (New York, 1964), xiii, 82–83.
2. *CB*, 4; *AT*, 5:147.
3. *Lev*, 469.
4. For all this the reader may consult B. Barry and R. Hardin, *Rational Man and Irrational Society? Introduction and Sourcebook* (Beverly Hills, London, New Delhi 1982). On the failure of the most recent attempts to establish rationality of collective action in Hobbes see: J. S. Kraus, *The Limits of Hobbesian Contractarianism* (Cambridge: Cambridge University Press 1993) pp. 316–18.
5. *Lev*, 82
6. *HR* 1:212; *AT* 9B: 16; see also *HR* 2:51; *AT* 7:159.
7. *HR* 2:48–51; *AT* 7:155–59.
8. See especially my last two books, *Doubt, Time, Violence* (Chicago, 1986) and *Violence in Modern Philosophy* (Chicago, 1989).

Part I

Chapter 1: The Self as a Power Center

1. *Lev*, 99.
2. *Lev*, 111.
3. *Lev*, 103.
4. *Lev*, 104.
5. *Lev*, 96.
6. *Lev*, 169.
7. Ibid.
8. *Lev*, 162–63
9. "The POWER of a Man, (to take it universally) is his present means to obtain some future apparent Good" (*Lev*, 150), where the "good" is identical with the "desirable."
10. *Lev*, 96.
11. *Lev*, 167.
12. *Lev*, 225; *EL*, 34.
13. *EL*, 34.
14. *EL*, 72; *De Cive*, 127.
15. Here lie the anthropological roots of the Hegelian dialectic of pure Being passing over into pure Nothing. See P. Hoffman, *Violence in Modern Philosophy* (Chicago, 1987), 80–84, 144–45.
16. *De Corp*, 94–95.
17. *De Corp*, 94.

18. *Lev*, 97.
19. *De Corp*, 95; *Lev*, 97.
20. *EL*, 15.
21. *Lev*, 97.
22. *EL*, 32.
23. *Lev*, 88.
24. *EL*, 34; emphasis added.
25. *Lev*, 161.
26. *Lev*, 186.
27. Ibid.
28. *Lev*, 128.
29. *Lev*, 111.
30. *Lev*, 171.
31. *Lev*, 131.
32. *Lev*, 223; emphasis added.
33. For more detail, see Hoffman, *Violence in Modern Philosophy*, ch. 1, sec. 3.
34. *EL*, 71.
35. *De Corp*, pt. 2, chaps. 9–10. Valuable material can also be found in *A Short Tract on First Principles* (in: *EL*, app. 1).
36. *De Corp*, pt. 2, p. 122.
37. *De Corp*, 129–31.
38. *De Corp*, 122.
39. In a clear reference to Aristotle's classical example of a future sea battle, Hobbes points his finger accusingly at those "who though they confess this whole proposition, *tomorrow it will either rain, or not rain,* to be true, yet they will not acknowledge the parts of it, as tomorrow it will rain, or *tomorrow it will not rain,* to be either of them true by itself" (*De Corp*, 130–31).
40. *De Corp*, 120.
41. *De Corp*, 124.
42. *De Corp*, 123.
43. *De Corp*, 132.
44. Especially pp. 2 and 35.
45. *Lev*, 150.
46. As S. I. Benn asks, "If power is the excess of power, what is it an excess of?" (S. I. Benn, "Hobbes on Power," in *Hobbes and Rousseau: A Collection of Critical Essays*, ed. Maurice Cranston and Richard S. Peters [New York, 1972], p. 210).
47. *EL*, 34

Chapter 2: The "Chaos of Violence"

48. *Lev*, 184.
49. This function of vanity is the pillar of Leo Strauss's interpretation of the entire political philosophy of Hobbes. See: L. Strauss, *The Political Philosophy of Hobbes* (Chicago, 1952).
50. *EL*, 36.
51. *EL*, 34.
52. *Lev*, 151.
53. *EL*, 43.
54. *EL*, 36.
55. *Lev*, 401.
56. *De Cive*, 5.

57. "But the most frequent reason why men desire to hurt each other, ariseth hence, that many men at the same time have an appetite to the same thing; which yet very often they can neither enjoy in common, nor yet divide; whence it follows that the strongest must have it, and who is strongest must be decided by the sword" (*De Cive*, 8).
58. *EL*, 71.
59. *Lev*, p. 161.
60. *Lev*, p. 185.
61. Ibid.
62. G. W. F. Hegel, *Lectures on the History of Philosophy* (New York, 1974), 3: 317.
63. *Lev*, 210–11; see, too, *De Cive*, 318.
64. *De Cive*, p. 7.
65. *De Cive*, p. 8.
66. *EL*, 40.
67. Ibid.
68. Ibid.
69. Ibid.
70. *Lev*, 184.
71. *Lev*, 203–5.
72. *Lev*, 204.
73. Ibid.
74. *Lev*, 205.
75. *EL*, 71, 73.
76. *De Cive*, 65. Cf., too, Hobbes, *Liberty, Necessity and Chance*, in *EW* 5:184.
77. Gregory S. Kavka (*Hobbesian Moral and Political Theory* [Princeton, N.J.], 1986, 137–70) builds his own "Hobbesian" theory on the assumption of the rationality and the reality of *large* defense groups as providing a relatively stable and sufficient security arrangement for individuals in the state of nature. But as Kavka himself acknowledges (162), this is a possibility that Hobbes himself never considered; and, Kavka acknowledges further, his own theory, although "Hobbesian," does not correspond to Hobbes's actual views (xii).
78. *Lev*, 186.
79. *EL*, 71, 73.
80. *Lev*, 215; *EL*, 93.
81. *Lev*, 196.
82. Ibid.
83. *EL*, 93; *De Cive*, 46.
84. *Lev*, 365–66; *EL*, 170–71.
85. G. W. F. Hegel, *The Phenomenology of Mind* (New York, 1966), 642–79.
86. *Lev*, 198.
87. "For he that performeth first, has no assurance that the other will performe after . . . therefore he which performeth first, does but betray himself to his enemy; contrary to the Right (he can never abandon) of defending his life, and means of living" (*Lev*, 196).
88. D. Gauthier, "Reason and Maximization," in B. Barry and R. Hardin, *Rational Man and Irrational Society*, 102.
89. *EL*, 93.

Chapter 3: The Laws of Nature

90. *EL*, 73; *De Cive*, 12.

91. A detailed refutation of it can be found in J. W. N. Watkins, *Hobbes's System of Ideas* (London, 1965), 57– 68.
92. *Lev,* 216; *De Cive,* 47.
93. Peace itself is "good" only in the sense that it is found desirable by each and every individual.
94. *Lev,* 215; *De Cive,* 46.
95. *Lev,* 682.
96. *Lev,* 115.
97. *EL,* 88.
98. *De Cive,* 44–45.
99. *Lev,* 214.
100. *Lev,* 211; cf., too, *De Cive,* 39; *EL,* 89.
101. Thus the step from the factual to the normative equality of the other is imposed upon me by the other's emergence as the ultimate limit of my *will.* It may be, as C. B. MacPherson claims (*The Political Theory of Possessive Individualism* [Oxford, 1962], 75–76), that the same step could also be interpreted as a law of reason: since the other is by nature equal to me, there is "no reason" (ibid.) to treat him unequally. Be this as it may, it hardly matters in the context of *Hobbes's* use of the laws of nature. For these laws are effective only insofar as they can influence human will; and while there may be no reason to treat the other unequally, there is certainly a will to do so. It is my will to treat the other as means to my ends that has to be blocked and educated to reality before I come to acknowledge the equality of the other *even if* such an acknowledgment would be, at the same time, an independently valid law of reason.
102. *De Cive,* 12–13.
103. *Lev,* 256; *De Cive,* 109–10.
104. *Lev,* 189.
105. *Lev,* 315, 189.
106. I say "in a certain way," for in chapter 21 the distinction between power and liberty is drawn differently. See below, 69–71.
107. *Lev,* 189.
108. *De Cive,* 36.
109. *Lev,* 185; emphasis added.
110. *De Cive,* 8.
111. *Lev,* 190.
112. *EL,* 71.
113. *Lev,* 189–90; emphasis added.
114. Ibid.; emphasis added.
115. *Lev,* 190.
116. Ibid.
117. Ibid.
118. Ibid.
119. If I *already* have the concept of laying down my rights, then I can think about the possibility of applying this concept to my relations with animals, even of making contracts with them—an idea which is to be rejected if only on the grounds that animals have no power of speech (*Lev,* 197). But the very concept of laying down my rights presupposes the concept of the other as the ultimate limit of my powers.
120. *Lev,* 190.
121. *Lev,* 191.

122. Ibid.
123. Ibid.
124. Ibid.
125. Ibid.; emphasis added.
126. Ibid.
127. Ibid.
128. Ibid.
129. Ibid.
130. Ibid.; emphasis added.
131. *Lev*, 192.
132. *Lev*, 199; emphasis added.
133. *Lev*, 192. It seems that for Hobbes a man can be said to be "weary" of life when he can't enjoy air, water, motion, and other necessities. Cf. *EL*, 189; *De Cive*, 39; *Lev*, 212.
134. *Lev*, 343.
135. Ibid.
136. *De Cive*, 25.
137. Indeed the laws of nature as actually existing *are* civil laws (*Lev*, 314).
138. *Lev*, 235–36.
139. *Lev*, 234, 293.
140. *Lev*, 207.
141. Working out the implications of his Hobbesian theory, Kavka argues (*Hobbesian Moral and Political Theory*, 127–88) that the choice of the sovereign in the state of nature is primarily such a coordination problem. Having already tasted the horrors of the state of war, the individuals agree that it is better to have any sovereign whatever than to lapse back into the state of nature; their coalescence around whoever gets elected is then a matter of self-interest of all the parties involved. There is one problem with this solution: individuals' understanding of their predicament as a coordination problem is taking place in a situation still defined by the passion of diffidence. Hence the entire difficulty of establishing a sovereign reemerges as the problem of first compliance (234–44). Prior to the establishment of effective controls by the sovereign it is irrational for anyone to obey him first—and yet he can not have such effective controls without some individuals' taking the risk of obeying him first.

   Can this difficulty of the first compliance be removed? Kavka himself seems to be of two minds on this issue. At times he suggests (244) that the danger to the first compliers is simply part of the human condition; which, if true, brings back the entire *ir*rationality of creating the sovereign. At times (387) he claims that "the problem is readily solvable," and he goes on to give the usual reasons for cooperative behavior: we are released from the obligation to cooperate only if we have grounds to suspect that the others will not cooperate (in this case cooperation means obeying whoever gets elected as the sovereign), we can not be free to refuse to perform our agreement (to obey whoever gets elected) unless other people give us grounds for suspicion after the making of the agreement (and they are not likely to do that on account of their fear to lapse into war), and so on. As I have argued earlier, given the passions (of diffidence) and the corresponding modes of reasoning actually prevailing in the state of nature, those reasons for cooperative behavior can not, on their own, secure cooperation.
142. G. W. F. Hegel, *The Phenomenology of Mind* (New York, 1966), 149–60.

Chapter 4: "The Mortall God"

143. *Lev,* 81.
144. *Lev,* 228; emphasis added.
145. *EL,* 40.
146. *De Cive,* ii.
147. *Lev,* 602.
148. C. B. MacPherson, introduction to *Leviathan* (Penguin Books: London 1968) 62.
149. If someone were to object, at this point, to my use of such holistic and organismic concepts to clarify the present issue, I would reply that I am in agreement with Hobbes's own language: "The Obligation of Subjects to the Soveraign, is understood to last as long, and no longer, than the power lasteth, by which he is able to protect them. For the right men have by Nature to protect themselves, when none else can protect them, can by no Covenant be relinquished. The *Soveraignty is the soule of the Common-wealth; which once departed from the Body, the members doe no more receive their motion from it*" (*Lev,* 272; emphasis added). See, too, *Lev,* 375.
150. A. Rapaczyński, *Nature and Politics, Liberalism in the Philosophies of Hobbes, Locke and Rousseau* (Ithaca, N.Y., 1987), 69–75, 97–98.
151. Hobbes himself says in *Behemoth* that "the power of the mighty hath no foundation but in the opinion and belief of the people" (*EW,* 6:184).
152. *EL,* 103.
153. Ibid.
154. See especially, *De Cive,* 88–89.
155. *Lev,* 260.
156. *Lev,* 602.
157. *Lev,* 229.
158. *Lev,* 221.
159. *Lev,* 232.
160. This is why animals, lacking the power of speech, can not form society through a contract (*Lev,* 100).
161. *Lev,* 82.
162. *Lev,* 217.
163. The distinction between the material and the formal definitions of authorization allows David Gauthier (*The Logic of Leviathan* [Oxford 1969], Chap. 4) to develop an interpretation of Hobbes in which the formal concept of authorization does the main work in organizing the argument of *Leviathan.*
164. *Lev,* 220.
165. *Lev,* 227.
166. *Lev,* 225–26; *De Cive,* 66–67.
167. *Lev,* 227; my emphasis added.
168. Ibid.
169. *Lev,* 191.
170. Hobbes first hit upon this difficulty in the *Elements of Law* (104), and, in that early treatise, he drew the conclusion that the transferring of strength and power to the sovereign can mean no more than relinquishing the right to resist him. Since *Leviathan* speaks of individuals actually "conferring" power upon the sovereign, the entire difficulty becomes all the more acute.

171. See H. Pitkin, *The Concept of Representation* (Berkeley and Los Angeles, 1967), 20–28.

Chapter 5: Obligation and Liberty

172. *Lev*, 184.
173. This novelty of man's obligation toward the sovereign was first brought out in clear terms by Michael Oakeshott in his celebrated introduction to his edition of *Leviathan* for the Blackwell's Political Texts series (Oxford, 1946, pp. vii–lxvi). He has been criticized by Warrender (*The Political Philosophy of Hobbes* [Oxford, 1957], 330–35) on the grounds that since no bridge is being provided between the obligations valid in the state of nature and the new, specifically moral, obligation, the justification of the latter "has to be regarded as an unanswerable question or a dogma" (335). The criticism may be at least partly justified, for Oakeshott does not rely, in his interpretation, upon the much needed notions of conversion and creativity; and without some such notions being put to work the novelty of moral obligation is indeed inexplicable and unjustifiable.
174. *Lev*, 238.
175. The argument and all the words in quotation marks are taken from *Lev*, 232. Cf., too, *Lev*, 264–65: "Nothing the Soveraign Representative can doe to a Subject, on what pretence soever, can properly be called Injustice, or Injury; because every Subject is Author of every act the Soveraign doth."
176. *Lev*, 201.
177. *Lev*, 202.
178. *Lev*, 193, 209.
179. See A. E. Taylor, *The Ethical Doctrine of Hobbes*, in *Hobbes Studies*, ed. K. C. Brown (Oxford, 1965), 37–39. D. D. Raphael's entire interpretation of Hobbes is based on such a view of the obligation to keep promises. See: D. D. Raphael, *Hobbes, Morals and Politics* (London, 1977), especially 32–40.
180. See above, 67–68.
181. *Lev*, 202.
182. Ibid.
183. Ibid.
184. Even in this case, however, the future master and the future slave first meet as equal and independent individuals, although what results from their encounter is a relationship in which the justice imposed by the master is very similar to the justice imposed by the sovereign (especially on the model of sovereignty by acquisition).
185. *Lev*, 215.
186. *Lev*, 202.
187. *Lev*, 230.
188. *Lev*, 227.
189. *De Cive*, 91–92; emphasis added.
190. *Lev*, 198.
191. *Lev*, 263.
192. Matthew 5:17.
193. K. R. Minogue, "Hobbes and the Just Man," in Cranston and Peters, *Hobbes and Rousseau*, 81.
194. For what follows immediately see: *Lev*, 216–17, 303, 312–15.
195. *Lev*, 388.
196. *Lev*, 238.
197. *Lev*, 376.

198. R. Polin, *Hobbes, Dieu et les hommes* (Paris, 1984), 120–21.
199. On account of his irresistible power coupled with our weakness, God rules over us by the right of nature (*Lev,* 397–98; *De Cive,* 206–9). To ask about the concept of man's obligation toward God is to ask whether this kind of rule falls under the concept(s) of obligation as defined and employed by Hobbes. I am inclined to agree with scholars who think that it does not. For supporting arguments, see: Gauthier, *The Logic of Leviathan,* 181–96; B. Barry, "Warrender and his Critics," in Cranston Peters, *Hobbes and Rousseau,* 37–46.
200. *Lev,* 99.
201. *De Cive,* 214.
202. *Lev,* 406; see, too, *De Cive,* 219.
203. *Lev,* 604.
204. *Lev,* 625; *De Cive,* 316.
205. *Lev,* 262.
206. Ibid.
207. M. M. Goldsmith, *Hobbes's Science of Politics* (New York, 1966), 57.
208. *EL,* 117.
209. Ibid.
210. Ibid.
211. *EL,* 61; *Lev,* 127.
212. *Lev,* 139.
213. *Lev,* 128.
214. *Lev,* 127.
215. *Lev,* 128.
216. *Lev,* 127.
217. *Lev,* 140.
218. *EL,* 62–63.
219. *Lev,* 263.
220. *Lev,* 263–64.
221. This paradox was first identified and discussed in a pioneering article by J. Roland Pennock titled *Hobbes's Confusing "Clarity"—The Case of "Liberty",* in *Hobbes Studies,* ed. K. C. Brown (Oxford, 1965), 101–16.
222. *Lev,* 198.
223. *Lev,* 263.

Part II

Chapter 1: The Demon & the Doubt

1. For more detail, see my *Doubt, Time, Violence* (Chicago, 1986), 1–21.
2. A. Kenny, *Descartes. A Study of His Philosophy* (New York, 1968), 35.
3. *HR* 1:148; *AT* 7:22.
4. Ibid.
5. H. Gouhier, *La pensée métaphysique de Descartes* (Paris, 1987), 115–16; and, especially, F. Alquié, *La découverte métaphysique de l'homme chez Descartes* (Paris, 1966), 176.
6. *HR* 1:145; *AT* 7:18.
7. Gouhier, *Pensée métaphysique,* 116; Alquié, *Découverte métaphysique,* 176–77.
8. *HR* 1:148; *AT* 7:22.
9. *HR* 1:148; *AT* 7:21.

10. *HR* 1:159; *AT* 7:36.
11. In most of the relevant passages of the Second Meditation, Descartes speaks only of a "deceiver" (*deceptor*), but he continues to describe him with the term *malignus*— and this is the very term Descartes used to establish the contrast between the deceiving God and the demon.
12. *HR* 2:49–50; *AT* 7:156–57.
13. *CB*, 3; *AT* 5:146.
14. "*Un honneste homme*," *Recherche de la Vérité par la Lumière Naturelle, AT* 10:511; Haldane and Ross render this as "any ordinary man," *HR* 1:314.
15. "At the same time I must remember that I am a man, and that consequently I am in the habit of sleeping, and in my dreams representing to myself the same things or sometimes even less probable things, than do those who are insane in their waking moments" (*HR* 1:145; *AT* 7:19).
16. *HR* 1:145; *AT* 7:19.
17. *HR* 1:5; *AT* 10:365.
18. Both the "*me ipsum fallam*" (*AT* 7:22) and the "*je me trompe moi-même*" (*AT* 9:17) are stronger and clearer in this respect than the English "I allow myself to be deceived" (*HR* 1:148).
19. *HR* 1:148; *AT* 7:22.
20. *HR* 1:147; *AT* 7:21.
21. "For all I know, may not that demon who tricked me be the one who created me?" (*CB*, 9; *AT* 5:151).
22. *HR* 1:145; *AT* 7:19.
23. *HR* 2:326; *AT* 7:537.
24. *HR* 2:277; *AT* 7:473–74.
25. O. Hamelin, *Le système de Descartes* (Paris, 1911), 117.
26. Ibid., 118.
27. "This last [demon] hypothesis is shown to be really an attempt to hyposthesize to an infinite degree a human failing of notorious universality" (J. L. Beck, *The Metaphysics of Descartes* [London, 1965], 201). See, too, Gouhier, *Pensée métaphysique*, 117.
28. *HR* 1:231; *AT* 8:16.
29. Commentators who adopt entirely different, indeed the very opposite, approaches to the *Meditations* agree that Descartes generates his methodical scepticism without relying upon his theory of the divine creation of eternal truths. See, for example, M. Gueroult, *Descartes selon l'ordre des raisons,* vol. 1 (Paris, 1968), 24; H. Frankfurt, *Demons, Dreamers and Madmen* (New York, 1970), 7.

It must be pointed out, however, that a key passage in the Third Meditation is not free of an ambiguity. On the one hand, it seems clear to Descartes that if he only sticks to what he perceives very clearly he can not be deceived: "Let who will deceive me, He can never cause me to be nothing while I think that I am, or some day cause it to be true to say that I have never been, it being true now to say that I am, or that two and three make more or less than five, or any such thing in which I see a manifest contradiction" (*HR* 1:159; *AT* 7:36). But, Descartes goes on, "in order to be able altogether to remove [the doubt], I must inquire whether there is a God as soon as the occasion presents itself and if I find that there is a God, I must also inquire whether He may be a deceiver; for without the knowledge of these two truths I do not see that I can ever be certain of anything" (ibid.). Thus, Descartes might be understood as suggesting here not only (1) the possibility that a deceiving God could actually have decreed that the

proposition two plus three equal five be false and that some other proposition
about the sum of two and three be true instead, but also (2) that this possibility
ought to be used as the reason for pushing our methodical scepticism to its
limits.

If this is what Descartes wanted to convey in the present passage, he would
certainly be out of step with the rest of the *Meditations*. However, even this
passage explores the supposition that it would be easy for God to cause *me* to err
(*HR* 1:158; *AT* 7:36). The rest of the passage should, perhaps, be read in the
same spirit: if God wanted to deceive me he would cause *in me* an erroneous
apprehension of the truth.

30. *HR* 1:147; *AT* 7:21; *HR* 1:220; *AT* 8:6.
31. R. Kennington, "The Finitude of Descartes's Evil Genius," *Journal of the History
of Ideas* 32 (July–September 1971): 441–46; H. Caton, "Kennington on Descartes's
Evil Genius," ibid. 34 (October–December 1973): 639–41; R. Kennington, "Reply
to Caton," ibid., 641–43; H. Caton, "Rejoinder: The Cunning of the Evil Demon," ibid., 643–44.
32. *HR* 1:150; *AT* 9:19; *HR* 1:151; *AT* 9:21.
33. Caton's entire case, as far as the text of the Second Meditation is concerned,
amounts to denying the correctness of Descartes's own approval of the translation of *summe potens* as *très puissant* or *extrêmement puissant* (rather than *tout-
puissant*). One can only wonder why Descartes did not see it that way when he
was checking the translation of the *Meditations* into his native tongue.
34. *HR* 1:148; *AT* 7:23.
35. *HR* 1:234; *AT* 8:20.
36. *HR* 1:221; *AT* 8:6.
37. See my *Doubt, Time, Violence,* chap. 1.
38. According to Sartre, who builds his theory of intersubjectivity with the Cartesian
cogito as its basis (J. P. Sartre, *Being and Nothingness* [New York, 1946], 251),
we can be certain only of our own being-for-other; we can never be certain
whether this or that object we perceive in the world is in fact another self (252).
39. See Hoffman, *Doubt, Time, Violence,* chap. 1.
40. *HR* 1:331–32; *AT* 11:328.
41. *HR* 1:148; *AT* 7:22.
42. *HR* 1:149; *AT* 7:24.
43. "What, then, can be esteemed as true? Perhaps nothing at all, unless that there is
nothing in the world that is certain".
44. *HR* 1:148; *AT* 7:23.

Chapter 2: "I am a Something"

45. "In the second *Meditation,* mind, which making use of the liberty (*libertate*)
which pertains to it, takes for granted, that all those things of whose existence it
has the least doubt, are non-existent, recognises that it is however absolutely
impossible that it does not itself exist" (*HR* 1:140; *AT* 7:2).
46. *HR* 1:42; *AT* 10:420.
47. *HR* 1:172; *AT* 7:54. *HR* 2:222; *AT* 7:374.
48. Ibid.
49. *HR* 1:150; *AT* 7:25, emphasis added.
50. Ibid.; emphasis added.
51. Ibid.
52. *HR* 1:152; *AT* 7:27.

53. Descartes dots the *i* when he explains the argument of the *Meditations* in the Second Replies. The truth that "I, while I think, exist" belongs to such truths which "we cannot doubt . . . unless we think of them; but we cannot think of them without at the same time believing them to be true" (*HR* 2:42; *AT* 7:145–46). As Bernard Williams has shown, for Descartes both the "I think" and the "I exist" are self-verifying. See B. Williams, *Descartes: The Project of Pure Enquiry* (New York, 1978), 73–77.
54. *HR* 2:241; *AT* 7:422.
55. *HR* 2:244; *AT* 7:427, emphasis added.
56. *HR* 2:310; *AT* 7:515.
57. *HR* 2:241; *AT* 7:442.
58. "If it is true that I doubt just because I cannot doubt that I do so, it is also equally true that I think; *for what is doubting but thinking in a certain way?* And in fact if I did not think, I could not know whether I doubt or exist. Yet I am, and I know that I am, and I know *because I doubt that is to say because I think*" (*HR* 1:322; *AT* 10:521, emphasis added.
59. *HR* 1:324–25; *AT* 10:524.
60. *HR* 2:207; *AT* 7:352.
61. *To Reneri for Pollot,* April 1638, *K.,* 52; *AT* 2:37–38.
62. Ibid.
63. *HR* 1:222; *AT* 8:7.
64. *HR* 2:52; *AT* 7:160.
65. *HR* 2:115; *AT* 7:246.
66. Sartre, *Being and Nothingness,* lii.
67. *HR* 2:115; *AT* 7:246.
68. Ibid.
69. "For by means of our natural light we know that a real attribute cannot be an attribute of nothing" (*HR* 2:53; *AT* 7:161).
70. "For it is so evident of itself; that it is I who doubts, who understands and who desires that there is no reason here to add anything to explain it" (*HR* 1:153; *AT* 7:29). Let us note, too, that the idea of myself is innate in me. See: *HR* 1:170; *AT* 7:51.
71. *HR* 1:224; *AT* 8:29.
72. When arguing for the "real distinction" between mind and body, Descartes will try to convince us—in the Synopsis and in the Sixth Meditation—that mind, as opposed to a body, represents an indivisible unity. While bodies are made up of parts capable of an independent existence, the contents of a mind can not exist on their own. And while a body changes beyond recognition or disintegrates altogether when the changes in its parts are sufficiently far-reaching, mind can preserve its unity and identity throughout all changes in its content. Consequently, in comparison with bodies, mind is a "pure substance" while bodies are substances only in relative sense (*HR* 1:141; *AT* 7:14).
    But this claim, even if sound, would not help us to solve the present problem. For even if our mental experience were to show that special "pure" unity, the latter would not need to be the unity of a *particular* substance. When I view myself as existing in that solipsistic world of doubt, where no other substances, mental or material, continue to exist with me, I am, to be sure, given access to a certain field of consciousness (for I continue to be aware of various thoughts, images, etc.), and I may even be in a position to perceive that field as bound up in an indivisible unity; but this would not, by itself, give me any right to consider

that unified field of consciousness as personal rather than impersonal.

73. The position I have outlined is taken by Gueroult (*Descartes*, 58–59). See, however, the very pertinent criticisms advanced against Gueroult's position by Alquié during their discussion at a Royaumont conference. In: F. Alquié, *Études cartésiennes* (Paris, 1982), especially 68–76 (originally printed in: *Descartes. Cahiers de Royaumont* Paris, 1957).

74. *HR* 1:221; *AT* 8:6.

75. *HR* 1:234–35; *AT* 8:19–20.

76. *HR* 1:235; *AT* 8:20.

77. See my *Violence in Modern Philosophy*, Chap. 1, sec. 4.

78. It is often overlooked that in Hegel the adversary the self struggles with is the self itself as posited outside: the "other" is both external and internal to the self; in struggling against another self I also struggle against myself. For an useful, if perhaps too one-sided, clarification of this "internal" status of the Hegelian other, the reader may consult an article by G. A. Kelly, "Notes on Hegel's 'Lordship and Bondage,'" in *Hegel, Selections*, ed. A. MacIntyre (New York, 1972), 189–217.

79. *HR* 2:116; *AT* 7:247.

80. *HR* 1:151; *AT* 7:26.

81. *HR* 2:210; *AT* 7:356.

82. *HR* 2:241–42; *AT* 7: 422–23.

83. *HR* 1:151; *AT* 7:27.

84. *HR* 1:152; *AT* 7:27.

85. *HR* 2:97; *AT* 7:219.

86. *HR* 1:246; *AT* 8:31.

87. *HR* 1:190; *AT* 7:78; *HR* 1:196; *AT* 7:85–86.

88. *HR* 2:99–100; *AT* 7:223.

89. *HR* 2:101; *AT* 7:225–26.

90. *HR* 2:100; *AT* 7:223.

91. *HR* 1:152–53; *AT* 7:27–28.

92. *HR* 1:151; *AT* 7:26.

93. *HR* 1:140; *AT* 7:13.

94. To Colvius, 14 November 1640, *K.*, 84; *AT* 3:247.

95. *HR* 2:101; *AT* 7:225.

96. To Mersenne, July 1641, *K.*, 105; *AT* 3:392.

97. *HR* 2:22–23; *AT* 7:121.

98. *HR* 2:99–100; *AT* 7:223.

99. "Two substances are said to be really distinct, when each of them can exist apart from the other" (*HR* 2:53; *AT* 7:162).

100. *HR* 2:101; *AT* 7:226.

101. *HR* 2:102; *AT* 7:226.

102. *HR* 1:190; *AT* 7:78.

103. *HR* 2:97; *AT* 7:219.

104. *HR* 2:98; *AT* 7:221.

105. For all of the above, see *HR* 2:97–98; *AT* 7:220–21.

106. I. Kant, *Critique of Pure Reason* (New York, 1965), A358–60.

107. *CB*, 11; *AT* 5:152.

108. *HR* 2:218; *AT* 7:368.

109. *HR* I, 245–46; *AT* 8:30–31.

110. *HR* 1:153; *AT* 7:28.

111. *HR* 1:232; *AT* 8:17.

112. *HR* 1:153; *AT* 7:28.
113. *HR* 1:153; *AT* 7:28–29.
114. To demand knowledge "by which we know that we know, and again that we know that we know and so *ad infinitum* . . . [is to demand] such knowledge [as] could never be obtained about anything" (*HR* 2:241; *AT* 7:422).
115. *HR* 1:153; *AT* 7:29.
116. Ibid.
117. *HR* 1:186–87; *AT* 7:73.
118. *HR* 1:190; *AT* 7:78.

Chapter 3: Self and God: Powerlessness and Power

119. This, of course, is Hegel's view.
120. *HR* 2:52; *AT* 7:161.
121. *HR* 2:67–68; *AT* 7:181.
122. *HR* 2:73; *AT* 7:188.
123. To Mersenne, 28 January, K., 93; *AT* 3:295.
124. *HR* 1:163; *AT* 7:42.
125. *HR* 1:159; *AT* 7:37.
126. See the explanation given in the Fifth Replies: *HR* 2:215; *AT* 7:363–64.
127. *HR* 1:159; *AT* 7:37.
128. *HR* 1:161; *AT* 7:40.
129. *HR* 1:166; *AT* 7:46.
130. *HR* 1:166; *AT* 7:45–46.
131. *HR* 1:171; *AT* 7:53.
132. *HR* 1:231; *AT* 8:16.
133. *HR* 2:39, 245; *AT* 7:141, 428.
134. *HR* 1:231; *AT* 8:16.
135. Kenny, *Descartes,* 135.
136. *HR* 1:166; *AT* 7:45.
137. *HR* 1:170; *AT* 7:51.
138. *HR* 1:168; *AT* 7:48.
139. *HR* 1:170; *AT* 7:51.
140. Replying to Burman's query concerning a passage in the *Discourse,* Descartes refers his young interlocutor to the argument of the *Meditations* which, he says, must be used to explain the *Discourse* passage. Elaborating upon what he said in the *Meditations,* Descartes tells Burman that "the infinite perfection of God is prior to our imperfections, since our imperfection is a defect and negation of the perfection of God. And every defect and negation presupposes that which it falls short and negates" (*CB,* 13; *AT* 5:153). We have already noted why the familiar points about the "defect" and the "negation" of the infinite perfection must be taken in conjunction with what the *Meditations* identify as the *aspiration* of the self to reach the infinite perfection. But there is a new point to be considered. Our knowledge of the infinite perfection of God is now said to be only "implicitly" prior to our knowledge of ourselves as finite and imperfect; "explicitly" we come to know our own finitude and imperfection prior to achieving our knowledge of God (ibid.).

This distinction between some features of our experience which are known "explicitly" as prior to, but remain "implicitly" dependent upon, the underlying principle or idea is not an ad hoc invention meant simply to put to rest Burman's objection. The distinction is embedded in the very procedures of the *Meditations* beginning with the discovery of the *cogito;* indeed as our discovery that we exist as thinking beings is the paradigm case for successful discoveries in metaphysics (*HR* 1:158; *AT* 7:35), the distinction at issue *must* be at work in my coming to know that I am on the basis of my knowledge that I think. In reflecting upon this discovery, I can grasp its underlying ground—the principle "whatever thinks, exists."

There are several difficulties with this type of solution and Descartes struggled long and hard with them. As we recall, in his Fourth Replies, Descartes claimed that the move from *cogito* to *sum* does not require any reflective cognition or demonstration. If this is true, then the "I think therefore I am" can not (or at least need not) represent a syllogism with the major premise "whatever thinks, exists." There is no room for such a reasoning on the prereflective level. In fact, at times Descarte suggests that when we try to cast the step from "I think" to "I exist" in the form of a syllogism, we misdescribe what is actually taking place. "He who says '*I think, hence I am, or exist,*' does not deduce existence from thought by a syllogism, but, by a simple act of mental vision, recognizes it as if it were a thing that is known *per se*" (*HR* 2:38; *AT* 7:140); and Descartes goes on to argue, in the same passage, that the move from "I think" to "I exist" *could* not be a syllogism, since our knowledge of universal principles is acquired through our knowledge of particular instances—and so my own knowledge of the proposition "whatever thinks, exists" must be derived from my prior grasp of the connection between my thinking and my existence. But then in what sense can the proposition "I exist" be said to *follow* (as in *cogito ergo sum*) from the proposition "I think"?

Once again, in the *Conversation with Burman* Descartes will explain (*CB,* 4; *AT* 5:147) that the major premise "whatever thinks, exists" is presupposed "implicitly" in my coming to know that I am on the basis of my knowledge that I am thinking. Thus, in the order of discovery I would come to know *my* existence from *my* thought; and only then would I be in a position, due to my grasp of that particular relation between thinking and existing, to grasp the principle that was implictly involved all along as the ground of my discovery that I am.

But there are problems with this explanation. For if the underlying principle is known only "implicitly," then how can I claim that when I come to know that I exist on the basis of my knowledge that I think, my discovery of my existence "follows" from its basis? The tension involved in Descartes's position comes out openly in *The Search After Truth.* In one and the same breath we are told by Eudoxus, "Is there anything in all this [and the reference is not only to the discovery of my existence from my thinking, but even to the further discovery that my essence consists in thinking] which is not exact, which is not legitimately argued, and well deduced from what precedes? And all that is said and done without logic, or rule, or a formula for the argument, but with the simple light of reason [*solo lumine rationis*]?" (*HR* 1:322; *AT* 10:521). Here Descartes does not dismiss only the *syllogistic* rules or formulas as guiding us in our discovery. He says the *no* rule or formula was involved. And yet, in spite of this, our knowledge is sound, due to our reliance upon the "light of reason."

This is the *lumen naturale* with the aid of which, we were told, Descartes made his first discoveries in the *Meditations* (*HR* 1:160; *AT* 7:38). This light is rational, and so when I apprehend something with its aid, I apprehend it as *immediately* true, but I must also be aware, at the very least, that some *rational* necessity is involved. When I move from the "I think" to the "I am," my knowledge does not appeal to any "rule" or "formula," but I am nonetheless aware that some rational basis must be involved in allowing me to take this step; and by reflecting on my discovery I become aware of the principle "whatever thinks, exists" or "he who *actually* thinks, exists" (*HR* 2:46; *AT* 7:151, emphasis added). (We may have to opt for this second formulation, or else we may find ourselves forced to conclude that Hamlet's "thinking" is sufficient to entail the existence of that fictional hero.)

My knowledge of the infinite perfection of God is "prior" to the knowledge of my own imperfection in a very similar fashion. When I reflect upon my imperfection, I see that it is due to my inability to tell what is the very origin of my ideas. By reflecting upon what is involved in my discovery of myself as imperfect in *this* sense I am led to my knowledge of the idea of God as the standard with which I (implicitly) compare myself and toward which I aspire.

141. *HR* 1:166; *AT* 7:46; *HR* 2:17; *AT* 7:112–13.
142. *HR* 2:218; *AT* 7:368.
143. Descartes did address this issue. There can be no contradictoriness in our clear and distinct ideas (*HR* 2:46; *AT* 7:152). But the idea of God is "the most true, most clear and most distinct of all the ideas that are in my mind" (*HR* 1:166; *AT* 7:46). On these grounds, and even given the limited content of our idea of God, we can conclude that it contains no contradiction (*HR* 2:47; *AT* 7:152). It would take us too far to reopen the issue whether (as Leibniz already objected) Descartes should have supplied an *independent* proof that the idea of God is indeed free of contradiction and whether such a demand could be accommodated, or even made legitimate, within the framework of Descartes's intuitionism.
144. *HR* 2:34–35; *AT* 7:135.
145. *HR* 1:162; *AT* 7:40.
146. *HR* 2:25; *AT* 7:123.
147. *HR* 2:35; *AT* 7:135.
148. *HR* 2:2; *AT* 7:92.
149. *HR* 2:10–11; *AT* 7:102–3; *HR* 1:226; *AT* 7:11.
150. *HR* 1:163; *AT* 7:42.
151. *HR* 1:161; *AT* 7:39.
152. *HR* 2:115; *AT* 7:246–47.
153. Williams, *Descartes*, 135.
154. *HR* 1:166; *AT* 7:45.
155. To say that an idea is "innate" to us means just that: we are born with a disposition to develop this idea (*HR* 1:442; *AT* 7:358). Like with any dispositional account, there will be problems with Descartes's account too, but at least Descartes is not asking us to believe that a child is born with an awareness of a host of ideas said to be innate.
156. *HR* 1:165; *AT* 7:45.
157. *HR* 1:165; *AT* 7:44.
158. Ibid.
159. *HR* 1:149; *AT* 7:24.
160. "The certainty and evidence of my kind of argument for the existence of God cannot really be known without a *distinct memory* [*en se souuenant distinctement*] of the arguments which display the uncertainty of all our knowledge of material things" (to Vatier, 22 February 1638, *K.*, 46; *AT* 1:560, emphasis added).
161. *HR* 1:165; *AT* 7:45.
162. *HR* 1:167; *AT* 7:46–47.

163. *HR* 2:221; *AT* 7:371.
164. *HR* 2:216; *AT* 7:365.
165. *HR* 2:37–38; *AT* 7:139.
166. *CB,* 18; *AT* 5:157.
167. *HR* 2:12; *AT* 7:106.
168. *HR* 1:445; *AT* 7:362; *HR* 2:12; *AT* 7:106.
169. *HR* 1:168; *AT* 7:48.
170. *HR* 2:58; *AT* 7:168.
171. *HR* 2:16; *AT* 7:111. See, too, *HR* 1:228; *AT* 8:13.
172. *HR* 1:169; *AT* 7:50. It is worth noting that this is an axiom known by the "light of nature" (HR 2:111; *AT* 7:241). We also know by the light of nature that whoever is aware of something more perfect than himself *can not* be the author of his being (*HR* 1:227; *AT* 7:12).
173. *HR* 2:14; *AT* 7:109.
174. *HR* 2:15; *AT* 7:110.
175. *HR* 2:219; *AT* 7:369–70.
176. *HR* 1:168; *AT* 7:49.
177. Ibid.
178. *HR* 1:169; *AT* 7:49–50.
179. *HR* 2:12–13; *AT* 7:106–7.
180. "We have in the notion of God absolute immensity, simplicity, and a unity that embraces all other attributes and of this idea we find no example in us" (*HR* 2:36; *AT* 7:137).
181. *HR* 1:170; *AT* 7:51.
182. F. Alquié, in *Découverte métaphysique.*
183. Alquié, *Découverte métaphysique,* 212–13.
184. *HR* 1:181; *AT* 7:65–66.
185. *HR* 2:55; *AT* 7:163–64.
186. *HR* 2:20; *AT* 7:117.
187. For what follows immediately, see: *HR* 2:20–21; *AT* 7:117–18.
188. Kenny (*Descartes,* 169–71) thinks that this right to make true predications about essences (i.e., about things which are not actual existents) is incompatible with the principles supporting the *cogito*—with the principle "in order to think one must exist" and with the underlying rule that every attribute must belong to a substance. Consequently, the ontological argument and the *cogito* can not both be true. For if the ontological argument is to take off the ground we must allow that some items (such as the pure essences) devoid of actual existence may be the subjects of true predications; but if we allow for this, then there is no reason why the predication of the property of thinking about an *X* would need to entail (as it is meant to do in the *cogito*) the actual existence of this *X*.

But this is only one more reason that, as I have already pointed out earlier, Descartes's formulation of the principle behind the *cogito* as "he who actually thinks exists" (*HR* 2:46; *AT* 7:151) is to be preferred above all the other formulations. Only actual, or actually occurring properties, need to be ascribed to existent subjects (our own thinking as we apprehend it in the moment of doubt being precisely such an actual, or actually occurring, mental property). In all other cases we are free to predicate all kinds of properties without eo ipso committing ourselves to the actual existence of the subjects of those predications.
189. *HR* 1:181; *AT* 7:66.
190. *HR* 2:186; *AT* 7:323.

191. *HR* 2:228; *AT* 7:382–383.
192. *HR* 1:242; *AT* 8:26.
193. *HR* 1:167; *AT* 7:47.
194. E. Gilson, *L'ésprit de la philosophie médiévale* (Paris, 1932), chap. 5, pp. 92–93.
195. *HR* 1:224; *AT* 8:10. In St. Anselm, let us note parenthetically, there are really two different proofs of the existence of God: first the proof that the concept of the supreme being implies existence and then also (especially in Anselm's reply to Gaunilo) the proof that the concept of such a being implies the necessary, eternal, and ubiquitous existence.
196. *HR* 2:8; *AT* 7:100.
197. *HR* 1:224; *AT* 8:10.
198. *HR* 2:21; *AT* 7:118.
199. *HR* 2:21–22; *AT* 7:119.
200. E. Gilson, *Études sur le rôle de la pensée médiévale dans la formation du système cartésien* (Paris, 1967), 226–27.
201. Ibid.
202. Williams, *Descartes,* 159.
203. "Poids," Alquié, *Découverte métaphysique,* 211.
204. "Renvoie," ibid., 220.
205. Alquié, *Études cartésiennes,* 113.
206. Alquié, *Découverte métaphysique,* 212.
207. Williams, *Descartes,* 167.
208. "The evidence of the *cogito* . . . expresses the incontestable experience of a mortal and changing self, situated in time . . . this self grasps itself as contingent, mortal, limited to an instant, without guarantee of any future" (Alquié, *Découverte métaphysique,* 189–90; my translation). Until recently, and at least since J. Wahl's classical study *Du rôle de l'idée de l'instant dans la philosophie de Descartes* (1920) it was almost taken for granted that Descartes views *all* thinking as composed of instantaneous acts. This is now less obvious thanks to J. M. Beyssade's impressive arguments to the contrary. See his *La philosophie première de Descartes. Le temps et la cohérence de la métaphysique.* (Paris, 1977), 135–53.

Chapter 4: Reason, Will, Power

209. *HR* 1:171; *AT* 7:52.
210. *HR* 1:103; *AT* 6:35, emphasis added.
211. *HR* 1:172; *AT* 7:53.
212. *HR* 1:231; *AT* 8:16, emphasis added.
213. *HR* 1:172; *AT* 7:54; *HR* 2:222; *AT* 7:374.
214. *HR* 2:245; *AT* 7:428. *CB,* 5; *AT* 5:147.
215. "Malice is incompatible with supreme power" (*CB,* 4; *AT* 5:147).
216. *HR* 2:41; *AT* 7:144.
217. Ibid.
218. *HR* 1:41; *AT* 7:145, emphasis added.
219. My reading of this key passage in the Second Replies is in line with the traditional interpretation of Descartes as committed to the correspondence theory of truth. I do not think that in this passage Descartes "denies that the truth he seeks consists in the correspondence of a belief to reality" (Frankfurt, *Demons, Dreamers and Madmen,* op. cit. 25). While "some one" may feign that fiction of an absolute falsity of all of our beliefs, Descartes himself will not take this supposition seriously. Quite the contrary. In a letter to Clerselier, meant as a reply

to Gassendi, Descartes will consider Gassendi's supposition that our thought may not be "the rule of the truth of things" only to reject it as "the most absurd and extravagant [*exorbitante*] error" at least in the cases of our clear and distinct perceptions (*HR* 2:128–29; *AT* 9:207–8). As for Descartes's commitment to the correspondence theory of truth, it is expressed clearly in a letter to Mersenne in which Descartes not only endorses our plain, prereflective notion of truth as conformity of thought with its object, but, in addition, considers this notion of truth to be so clear that it needs no definition (to Mersenne, 16 October 1639, *K.*, 65–66; *AT* 2:59).

220. To Mesland, 2 May 1644, *K.*, 151; *AT* 4:118.
221. To Mersenne, 15 April 1630, *K.*, 11; *AT* 1:145.
222. To Mersenne, 6 May 1630, *K.*, 13; *AT* 1:149.
223. *HR* 2:248; *AT* 7:431–32.
224. To Mersenne, 6 May 1630, *K.*, 13; *AT* 1:149.
225. Ibid.
226. *HR* 1:228; *AT* 8:14. See, too, to Mersenne, 27 May 1631, *K.*, 15; *AT* 1:153: "In God willing, understanding and creating are all the same thing without one being prior to the other even *conceptually.*"
227. *HR* 1:180 *AT* 7:65.
228. *CB*, 22; *AT* 5:60.
229. *HR* 1:264; *AT* 8:51.
230. On one end of the spectrum, M. Gueroult (*Descartes* 2:23–32) lists a rather large number of such "absolute impossibilities" flowing from God's omnipotence and limiting his choices; on the other end of the spectrum, H. Frankfurt argues that there are no such limits at all (H. Frankfurt, "Descartes on the Creation of the Eternal Truths," in *Philosophical Review* 86 (1):222–42.
231. Frankfurt, art. cit. 238–39.
232. This is the view of J. Bouveresse. See his "La théorie du possible chez Descartes," in *Eternal Truths and the Cartesian Circle,* ed. W. Doney (New York, 1987), 330–31.
233. To Mersenne, 15 April 1630, *K.*, 11; *AT* 1:145.
234. *HR* 2:251; *AT* 7:436.
235. To Arnauld, 29 July 1648, *K.*, 236; *AT* 5:224.
236. *HR* 2:227; *AT* 7:381.
237. *HR* 2:248; *AT* 7:432.
238. *AT* 2:628; reprinted in *Descartes. Oeuvres philosophiques,* ed. F. Alquié (Paris, 1973), 2:153.
239. *HR* 2:222; *AT* 7:373.
240. Ibid.
241. *HR* 1:167; *AT* 7:47.
242. *HR* 2:56; *AT* 7:166.
243. *HR* 1:175; *AT* 7:57.
244. Ibid.
245. *HR* 1:233; *AT* 8:18.
246. Ibid.
245. *HR* 1:233; *AT* 8:18.
246. Ibid.
247. Descartes speaks, in this connection, not just about the earth and its elements, but about the stars and the heavens "and all other bodies that environ us" (*HR* 1:119; *AT* 6:62).

248. To Chanut, 1 February 1647, *AT* 4:608; reprinted in: *Descartes. Oeuvres philosophiques,* ed. Alquié, 3:716.
249. *HR* 1:175; *AT* 7:57.
250. Ibid.
251. To Christine of Sweden, 20 November 1647, *K.,* 228; *AT* 5:85.
252. *HR* 1:235; *AT* 8:20.
253. *HR* 1:175; *AT* 7:57.
254. *HR* 1:233; *AT* 8:18.
255. *HR* 1:401; *AT* 11:445.
256. *HR* 1:350; *AT* 11:359.
257. *HR* 1:355–56; *AT* 11:368–70.
258. *HR* 1:354; *AT* 11:367.
259. *HR* 1:401–2; *AT* 11:445–46.
260. *HR* 1:403; *AT* 11:448.
261. "To will and to be free are the same thing" (*HR* 2:75; *AT* 7:111).
262. *HR* 1:175; *AT* 7:58.
263. *HR* 1:176; *AT* 7:58.
264. *HR* 1:175; *AT* 7:58.
265. *HR* 1:176; *AT* 7:60.
266. *HR* 1:406; *AT* 11:452–53.
267. In what follows immediately, I am commenting on *Principle XXXV* of the *Principles of Philosophy* (*HR* 1:233; *AT* 8:18).
268. *HR* 1:403; *AT* 11:449.
269. *HR* 1:401; *AT* 11:446.
270. I. Kant, *Religion Within Limits of Reason Alone* (La Salle, Ill., 1960), 19–20.
271. *HR* 1:176; *AT* 7:58.
272. *HR* 1:358, 406–7; *AT* 11:374, 454–55.
273. *HR* 1:115–16; *AT* 6:55–56.
274. *HR* 1:176; *AT* 7:59.
275. *HR* 1:175; *AT* 7:58.
276. *HR* 1:175; *AT* 7:57.
277. *HR* 1:175; *AT* 7:58.
278. *HR* 1:121; *AT* 6:64.
279. Beck, op. cit. 200.
280. To Mesland, 9 February 1645, *K.,* 159–60; *AT* 4:173.
281. *HR* 1:90; *AT* 6:15; *HR* 2:126; *AT* 9:204.
282. To Buitendijck, 1643, *K.,* 144; *AT* 4:63.
283. To Mesland, 9 February 1645, *K.,* 160; *AT* 4:174.
284. *HR* 1:234; *AT* 8:19.

Works Cited

Alquié, F. *La découverte métaphysique de l'homme chez Descartes*. 2d ed. Paris: Presses Universitaires de France, 1966.

———. *Études cartésiennes*. Paris: Joseph Vrin, 1982.

Barry, B., and Hardin R. *Rational Man and Irrational Society? An Introduction and Sourcebook*. Beverly Hills, Calif.: Sage, 1982.

Barry, B. "Warrender and His Critics." In *Hobbes and Rousseau. A Collection of Critical Essays,* edited by M. Cranston and R. S. Peters, 37–65. Garden City, N.Y.: Anchor Books, 1972.

Beck, J. L. *The Metaphysics of Descartes*. London: Oxford University Press, 1965.

Benn, S. I. "Hobbes on Power." In *Hobbes and Rousseau. A Collection of Critical Essays,* edited by M. Cranston and R. S. Peters, 184–212. Garden City, N.Y.: Anchor Books, 1972.

Beyssade, J. M. *La philosophie première de Descartes. Le temps et la cohérence de la métaphysique*. Paris: Flammarion, 1977.

Bouveresse, J. "La théorie du possible chez Descartes." In *Eternal Truths and Cartesian Circle. A Collection of Studies,* edited by W. Doney, 315–22. New York: Garland Publishing, 1987.

Caton, H. "Kennington on Descartes's Genius." *Journal of the History of Ideas* 34 (October–December 1973): 639–41.

———. "Rejoinder: The Cunning of the Evil Demon." *Journal of the History of Ideas* 34 (October–December 1973): 643–44.

Descartes, R. *Descartes' Conversation with Burman*. Translated with an introduction and commentary by John Cottingham. Oxford: Clarendon Press, 1976.

———. *Descartes. Philosophical Letters*. Translated and edited by A. Kenny. Oxford: Clarendon Press, 1970.

———. *Descartes. Oeuvres philosophiques*. Edited by F. Alquié. 3 vols. Paris: Garnier Frères, 1963–73.

———. *Oeuvres de Descartes*. Edited by Ch. Adam and P. Tannery. Paris: Cerf, 1897–1931.

———. *The Philosophical Works of Descartes*. Edited by E. Haldane and G. R. T. Ross. 2 vols. Cambridge: Cambridge University Press, 1972.

Frankfurt, H. *Demons, Dreamers and Madmen. The Defense of Reason in Descartes's Meditations*. Indianapolis: Bobbs-Merrill, 1970.

———. "Descartes on the Creation of the Eternal Truths." *Philosopical Review* 86, no. 1 (January 1977): 36–57.

Gauthier, D. *The Logic of Leviathan*. Oxford: Clarendon Press, 1969.

———. "Reason and Maximization." In *Rational Man and Irrational Society? An Introduction and Sourcebook,* edited by B. Barry and R. Hardin, 89–105. Beverly Hills, Calif.: Sage, 1982.

Gilson, E. *L'ésprit de la philosphie médiévale*. Paris: Joseph Vrin, 1932.

———. *Études sur le rôle la pensée médiévale dans la formation du système cartésien*. 3d ed. Paris: Joseph Vrin, 1967.

211

Goldsmith, M. M. *Hobbes's Science of Politics*. New York: Columbia University Press, 1966.

Gouhier, H. *La pensée métaphysique de Descartes*. 4th ed. Paris: Joseph Vrin, 1987.

Gueroult, M. *Descartes selon l'ordre des raisons*. 2 vols. Paris: Aubier, 1953.

Hamelin, O. *Le système de Descartes*. Paris: Felix Alcan, 1911.

Hegel, G. W. F. *Lectures on the History of Philosophy*. 3 vols. New Jersey: Humanities Press, 1974.

———. *The Phenomenology of Mind*. New Jersey: Humanities Press, 1966.

Hobbes, T. *Behemoth*. In *The English Works of Thomas Hobbes,* edited by W. Molesworth, vol. 6. London 1840. Reprint, Scientia Aalen, 1962.

———. *De Cive or. Philosophical Rudiments Concerning Government and Society*. In *The English Works of Thomas Hobbes,* vol. 2. 1840. Reprint,

———. *De Corpore*. In *The English Works of Thomas Hobbes,* vol. 1. 1840. Reprint,

———. *The Elements of Law, Natural and Politic*. Edited by F. Tonnies. 2d ed. London: Frank Cass and Company, 1969.

———. *Leviathan*. Edited by C. B. Macpherson. London: Penguin Books, 1968.

———. *The Questions Concerning Liberty, Necessity, and Chance*. In *The English Works of Thomas Hobbes,* vol. 5. 1840. Reprint,

Hoffman, P. *Doubt, Time, Violence*. Chicago: University of Chicago Press, 1986.

———. *Violence in Modern Philosophy*. Chicago: University of Chicago Press, 1989.

Kant, I. *Critique of Pure Reason*. New Jersey: Humanities Press, 1965.

———. *Religion Within the Limits of Reason Alone*. New York: Harper and Row, 1960.

Kavka, G. S. *Hobbesian Moral and Political Theory*. Princeton, N. J.: Princeton University Press, 1986.

Kennington, R. "The Finitude of Descartes's Evil Genius." In *Journal of the History of Ideas* 32 (July–September 1971): 441–46.

———. "Reply to Caton." In: *Journal of the History of Ideas* 34 (October–December 1973): 641–43.

Kelly, G. A. "Notes on Hegel's 'Lordship and Bondage.'" In *Hegel. Selections,* edited by A. MacIntyre. New York: Anchor Books, 1972.

Kenny, A. *Descartes. A Study of His Philosophy*. New York: Random House, 1968.

Kraus, J. S. *The Limits of Hobbesian Contractarianism,* Cambridge: Cambridge University Press 1993.

MacPherson, C. B. Introduction to *Leviathan,* by T. Hobbes, 9–63. London: Penguin Books, 1968.

———. *The Political Theory of Possessive Individualism. Hobbes to Locke*. Oxford: Oxford University Press, 1962.

Minogue, K. R. "Hobbes and the Just Man." In *Hobbes and Rousseau. A Collection of Critical Essays,* edited by M. Cranston and R. S. Peters, 66–84. Garden City, N.Y.: Anchor Books, 1972.

Oakeshott, M. Introduction to *Leviathan,* by T. Hobbes. Edited by M. Oakeshott, vii–lxvi. Oxford: Basil Blackwell, 1946.

Pennock, J. R. "Hobbes's Confusing 'Clarity'—The Case of 'Liberty.'" In *Hobbes Studies,* edited by K. C. Brown, 101–15. Oxford: Basil Blackwell, 1965.

Pitkin, H. *The Concept of Representation*. Berkeley and Los Angeles: University of California Press, 1967.

Polin, R. *Hobbes, Dieu et les hommes*. Paris: Presses Universitaires de France, 1984.

Popkin, R. H. *The History of Scepticism from Erasmus to Descartes*. New York: Harper and Row, 1962.

Rapaczyński, A. *Nature and Politics. Liberalism in the Philosophies of Hobbes, Locke and*

Rousseau. Ithaca, N.Y.: Cornell University Press, 1987.

Raphael, D. D. *Hobbes. Morals and Politics.* London: George Allen and Unwin, 1977.

Sartre, J. P. *Being and Nothingness.* New York: Philosophical Library, 1957.

Strauss, L. *The Political Philosophy of Hobbes.* Chicago: University of Chicago Press, 1952.

Taylor, A. E. "The Ethical Doctrine of Hobbes." In *Hobbes Studies,* edited by K. C. Brown, 35–55. Oxford: Basil Blackwell, 1965.

Warrender, H. *The Political Philosophy of Hobbes.* Oxford: Clarendon Press, 1957.

Watkins, J. W. N. *Hobbes's System of Ideas.* London: Hutchinson University Library, 1965.

Williams, B. *Descartes. The Project of Pure Enquiry.* Harmondsworth: Penguin Books, 1978.

Index

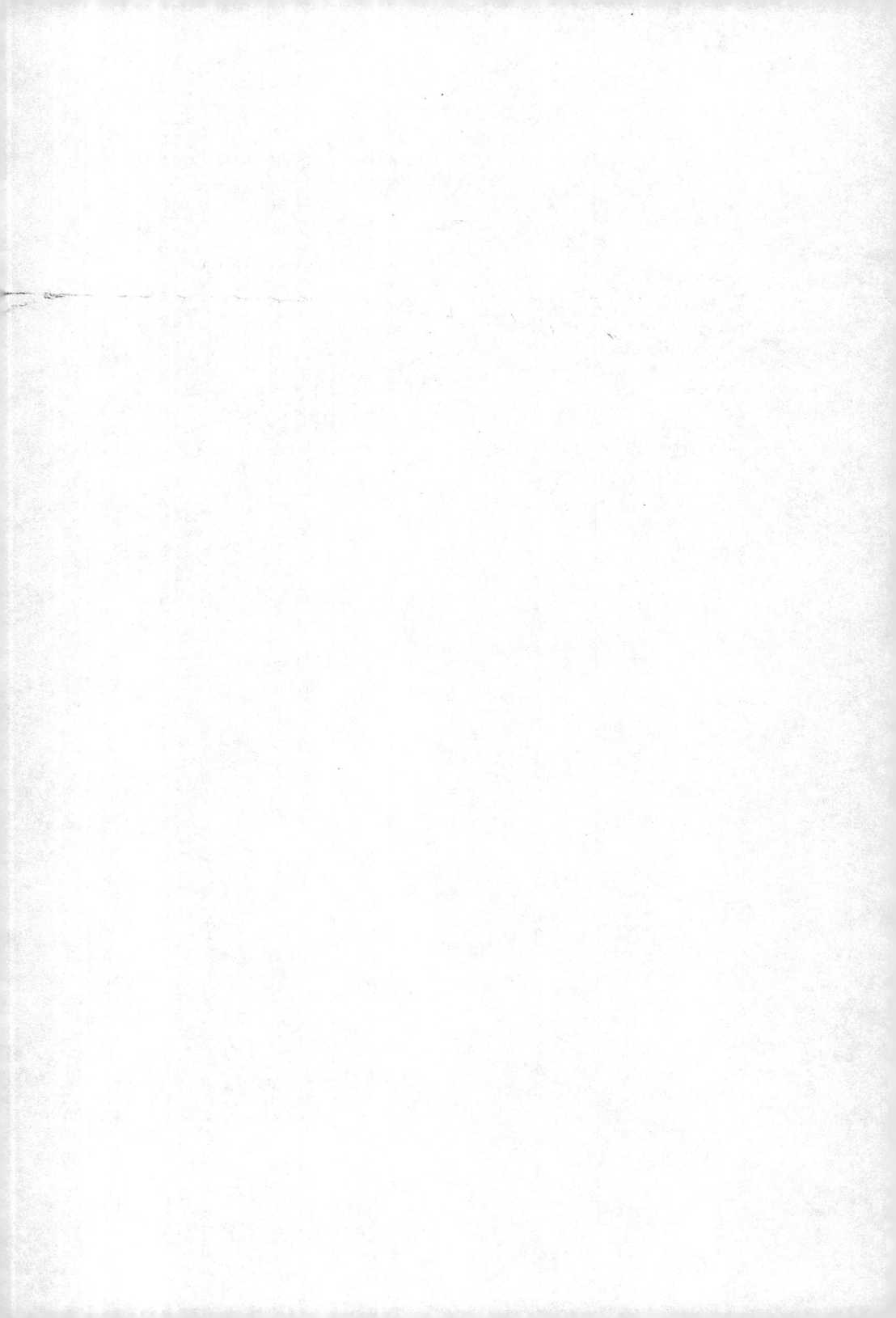